FROM A TRAMP'S WALLET

Douglas W. Freshfield (1903)

FROM

A TRAMP'S WALLET

HERVEY FISHER

A LIFE OF
DOUGLAS WILLIAM FRESHFIELD,
D.C.L. M.A.
1845–1934

Explorer, mountaineer, writer and scholar
One time President of the Royal Geographical Society
Gold Medallist of the Royal Geographical Society
President of the Alpine Club

There are, who love the silver heights,
The silver heights above the lawn,
Who spurn the lowland's tame delights,
Sworn fellow-travellers with the dawn;
Pursuers of no earthly goal,
They leave the slopes of maize and vine,
Outclimbing pasturage and pine,
To seek beyond the mountain line
That far-sought country more divine,
Where life is whole.

From 'A Tramp's Wallet', by D. W. Freshfield

THE ERSKINE PRESS

2001

First published in 2001 by
The Erskine Press, The Old Bakery, Banham, Norfolk NR16 2HW

© Hervey Fisher, 2001
This edition © The Erskine Press, 2001

ISBN 1 85297 069 3

British Library Cataloguing-in-Publication Data
A catalogue record of this book is available
from the British Library

Typeset by Waveney Typesetters
Wymondham, Norfolk
Printed in England

CONTENTS

Kanchenjunga

AUTHOR'S PREFACE

I am sure that the geographers and geographical historians within Kensington Gore must feel that I am in no way qualified to write the life of a distinguished past President and Gold Medallist of the Royal Geographical Society. I can only agree and say to them and to members of the Alpine Club that if they are disappointed with what I have written then I would be only too pleased to see a more learned work provoked by my effort that might do proper justice to the serious work undertaken by Douglas Freshfield.

I was introduced, as it were, to Freshfield by my grandmother, Janie, his daughter. Janie told me that she had always had great love and respect for her father and felt that he had in many ways been both underestimated by his family, and misjudged by some of his contemporaries. In some respects his great wealth had cut him off both from the younger generations, and from those who shared his mountain enthusiasms but had to earn their livings at the same time and did not feel that he made enough use of his freedom. My sisters and I owed a great deal to our grandmother, and, after long discussions with her about her father, I felt that the best I could do for her was to introduce him as a unique person, an explorer and mountaineer and an author of travel books whose name should be known and appreciated beyond specialists in mountain history.

Freshfield represented all that is best in the Victorian era. He had his faults, and I have not attempted to disguise them. They were the faults of his times, just as we in our time carry the faults of ours. In order to try to reveal something of the true nature of the man I have set him firmly in his family circle, which was interesting in ways that have little to do with mountaineering and much to do with the intellectual and artistic life of London and Freshwater on the Isle of Wight.

I had a great deal of help from Janie, and also from her sister Katherine, to whom I was indebted for many of her father's papers and his mother's notes on their travels in the very early days. In the box from her attic which she gave me I found the water-colours done by Douglas's mother of the mountains they explored and many examples of her father's writings. The same box contained such treasures as his letters to his mother on the first trip to Egypt and the Caucasus and early letters home to his wife when he was travelling without her.

Freshfield was a great exponent of accurate and vivid descriptive writing, and for this reason I have allowed him to speak for himself whenever it seemed proper to do so. Any armchair traveller cannot fail to be moved and impressed as he was when traversing the Caucasus or battling round Kanchenjunga; and modern visitors could do worse when walking in the Italian Alps and Dolomites than to carry his book with them.

I am indebted to Freshfield's granddaughter, Lady Magdaline Macnaghten, for the loan of her grandmother's diaries and giving me the opportunity of copying some of her letters.

My thanks are due to the Royal Geographical Society for permission to use their library when researching the period of Freshfield's Hon. Secretaryship. My grateful thanks are also due to Joanna Merz who a long time ago read the first draft and made many helpful comments and suggestions, corrected spellings, as well as allowing me to read her narrative of her climb on the San Grasso D'Italia in the 'Footsteps of Douglas Freshfield'.

I must also thank R. W. Harris of Freshfield's, the internationally renowned solicitors, for his kind help and for sending me a copy of 'A History of Freshfield's', which gave me an insight into the early family history. Grateful thanks are also due to The Julia Margaret Cameron Trust of Dimbola, Isle of Wight, for their assistance in finding and allowing me to use a contemporary picture of Dimbola.

Many others have helped me, both members of his family as well as members of the climbing fraternity, both as to matters of fact as well as with anecdotes that have helped to paint a more vivid picture of this most shy of men.

My grateful thanks are especially due to Signore Lodovico Sella and the Fondazione Sella of Biella, Italy for the trouble taken to reproduce pictures taken by his forebear of the elusive Freshfield, as well as permission to use some of the grand photographic mountain scapes taken by Vittorio both in the Caucasus and in the Himalayas. Lodovico told me that when Vittorio returned from his visit to

Freshfield to assist with the illustrations for *The Exploration of the Caucasus* he was full of the treasure-filled 'palace' in which the Englishman lived. He felt obliged to invite his host to make a return visit to his home, and was much relieved when Freshfield was unable to accept as he felt that Freshfield would not care much for the Sella home. Probably a misjudgement as Freshfield was most unlikely to feel, let alone show, disapproval on that score. And last but not least my thanks to Molly – who made me finish it when I had given up!

Hervey Fisher
September, 2001

CHAPTER 1

Deep within the sombre cyprus and rhododendron groves of Brookwood Cemetery in Surrey, almost undetectable amidst long grass and seedling birches, there is a singular private grave plot. It is solitary and long undisturbed, down towards the wild heath and woodland on the periphery of the great Victorian necropolis. Here the sound of traffic hardly penetrates. Wild deer wander, shyly curious of intruders; a grass snake suns itself in the heather amongst the scattered stones of a forgotten Governor General's final display of pomp, and through the pine tops a crowd of tits and finches hunt with faint but audible chatter.

The once elaborate wrought-iron fence surrounding this plot is rusting away, intertwined and perhaps supported by heather and honeysuckle. The paint has gone from the crested shields that decorated the low double gates. One of these gates is partially open so that it is possible to enter the overgrown interior, holding the thorns to one side and at the same time treating the gate with care so as not to detach it from its decayed hinges. In the middle of the plot, partially obscured by moss and leaves, but still showing its sharply carved Carrara, there is a low sarcophagus. Push back the bramble, brush off the moss, and read the deeply incised lettering:

'I WILL LIFT UP MINE EYES UNTO THE HILLS'.

Here then is the first clue that we have found what we sought. Clear the debris from the top of the tomb and there are two medallions. The upper reads:

AUGUSTA CHARLOTTE FRESHFIELD
1847–1910

and the lower:

DOUGLAS WILLIAM FRESHFIELD
1845–1934

It is the remains of one of that extraordinary breed of Victorian mountaineer explorers that lie here with those of his wife, a good many miles from their own parish, removed from the familiar scenes of their family life. So why here? Can it be that by half closing the eyes to obscure the scattering of other monuments, it is possible to imagine that this is some remote corner in the foothills of the Caucasus? Looking up between the branches of the giant Douglas fir overhead is there perhaps some ghostly glimmer of the remote ice peaks that had lured and seduced him with an attraction capable of absorbing a whole life? Like Little Kay it was the Snow Queen that he sought and loved, far off, a cold and shimmering beauty. But the shaft of ice that undoubtedly entered his eye at a very early age, did not quite pierce the heart. He was to meet his human Snow Queen too, and maybe there was that quality in her that attracted him, for he remained true to them both. But his love for mountains bore remarkable fruit, for even today there are those who will follow in his footsteps, gripped by his graphic prose, vivid, sometimes alarming, deeply impressed by the natural grandeur and beauty encountered on the way.

But our research has told us there should be more to find here. We push deeper within the enclosure, and there up against the rear fence, nearly hidden behind overgrown Irish yews and uninvited saplings, there is a hint of more white marble. This time it is an upright plinth some twelve feet high, of marble and green bronze, with a decorated pedimented top. At its centre there is a medallion, the sculptured head of a boy of about twelve years, most certainly a portrait. It is surrounded by a frieze of birds; a thrush returns to her nest of eggs; small birds and animals worry their way through a pattern of foliage, all because of the monument's upright angle almost unblemished by the stains of time. Below the portrait two child-like winged and naked angels support a shield bearing the name 'Henry Douglas Freshfield'. Below that again there is a bronze scroll with details of the death and the message of love and admiration of the parents for the child.

One is struck how this neglected and private place, even after nearly seventy years since its last incumbent was laid to rest, still exudes an aura of stolid wealth and cultivated taste. Everything is exquisitely chosen and executed. There is an air of permanence which is not belied by the neglect all around. One can feel that it will be a long time before the peculiar spirit that has been so carefully imprinted here will fade and become unrecognizable to anyone who takes the trouble to push his way in, pause, and reflect and imbibe its message. It is to be hoped too Douglas Freshfield himself would have derived some wry amusement from the fact that this great bastion of the Victorian upper class dead should have had its carefully planned and exclusive final resting place invaded, so as to become in part one of the largest Moslem graveyards in the country. For the illusion, if that was the intention, of a remote Caucasian glade is wearing a little thin now; the traffic noise never really fades, and no doubt the developer's excavator is not far away.

During the last few years of the nineteenth century and the first decade of the twentieth, the mansions newly built amongst the leafy bowers of Campden Hill rivalled the great London houses of the landed aristocracy in the town below in the glittering gaiety and sophisticated artistry of the dances given to celebrate the launch of precious daughters into an adult world.

But we do not have to watch from the pavement as the girls in shimmering white or pink satins run laughing through the archway and towards the marble stair just visible from the outside in the home of this writer and explorer and his remarkable wife. For we have an eye witness to just such an evening within that very house. The memory was to stay with the writer for many years, as it would with any young woman with a lively imagination and well developed powers of description. She tells of their long, white kid gloves, elegant waists and sprays of flowers on the left side of their bodices, their hair coiled on the napes of their necks and trains swirling about their feet. She tells of the house, richly furnished with Italian shrines, caskets, cabinets, marquetry; the William Morris wallpapers; the pictures by Leighton, Burne-Jones, and many Pre-Raphaelites, as well as works by great artists both English and European.

The young, of whom their fascinating, artistic hostess was very fond, were happy as they swirled to the strains of the 'Valise'. They had every right to be, for Mrs Douglas Freshfield, thinly disguised in her niece's description as Mrs Tallboys, had a knack of mixing her adored young with such luminaries as Joseph Joachim, the great violinist of his day, with George du Maurier[1] or perhaps Mr Watts[2] himself.

Such parties at 1 Airlie Gardens, for a 'coming out' ball or a birthday for one of Mrs Freshfield's daughters or nieces, were generally composed of an unlikely mixture of guests. Their host, quietly sitting in his study along with others of the serious minded and distinguished elite, would not have seemed at first meeting a likely promoter of such gaiety. But amongst the young there could have been the Duckworths, the step-sons and step-daughter of his old friend Leslie Stephen. Perhaps looking on, with a somewhat colder eye, would be Stephen's own daughters by his second marriage, Vanessa and Virginia,[3] whose mother was a link with Mrs Freshfield's early days in London. Mingling with the guests would have been Henry James ('such a shock seeing him without his beard') and dear old Joseph Joachim much adored over many years by his hostess. There too almost invariably, Annie Thackeray, tirelessly devoted to promoting her famous father's memory and incidentally married to her cousin, Mrs Freshfield's brother, Richmond Ritchie. Her nephews and nieces added to the mix. Molly Ware Cornish[4] who left us her vivid description, herself would marry a young man who would eventually become a distinguished literary critic, but in so doing she would cross into the world of Bloomsbury and the Cambridge Apostles. At the same time one of her sisters was to marry such an establishment figure as a future Admiral, who, incidentally would become the victim of a much publicized practical joke perpetrated by some members of what came to be known as 'Bloomsbury' against him and the Royal Navy.[5] As a young woman Mrs Freshfield had

[1] George du Maurier, 1834–96, black and white artist and novelist. Best known novel *Trilby*.

[2] G. F. Watts, artist. Live for many years with the Princeps at Little Holland House. Married Ellen Terry.

[3] Vanessa Bell and Virginia Woolf respectively.

[4] *A Nineteenth Century Childhood* – Mary MacCarthy. Published by William Heinemann 1924.

[5] Described in numerous biographies associated with 'Bloomsbury' as the 'Dreadnaught Affair'.

herself mingled with those of both genders who were just starting to question the accepted values of her time, especially as far as women were concerned; just as now in the same way a much stronger current was flowing through the veins of some of the young women, and a few of the young men, to be found at these gatherings.

This mix of generations and backgrounds to be found on such occasions represented the combined tastes of both host and hostess. Mrs Freshfield brought to the circle a heady mix of India, Paris, and the artistic informality of Little Holland House[1] that had once stood so close by Campden Hill, and Douglas Freshfield himself, who shared her interest in continental travel, and the art and literature of the day. Intellectually they both enjoyed a richness of taste which he had the money to indulge, though he sprang from the very different background of the City, and in particular the Law.

So what then had inspired Freshfield from childhood in his passionate search for remote heights. He was a man of wealth and talent who had acquired an intelligent and lovely wife, but it was a choice that was inspired by the remoteness of some distant peak, to which indeed he had likened her.

Perhaps one way to give a picture of the antecedents of the young Douglas Freshfield would be to christen them the 'Forsyte' strand of Victorian society. Grim harvesters of new wealth, these respectable men managed new and complex manifestations of an industrial age when lawyers grew fat on the fortunes hammered out by the sweat and cunning of others. They made money out of the ramifications of Empire; sometimes they married old names and old money, but they never formed an aristocracy in spite of honours, art collections and county appointments as High Sheriff. Galsworthy's only fault was that he allowed them no redeeming features at all, so great was his contempt for the 'new' money they represented. But then he himself was a later familiar of the other phenomena of Victorian class structure, the new intellectuals, the seekers after artistic as well as scientific truth.

Douglas, as the only child of wealthy parents of the 'Forsyte'

---

[1] Presided over by another Indian connection Mrs Princeps, and her husband – later to move to Freshwater, Isle of Wight where her sister Julia Margaret Cameron, pioneer photographer, lived. Mrs Princep was another of the well known Pattle sisters.

image, might have been spoiled had it not been for his truly remark-able mother, Jane Quentin Freshfield (*née* Crawford). Her family background was very similar to that of her husband save that originally they were Scots. Indeed, her whole outlook would appear at first sight to have been most typical of her kind. Shackled willingly to the duties of household management, disciplining servants and keeping a firm hold over the rascally tradesmen of London, she nevertheless evinced an unlikely passion for climbing mountains. It was she who, apparently quite deliberately, instilled in her son what became, at times, an almost obsessive desire to climb, explore and write about mountains.

One can find nothing and nobody raffish in either the Crawford or the Freshfield families of that time. They achieved their solid backgrounds through the Inns of Court, Parliament and the Shires. They had acquired small country estates and substantial town houses. In many guises they are described by Trollope, Dickens and Thackeray as well as Galsworthy, and although some of them may have been, then as now, less than honest, it cannot be imagined that they ever did anything frivolous, and certainly the Freshfields had great integrity and in no way conformed to the 'Soames Forsyte' image. They took silk, represented their wards in Parliament, believ-ing that in so doing they were discharging their obligation to their fellow man. However the fact that Freshfield money was new money would have been very apparent to the old establishment in the middle years of Victoria's reign. In those times there were several young lawyers who started their careers in the hurley-burley of the Freshfield chambers to fill, in due course, such august offices as that of Lord Chief Justice. Today the firm remains one of the leaders in the City. But young Freshfield's great-great-grandfather James had been a London clockmaker. Born in the Isle of Wight, as far as we know in a family that knew real poverty, he came to London hoping to make a living. The clockmaking failed and he was forced to spend some time in debtor's prison. All the more remarkable then, that one of his sons, having at first been apprenticed as a clockmaker, should have made the wise decision to have himself articled to a solicitor, Thomas Thompson. From there, while still in his twenties and having already married a woman who's family were without wealth or influence, he secured for himself a position with a leading City firm, Winter and Kaye. That there was influence is undoubted, for becoming associated with the Clapham Sect and intimately involved with their business and personal affairs became not only a stepping-stone for James himself, but brought further substantial business to an already important firm. It was this same sect which imparted the strict and somewhat joyless outlook on life upon which later generations would pour scorn. There was one surprising outcome which came about after James Freshfield had become senior partner and had given his name to the firm which was to become famous. As he acquired wealth he was able to purchase a substantial house north of the City where he was reported to have shown great good taste in the richness of its furnishings. It must have been from here that his sons and ultimately his great-grandson Douglas inherited their own particular sense of discrimination in such matters. James Freshfield lived to a great age, and it must be said that he was much liked and respected. Amongst his closest friends was Lord Stanhope and affectionate correspondence was carried between them over many years. In old age he developed a habit of expressing his gratitude for each year of life completed in a series of notes written to himself that are touching in their sincerity and sense of spiritual fulfilment.

Douglas's father, Henry Ray Freshfield, was born in February 1814, and married Jane Quentin Crawford in 1840. Henry Ray, as he was generally called, did well. After Charterhouse he joined Freshfield's, which had been, since his grandfather's day in 1770, officially connected with the Bank of England.[1] In a few years Henry Ray had been made joint solicitor to the Bank with his brother and was well on his way to a fortune. He wielded considerable influence. The future Lord Chief Justice Coleridge and the future Sir Fredrick Pollock were both set on their way by Henry Ray, both remaining friends with Douglas in later years. Coleridge became one of the regulars at the 'court' at Farringford, where Douglas himself was welcome mainly through his wife's connections with the coterie on the Island.

[1] During the Napoleonic wars the country's reserves of gold bullion had been severely depleted and it was decided to issue paper money rather than gold coins. There followed a spate of forgeries, with conviction for such an offence being death. The official solicitors to the Bank were thus engaged in a huge increase in litigation in the prosecution of these felons.

Henry Ray Freshfield

Henry Ray's father, like his grandfather also called James William, was Conservative member for Penryn from 1835 to 1841, and later for Boston. He kept meticulous accounts of his family income and expenditure, including annual comparative summaries of the amount of wine, sherry and port consumed, but otherwise he does not seem to have made any great public mark upon the world. His official position in The Firm made him the intimate of many of the great names, political and society, of the period, and at the same time he was directly involved in the fast increasing legal involvements of the Bank. We know that the silver buttons on the footmen's uniforms came to more than the annual stipend of the same foot-men, but his comments on the accounts do not mention this strange anomaly. All the same it is clear that the servants and dependants were not only well looked after, their medical ailments cared for, and the names of butlers, coachmen and cooks mentioned generously in wills, but there seems to have been a certain reserved friendship between the senior men of the staff and their masters in each genera-tion. Family documents show that they had laid claim to descent from a Norman family called Frescheville that had come over with King William, and they proudly displayed a coat of arms which proclaimed the fact. The newly enriched Freshfields apparently searched churches for tombs and records to discover their ancestry and prove themselves as well-rooted stock. But their family origins remain humble and their rise to affluence and positions of influence was rapid, having been mainly accomplished in a single generation. That Henry Ray's great-grandfather was the twice bankrupt London clockmaker who had spent time in the Fleet Prison was a matter that was passed over in the correspondence between the brothers of a later generation as they tried to prove descent from Baron Freshfield of Derby.

In early middle age Henry Ray decided the time had come to step back from the City and take up a new life as a country gentleman. From Lord Colchester he bought a substantial mansion and estate, Kidbrook Park near Forest Row in Sussex.

From his portrait, dressed as Sheriff in knee breeches, velvet coat and lace cravat, he certainly looked the part – a 'Washington Irving' figure, benevolent and avuncular. It may be dangerous to judge a man from his lengthy obituaries in the local press or *The Times*, but

The Morteratch Glacier and Bernina range by 'Jane Q'.

one hears nothing to his detriment from any quarter. He shouldered his local responsibilities – serving as magistrate and sheriff, and there is every reason to believe that he was a much loved and respected figure.

Poor man! It is hard indeed to imagine him torn from his comforts and exalted station in life at home, to suffer the indignities of flea-ridden shacks, icy torrents, obstinate mules and dangerous crevasses that constituted Switzerland at that time. Only the railway had arrived, not much else. The trains brought the English, especially the English mountaineer explorer, but the Swiss were only just beginning to make a profit from providing creature comforts.

'Jane Q', as the whole family came to know her, was a tall, big-boned woman with the determination, courage and willpower that reflected her highland ancestry. She ruled her household as a general in the field, entertained her husband's associates and probably frightened the servants and tradesmen. But once or twice a year, taking her indulgent and for the most part unprotesting husband with her, she entrained for the Alps. There, despising the more normal and seemly occupations for a woman of her class and nationality such as sitting beside some valley stream admiring the view, possibly reading a book of popular verse, she bullied husband, guides and peasants alike into acquiescing to her wishes. She spurned the meadows for glaciers snowfields and rocks in order to achieve pass and summit.

In one respect she did follow convention when on her alpine pursuits. Even in the days when most gentlewomen had little else to do but develop their latent talent as watercolourists, the few remaining examples of Jane Q's work show a sense of drama and scale that arrest the eye, and some would be pasted into their record of each holiday.

But Jane did more than climb mountains and paint. She wrote and published books describing her walks and climbs, encouraging others to follow – and this at a time when to 'live rough' would be considered unseemly. Mountaineering was mainly held to be an unsuitable sport for ladies, certainly amongst those of her background. There was the question of dress for one thing. No one could deny that sweeping skirts, hoops and flounces were most unsuited for scrambling over ice and rocks. At the same time, in an age when it was indecent to show an ankle, there was hardly any garment of a

A tail piece drawn by 'Jane Q'.

suitable nature that a lady could wear. Perhaps it was the very thought of such an unlikely apparition amongst the peaks and passes, and within the confines of primitive alpine huts, that might prove too much for the sensitive. What else could have prompted her to publish only under the sobriquet 'A Lady'.[1] From her diaries of those summer expeditions, some of them lasting two months or more, she later wrote in morocco-bound note books a narrative of their days. Beautifully written, without a single correction, illustrated with maps drawn by herself, and sometimes with water-colours, these precious records were an example that her son would follow, although without her meticulous care, as hers were the final product, whilst he was aiming for publication.

Jane Freshfield was not unique. There are familiar photographs of skirted ladies roped together, armed with tall alpenstock, bestride crevasses. Poor little Maria Paradis is discounted, having been forced unwillingly to the summit of Mont Blanc for what

[1] *Alpine Byways* – published by Longman, Green, Longman & Roberts – London 1861.

Jane Quentin Freshfield, 'Jane Q'.

might have been termed a publicity stunt. It was not until nearly
thirty years later, in 1838, that the first woman climbed to the
summit of that mountain for sport – Henriette d'Angeville. The
few English women that had started wandering in the higher
regions of the Alps, in the footsteps of the divines and academics
that had blazed the trail, called forth a good deal of criticism from
those who stayed impeccably at home, or visited the sanctuaries of
art in Florence and Venice. Perhaps Jane Q played a part, with her
unquestionable social standing, in encouraging a generation of
young 'ladies' to follow their brothers and cousins into the mysterious mountains, to suffer cold and near exhaustion and to share
with them the sublime views of sunlight, cloud and distant snows
that had been so raved about at home.

The Freshfield's son and only child was born on 27 April 1845,
and was christened Douglas William. He seems to have been a
solemn, serious-minded child with kindly manners and a repressed
sense of fun. In contrast with the later outpourings of his wife over
his own children and their doings, there is little to go on when it
comes to the nursery years and early schooling of Douglas. His
mother doted on him, but at the same time was determined to instil
in him a feeling for serious adventure, and the manly qualities of
stoicism and indifference to hardship. What little has survived of his
years at Eton and university in the form of his mother's notes and his
stilted letters could be interpreted as showing an over-serious nature
and a lack of close friends. In those days of rigid class this could be
accounted for at least in part by the Freshfield origins. This was the
time of the 'young bloods', with their cultivated extremes of accent,
love of hard riding and rough sport, which would have been anathema to the Freshfields. Though they were now inheritors of great
wealth it was the stern moral influence of the Clapham Sect that still
strongly affected their private as well as their public lives. This may
well account for Douglas's alienation from his young contemporaries and in later life he never became involved in any form of religious activity, though the pall that it cast remained with him.

It is difficult to believe that Jane Freshfield did not embark on a
carefully thought out pre-determined course in organizing his introduction and education in mountain craft which perhaps owed something to her Scots ancestry. It is hardly surprising therefore that he

should have been introduced to mountains at a very early age. At five he was taken to Snowdon, his first sight of a mountain; at seven to the Lake District; and at the age of nine to Chamonix and Mont Blanc. For the most part he seems to have enjoyed himself, even if he did weep from cold when being taken over the Gemmi.

Harder too to understand or discover in her past any clue as to why Jane Q had come to look upon mountain climbing with such passionate interest, given her class and conventional upbringing. It does not seem to fit her general regard for the position of a wife in all the other aspects of her life. Still more difficult is it to understand why she so single-mindedly devoted Douglas's early years to such a regime. But his mother's overbearing manner had its effect on the boy. He became shy and withdrawn, concealing feelings and not showing emotion. From then on and for the remainder of his life he found it difficult, and seldom made any attempt, to speak of his inner feelings; something of which he was himself aware and once or twice confessed to. But under the shyness there was cloaked an inherited core of iron determination tempered by a secret kindness to individuals. Even as a schoolboy he was prepared to argue with force, publicly if necessary. There was perhaps a tinge of arrogance in the way he learned to listen to an argument and then go his own way without bothering to state his case or allow dissension – a quality that was to cause a good deal of annoyance to others.

Jane Q had done her work well. Each year, with Douglas, the routes and objectives for the next annual visit to the mountains were plotted. Many years later Douglas once admitted that he often forgot faces, but after that first sight of Mont Blanc, he never failed to remember and recognize individual mountains.

But there was another side to him, with which his mother was out of sympathy, and which would later attract the attention of Gussie Ritchie. Their two quite different worlds were to brush together for the first time when Douglas went to Eton where the Ritchies had a number of connections. At the school it was soon apparent that he had a quick and scholarly mind; so much so that his father began to see for him a brilliant future at the bar. However within himself he had begun to develop more romantic feelings for poetry and literature, tinged with the scholarly colourings of classical Greek that were fashionable at the time. In the end his rare outbursts of emotion could only be given expression through the medium of poetry. In a letter from his headmaster at Eton to his father his scholarly and literary interests were praised, as well as his attainments as head of his house.

But away from school it was his mother's passion that dominated. The early visits to the mountains could hardly be described as climbing expeditions, though they explored many of the lesser known higher valleys and passes, and ascended some of their well-known and easier peaks. They attempted nothing, as Mrs Freshfield says, that might be deemed unfeminine on her part, or which would place undue responsibility on their guides and companions. However there were unscheduled excitements, sometimes provided by unbroken horses hired by opportunist villagers. But sprains were effectively cured by the arnica which Mrs Freshfield always carried, and they seem never to have been the worse for their mishaps. Henry Freshfield suffered for this indulgence of his wife and son. More than once he was personally unlucky, and even more often he was himself a horrified audience to the antics of his little family. They were usually accompanied by Michael Couttet, one of the best veteran guides of the time, who was generally charged with giving Douglas his training in mountain craft. On one occasion poor Henry watched in helpless alarm as his wife and son were propelled down the Titlis in a glissade that seemed to hurl them directly towards a crevasse below. Real danger was never far away. Three Englishmen were killed on a route that the Freshfield party had travelled only a few hours before.

Throughout the years 1854 to 1862 these family tours continued, but during that short time interest in mountain climbing had increased almost to fever pitch. English lawyers, school masters and professional men of all kinds roamed the Alps in search of virgin peaks and passes against which to test their skill. Like big game hunters they raced each other for the most prized trophies, plotting and planning in secret to steal a march over rivals, especially if they were German. To us there is a powerful smell of arrogance in the way the English made the Alps their playground. These shabbily dressed men of letters and academia assumed sway over the natives and regarded this country as their prior right. But the schoolboy Freshfield read of their exploits with mounting interest and impatience, longing to make his mark before it was too late. Already in 1857 had come the foundation of the Alpine Club under the presidency of John Ball, and notwithstanding the primitive inns, the inaccessibility through lack of railways, and even, in many parts, roads and carriages, the mountain peasants began to get used to Englishmen who appeared suddenly in their midst, coming from regions far above, supposed to be inhabited only by ghosts and spirits. In the end, of course, those same peasants would turn the situation to their great advantage and wreak their revenge.

There remained a singular prize for an aspiring schoolboy mountaineer. In 1863 Douglas was just eighteen and Chamonix was still little more than a cluster of houses round the church, though it is true that there were one or two large new hotels, standing isolated in the midst of the river plain, dwarfed as today by the highest ranges in France and Switzerland. At that time there had still been less than thirty recorded ascents of the summit of Mont Blanc, and every fresh attempt was the subject of intense interest and speculation in the town, amongst the inhabitants, the guides, and visiting climbers. To ascend the mountain – the highest in the Alps and in Europe – while the number of successful attempts was still in low figures, was a matter of moment. Here was a worthy chance to throw off the mother's apron strings, or rope, and make a manly expedition, and at the same time achieve the record of being the first schoolboy to reach the prized summit.

Douglas had never shown interest in any of the usual field sports, nor in any of the outdoor activities of his contemporaries at school. In appearance he was tall but somewhat ungainly, and although he had never suffered any illness he did not look particularly strong. The impression is that he was studious, and although not unpopular, he did not share many of the pursuits and ambitions of his peers. His father's intention that he should read law did not enthuse him in the least. However, a number of the younger masters at Eton showed more than a passing interest in the new craze for mountain exploration and climbing, as did a number of his contemporaries, and there is evidence that he not unnaturally wanted to impress his school in the sphere in which he had special prowess and opportunity.

Today, when children under ten are wafted to the very tops of mountains, and use what were once the almost unattainable heights as a playground, it is an effort to imagine the conditions that prevailed in the middle of the twentieth century. Chamonix was gaining popularity, and several large hotels had been built, but it was still an outpost. A mountain climb started at the very foot – sometimes not much above sea level. There was no cable car or other means of transport to convey the climber to the place of final assault. Conditions were similar to those that now exist in far remoter parts of the world. Apart from the ice axe, rope and alpenstock, climbing equipment was non-existent, and protective clothing was on a par with that of a gamekeeper or country sportsman in England. In Europe today, the climber with all his specialized equipment seeks out the most difficult and most challenging routes. The art of mountaineering then was to plan the safest and most sure way of achieving the desired goal.

Another great spur to the mountain explorer was the scientific one. Not only was the opening of the ranges of remote regions geographically interesting, but a whole catalogue of other physical sciences were at their fascinating beginning. How had the mountains themselves been formed? What caused glaciers? How fast, and why, did they move? The industrial revolution had given the men of a new intellectual class the chance to question and explore many of the till then unsuspected aspects of their surroundings. To some extent this meant that the new members of the Alpine Club could take their pleasure with serious intent, and it was this same seriousness which was the hallmark in the planning and execution of the major expeditions which were conducted, for whatever reason, in the period.

Mrs Freshfield herself put the whole ethos in a nutshell, and incidentally sheds a little light on her motives in giving Douglas the upbringing she did, when she wrote: 'The higher regions of the Swiss Alps have been, not ineptly, called "the playground of England", where the energy, enterprise and endurance of [her grown-up sons] find ample scope for exercise amidst "Peaks, Passes, and Glaciers;" the pursuit of health and manly amusement being, in many well known instances combined with a keen appreciation of the beauties of nature, and the enthusiastic devotion to scientific research, and the study and development of the long unexplored mysteries of creation, which present themselves in the world of eternal ice and snow.'[1]

[1] Michel Couttet accompanied the Freshfields during Douglas's childhood, and was a famous veteran of the mountains. When he died in 1887 Freshfield wrote, as was his custom, a poem in his honour. Couttet was the father of Ruskin's famous guide, Joseph.

But these days of exclusivity were already numbered. The railways would move further and further into the mountain ranges; roads were being extended and hotels built. On every visit Douglas and his mother remark on the opening of new inns in higher and more convenient positions to ease access to hitherto remote areas. The local people were about to cash in on their until then unrecognized national asset. Soon it would be the package tour bringing thousands rather than a few dozens, and also bringing many differing nationalities. And, horror of horrors, the Swiss themselves might actually consider trying to achieve the summit of one of their own mountains on their own behalf and not as guide and porter to English gentlemen. So young Douglas was following, rather than setting, an example. But it was near enough to the start of the whole growth of the sport for him to be familiar with the writings and activities of the pioneer heroes of the day.

Seven years before, when climbing with his mother, Douglas had met a young guide who was to become the lifelong friend and companion of nearly all his expeditions. Close by the path leading out of Chamonix to Mont Blanc was the cottage where François Joseph Devouassoud lived. Strong, swarthy and capable, every year he was to await the arrival of his friend, who later would often bring with him his wife and children. Sometimes the broad shouldered mountaineer would carry one or other of the latter on his back, to picnic in the high meadows. It was to Freshfield's immense credit that, unlike most of his contemporary climbers, he never treated François as a mere servant. Together they were to range far beyond the Alps – François being the first alpine guide ever to do so. They would share hardship and difficulty with stoicism and, on François part, not a little panache.

The story of the Chamoniard guides was already a long and distinguished one. In the middle of the previous century, and before the French revolution, the nearest centre of civilization was Geneva, well within sight of the highest snows. But the inhabitants showed no enthusiasm to penetrate any further into the valley of the Arve than Sallanches and certainly not for pleasure. The area around Chamonix in its narrow valley was isolated by its huge enclosing mountains and glaciers and approachable only by the worst of tracks. The people of the village were pestered by the so called 'bohemians' – robber gangs that roamed the forests. Freshfield tells us in his life of the philosopher and mountain traveller, Horace Benedict de Saussure: 'Chamonix was thought of at Geneva, as far as it was thought of at all, as a forbidding district inhabited by a peasantry of a more or less uncouth, if not dangerous, disposition' In 1741 it was a party of young Englishmen who made a foray into the region and made known the 'miracles of nature' to be discovered in Savoy. The door to Chamonix was opened; more and more travellers found their way to the foot of the giant glaciers and the lower regions of Mont Blanc itself. The peasants of the village found a new method of making a reasonable living that far exceeded the precarious trade in butter on which they had relied in the past. The families of the early guides developed through many generations a reputation for professionalism and skill that was and is unrivalled. The descendants of the guides that accompanied de Saussure, Paccards, Devouassauds (five of them) and four Balmats in 1784 were familiar to climbers throughout the next century. Familiarity with a mountain can never breed contempt, Mont Blanc certainly not excepted. François once remarked to Freshfield: 'One is always content to be back safely from Mont Blanc'. Freshfield himself tells of a later climb on that same mountain: 'I shall not forget a morning of storm on the Aiguille du Gouter when, wrapped in Scotch plaids, W. F. Donkin and I rushed down the cliffs through mists which, urged by a southwest gale, raced past us in a wild procession'.

However, on this occasion the arrangement had already been made that the expedition, which was to start with the crossing of the Col du Geant, was to be in the charge of the family's regular guide to date, Couttet. For this first phase there were to be two more Englishmen, Mr Dodson and Captain Campaign as well as François. They arrived in Chamonix without mishap, though they apparently had to deal with some fairly tricky work on the glacier.

For several years now, when exploring the region with his mother, they had together kept meticulous journals of their travels. Douglas wrote the narrative, and drew the mountain ridges from the vantage points they reached, while his mother provided illustrations in watercolour. Rather in the manner of a scrapbook, they would also include picture postcards of famous views, as well as the occasional photograph. Although this adventure was done without his mother, the illustrated narrative was still produced and is remarkable for the maturity of its style, its accuracy and the power of description. Of the start of the journey over the Col du Geant he wrote: 'There was no moon as we walked up the valley past La Saxe, and the great battlements we hoped to surmount towered grimly in front, with their turrets seeming to rise far away among the stars. Soon the moon rose, throwing a cold gleam over the icy skirts of the "Monarch", and bringing out into sharp relief the dark crags of his satellites.' Here already we find the mixture of drama and helpful guide lines that in his later writings gave, and still give, so much pleasure to followers in his footsteps.

In this same narrative we find also the well developed sense of the English chauvinist: 'and the third (party) of a German professor and his two attendants. The professor was a most comical figure, being as thin as a lathe, with long fair hair streaming down his back; and, although he had ascended Piz Morteratsch in the Bernina district, he did not look much fitted for hard climbing.' German attempts at mountaineering came in for ridicule more than once in those early years.

They waited quietly making their final arrangements, joining forces with François and securing the services of a porter. The latter had already been to the summit five times in that season – one wonders whether these ascents figured in the official count of successful attempts. They kept their intentions quiet so as not to arouse speculation and unwelcome interest.

The weather on the day selected for their attempt was unsettled, but they did not consider it bad enough to prevent their going at least as far as the 'Grandes Mulets'. By then of course several routes to the summit were well known, and there was little in any fresh ascent to excite modern interest. They reached the rough hut near the 'Grandes Mulets' in six hours – quite good going then or at any time. They were in for an uncomfortable night as, in spite of the normal convention, previous parties visiting the hut had failed to leave any wood, and the quantity which their party had gathered on the lower slopes was quite inadequate. They lit the stove and placed the two covers alternately on the floor as a foot warmer until the supply ran out. It had begun to snow and the wind whistled through the numerous cracks in the walls, which meant that they had to pace

Hotel Imperial des Grandes Mulets.

to and fro for the rest of the night trying to keep warm with the help of a bottle of brandy. However, when they finally emerged at a little before four o'clock the weather had improved slightly and the guides seemed to think it possible that they might succeed. They roped together with François leading, 'tenderly nursing a most disreputable Guy Fawkish-looking lantern', and made their way over the slippery rocks, powdered by a fresh fall of snow. Later, in daylight, as they climbed the last steep ascent to the Grand Plateau a tremendous avalanche crashed from the ice cliff to the side of them, and thousands of tons hissed across the plain to the very tracks they had left only a few minutes before.

They faced a very strong and bitterly cold wind as they cut steps up the Mur de la Cote. Here the unfortunate porter declared that they would all suffer frostbite and that he would go no further. The

The Eton schoolboy who climbed Mont Blanc.

others however felt that the summit was now attainable and told him to remain and await their return – not an inviting prospect and an invitation that he ignored.

Douglas himself describes the final stages of this, his first memorable climb. 'On the top of the "Mur" lies a small plateau, and then the slope again steepens, forming the "calotte" or final dome of the mountain. Up this we climbed slowly, in the teeth of the wind, which, however, was not as violent as on the "Mur". By kicking my feet well into the hard snow at every step, and keeping my hands in my pockets, I did not feel the cold painfully. Progressing steadily in this way without any halts we passed the Petites Mulets, a group of rocks which protrude from the snow, the highest on this side of the mountain.

'I now for the first time felt confident of success, for the violence of the wind had been such that I feared it might increase and become unfaceable; but our work was now done. Looking back, the crest of Mont Maudit had sunk beneath our feet, and in a few minutes more we were all standing on the narrow saddle-shaped ridge which forms the actual summit of Mont Blanc. It was just half past ten; so that we had been six hours, exclusive of halts, from the Grandes Mulets. It was far too cold however to linger on the crest; so descending a few feet on the south side, we sat down on our alpenstocks, sheltered from the northern blast, and rubbed our hands with brandy, whilst we gazed on the wondrous panorama outspread beneath us.'

The return down the mountain was a long, uncomfortable grind; not dangerous nor as difficult as the Col du Geant. Douglas had acquired a very swollen and painful ear as a result of the cold wind and this prompted François to tell them of the tail of a spitz, the first canine climber to reach the summit. The dog had apparently been keen to be the first of the party to reach the summit and had trotted merrily ahead. However, as the dog climbed higher, the air grew colder, and its normally tightly curled tail had slowly unwound 'until it blew out in a stiff streamer, frozen, straight and hard as a poker.'

The party returned in triumph to Chamonix. Couttet 'levieux' regaled the more junior guides with tales of their suffering and hardship, and the next day the chief guide presented them with a 'highly coloured representation of a party on the summit, from which it might reasonably be inferred that the great object of the ascent was to drink brandy.' Thus ended the thirty-third ascent of Mont Blanc, and the first by a schoolboy. Couttet now considered that this portage had completed Douglas's mountain education, and no doubt, back in England, his mother knew with pride that the young eagle had fulfilled all her expectations and would henceforth soar in skies of his own choosing. Certainly at this point she seems to have abandoned more adventurous 'rambles', contenting herself with less strenuous expeditions and the duties related to her husband's home and position.

On his return to Eton a public announcement of this achievement was made before the whole school. Douglas was embarrassed, but his mother was no doubt, rightly, delighted.

CHAPTER 2

In stark contrast to the relatives and their friends that he was later to acquire through marriage, there is a singular absence of the normal trivia that would generally be part of the life of a wealthy young man, just left Eton, and studying at Oxford. Though he did not have any desire to practise law, he apparently did not find the work at University particularly irksome or difficult. He belonged to literary societies, and took part in debates, but his enthusiasms were never more surely revived than when the prospect of returning to the mountains loomed seasonally nearer.

Oxford however provided him with a new circle of friends as keen on mountaineering as he was himself, amongst whom C. C. Tucker and, most importantly, A. W. Moor were to remain friends and companions for many years. Some idea of the affection in which Douglas held the University is shown in a letter he wrote to Augusta Ritchie when visiting Tucker's rooms after Douglas himself had returned from his first visit to the Caucasus. 'I have been arraying myself in a huge sleeved bachelor gown, dining at high tables, drinking wine in oakpanneled (*sic*) common rooms and reflecting on all that I have scaped by not having worked harder and perhaps scrambled into a fellowship. It seems oddly familiar to come among the old "shop" again and hear people talking as if they were quite excited about it, of Plato's syntactical method, or the last new translation of the *Ethics*. Tucker has got very nice rooms in college looking out on the High Street …' and he rambles on about old friends, a much respected don who has died, and the antics of freshmen punting on the river, in a manner that he never seems to have done about the Eton that his housemaster had once unsuccessfully tried to persuade his father that he should not leave a year early, an argument that Douglas won.

The fever to accomplish 'firsts' was still raging, and Douglas was ready to be swept along with its tide and secure his place in the record as an alpine pioneer. In time this mode of mountaineering was to lose its appeal, and he would eventually become an opponent of those who tackled the mountains in a frame of mind that had more to do with athletics than with exploration. This first season he arranged to meet François and two English friends and planned a very formidable tour. The weather throughout was kind to them and they accomplished a considerable list of first ascents. They worked their way from Thonon on the shores of Lake Geneva, to Trente; they climbed Monte Rosa, Alphubeljoch, Rheinwaldhorn, and made a first crossing and ascent of Monte Sissone. Of this whole extensive tour perhaps the most interesting section was the ascent, the first ever, of La Presanella, if for no other reason than that it was the first time that the Italian Dolomites had been suggested as a possible alternative to the well trodden routes of the Swiss, French, and German heights.

In his collected and bound story of the whole expedition his two companions are referred to cryptically as W and B. Soon after they had started their adventure they were faced with the Mer de Glace where B, Freshfield writes icily 'insisted on larking over all the crevasses that came our way – an amusement to which green hands are rather given, one hazardous to yourself and disagreeable to your companions when the performer is one who does not always look before he leaps.' B comes in for a good lecturing from both guide and leader in the evening. However B seems to be somewhat accident

Presanella from the Pizzo della Fare.
1865.

Douglas Freshfield's sketch of La Presanella from the start of their climb.

prone while he remains with them for the first part of their journey, to the extent that whilst daydreaming on the march he manages to walk directly into a wall and knock himself flat on the ground. Falling debris from high mountain slopes gave the appearance of being aimed directly at him and on one occasion he had a very narrow escape when a large boulder passed close by his head with the velocity of a cannon ball.

Their expedition was not without its moments of danger, the lesser being having to share a mountain shepherd's supper of half cooked boiled marmot, and, what was worse, having to pay through the nose for it. But one of the greater being as they climbed the 12,800 foot Piz Palu – a first ascent. They had been joined by Fluri, a veteran mountain guide who it appears managed to tease the younger François, but by way of keeping the peace allowed François to choose the route to the summit. The way down occasioned much step cutting and rope work and if at this point Freshfield makes light of the fact that his alpenstock is knocked from his hand and slides away over the lip of a crevasse, the illustrated version of his privately printed book of the journey has at this point a full page engraving of a most terrifying crevasse, the jaws of which, framed with icy teeth, hang over the party. Whether this represents this actual occasion or was inserted to indicate an approximation is hard to tell, but it certainly looks impressive. In the end the redoubtable François is lowered by rope to retrieve the errant pole.

Freshfield was always to remember the climbing of Presanella as the high point of the tour. The country track up which they had climbed to the border of the Austrian Empire suddenly became a military highway at the frontier, and in the pouring rain that had accompanied them all day, they made their way to the Tonale Hospice, in the hope of finding somewhere to dry their clothes and obtain a night's lodging. They discovered, however, that the single room was crowded with workmen who were constructing a neighbouring fort, and they had to sit in a corner in their steaming clothes and wait until these men had been fed and had departed to a barn to sleep. Englishmen were still rare in the district and they were civilly treated by the men as they waited, lit by the lurid flames, eagerly watching the progress of their supper. François elected to sleep in the barn, but in the morning complained bitterly that the snores of the

workmen had kept him awake. Getting dressed proved equally difficult as they were forced to dive repeatedly under the blankets to
preserve their modesty as the servant girls kept dashing through the
climber's room, there being no other way from the kitchen to the
front of the house.

As the weather looked none too settled they decided to continue
down the valley to Pizzano in order to try to discover the best route
to their mountain. They passed a formidable blockhouse mounting
seven guns, and shortly afterwards the mists parted to reveal a
snowy peak at the head of the glen to their right. The lower slopes
were clothed in forest which reached as high as a considerable glacier. They decided to see if there was a shepherd's hut at the top edge
of the trees from which they could make their attempt on the following day. When they reached Pizzano they had trouble with the
police, who declared that François, having no passport, must return;
but as the route to the mountain lay, for the first part, up the track to
the frontier, they merely had to pretend to comply with the order.

While they breakfasted they made certain enquiries, and were told
that a 'German professor' had essayed the mountain the year before
and had declared it impossible. The local peasant who had accompanied the professor was found, and agreed to lead them to the
mountain. By midafternoon they had secured provisions, and, in
weather that had improved, set off.

As they had hoped they found a shepherd's shelter; a rough shed
open at one side, festooned with sheep corpses hung to dry over a
smouldering fire. The three shepherds that were in residence were
happy to make room for them, one of them being out on patrol at
all times for fear of the bears that were known to be prowling
around. François seemed fated to spend disturbed nights in Austria,
for while Douglas and his companion slept on a bed of hay, François
had spotted a veteran goat staring down at them from the loft, eerily
lit up by the flames. He scrambled up, and persuaded the goat to
settle beside him and keep him warm. Later in the night his companion became boisterous, quarrelled with him, and hoofed the poor
climber out.

They started at three in the morning, following the Pizzano porter,
who had previously accompanied the professor, up a track that led
along the west side of the glacier to where it finally gave out amongst

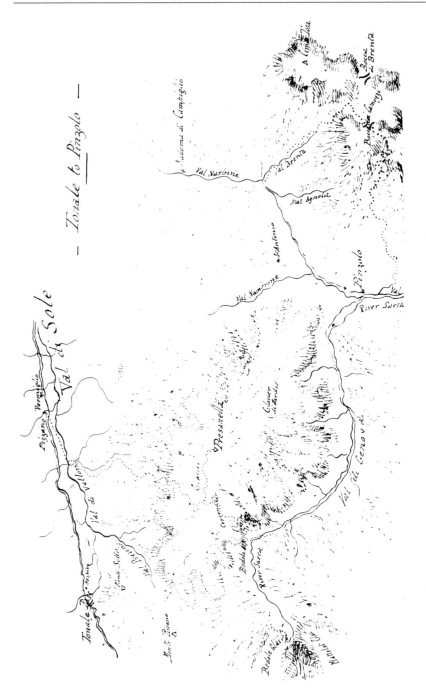

The climb of Presanella and the Val di Genova drawn by Jane Q.

the rocks. After scrambling to the right through the rocks for some distance Douglas decided, against the advice of the porter, that their best route was on the glacier, and led his party back on to its surface. They had to cut some steps before they reached fairly smooth going, where they paused to eat breakfast. After a break and some discussion, the ascent was resumed and half an hour's brisk walk brought them to the col at the head of the glacier. Here they stowed their knapsacks and provisions, taking enough for refreshment on the summit.

The next stage consisted of steep névé intersected with crevasses, but eventually they gained the ridge that encloses the Nardis glacier to the south-east, and forms the wall that links the twin summits when seen from the northern side. Progress along the wall proved treacherous and further steps had to be cut. With their alpenstocks they dislodged the coping of snow that hung over the precipice sending it whirling away down to the glacier a thousand feet below. François was in the lead cutting steps when eventually, with relief, they stepped onto a small plateau below the final peak. 'We cut across a steep ice slope,' Freshfield afterwards wrote, 'and in five minutes stood upon some broken rocks at its farther end, which ran up the southern face of the mountain. Here we had to wriggle around an awkward rock which required some circumspection; it was too much for our porter, who had thrown off the rope and was now fain humbly to beg to be reattached. Having tied the man up again, we hauled away and got him half way over; there he stuck, clinging on to the rocks like a distressed starfish.' Eventually they freed him and persuaded him up the last rocks to the summit; he must certainly have felt that he had earned the twenty francs that the trip paid him, though he did have a tale to tell that would make him the hero of the village for years to come.

The ascent had been made from the north side of the range, and having bid farewell to their brave guide, and spent some time admiring the views and consuming their lunch, they set off to descend, on the southern side, into the Val Di Genova which is encircled to the north, west, and south by Presanella and the skirts and glaciers of Adamello, to be climbed a year later by Douglas and a party which included a colourful porter, a poacher by trade, and a real dandy who carried a brush for his whiskers and a watch chain decorated with silver mounted charms. This narrow, beautiful and unspoiled valley remains much the same to this day, having been turned into a nature reserve. The Alps are untouched by the ubiquitous scars of ski lifts; the chalets still the summer abodes of mountain shepherds and drovers, and the icy torrent of the glacial waters yet tumble untrammelled down the five giant steps that mark each stratum of the rocky descent. 'Diverging a few yards from the path, we gained a spot where the Sarca, rushing down over the rocks, suddenly sprang boldly into the air, and was lost to sight in a cloud of foam. A bridge of one unsmoothed log crossed the stream at the edge of the precipice, looking the more slender and precipitous from its strange position'. It may not be the same log, but it's exact position and its successor are easily identifiable today. It was three hours hard walking to the village of Pinzolo at the end of the Val, and here we discover just how rare such visitors were, especially descending, as Douglas did, from the other side of their dominant mountain. They passed the little church of St Stelano standing on its rocky buff, and where, a few years later on a subsequent visit, Douglas was to translate the long inscription beneath an unusual fresco from the Latin, for the benefit of the villagers as well as their priest, who until that time had no idea of the historical story of Charlemagne in the locale represented in the mural.

In Pinzolo they discovered a typical mountain inn kept by Signor Bonapace. A deep dark archway leading off the street led them up a stone stairway into a dark hall crowded with benches and tables. 'Out of it open still gloomier inner chambers. In one a feint glimmer of bright copper, a sound of hissing, and a bustling of Martha's, reveal the kitchen; in the other at the foot of an enormous family bed, leaning over a table sits the master of the house.' Sleeping accommodation was a large dormitory which boasted two washbasins, apparently considered 'to fulfil every possible requirement for night accommodation'. Today the great-great-grandson presides over a large comfortable modern hotel not so very far distant from the site of that of his forebears. The present Signor Bonapace advertises the fact that it was that first visit of Douglas Freshfield, and his subsequent lyrical descriptions of Pinzolo and its surroundings, that first opened the remote valley to visitors, and established its prosperity. Over the years Douglas and his wife and family returned many times to stay at the new Bonapace Hotel, and wander in the unspoiled meadows along the sparkling streams. However beneficial to the local economy the rapid development of the winter ski resorts may be, summer walkers today have to climb a long way to find unscarred meadows, unless it be in the nature reserves that have at last been established.

The careful notebooks of his past travels and climbs bore fruit. On his return in 1864 Douglas wrote a book describing his adventures for that season. The main object was to open the way for others to discover the same delights, or, if unable to do so, as with all travel books, share vicariously in the sights, sounds and discomforts as well as the pleasures of the way. Later in life Douglas was to describe the process of writing as a task which did not come naturally to him, and that he needed to go through the process of rewriting many times. The actual evidence we have does not bear this out in quite the fashion he indicates. It seems that the method he adopted remained the same from the first of his books to the last. He would keep a rough journal in which he recorded the events of the day, and make summit sketches of neighbouring ranges if they were sufficiently novel to him, and periodically these notes were transferred to a 'tidy' version. There was another important step in that the 'tidy' version was quite often substituted by letters home, in the early days to his mother, and later to his wife and children. Considerable portions of these letters appear almost word for word in the published books which followed, or in articles in the *Alpine Journal* and the *Journal of the Royal Geographical Society*. Obviously, in his major works concerning his visits to the Caucasus and the Himalayas, events on the ground are described in very much of the original wording.

His first full length climbing and travel book appeared after his return in 1864. It was privately published, and illustrated in the same 'scrap-book' manner as the earlier journals of the expeditions with his mother. Although gauche in some places and a little bombastic in others, it conveys clearly his ability to create the full flavour and feeling of remote high places, the people in them and the detailed topography. It shows traces of the style he was to develop so successfully in his informal guides to remote walking and climbing in the more accessible areas, in such books as *The Italian Alps* and *Below The Snowline*, as well as his more important contributions to the literature of serious exploration.

By the time he had returned from the Caucasus for the first time he had developed a good eye for detail, and the power to transpose this to the page; but most interesting was his highly developed 'sense of location.' He was never, so far as is apparent, totally lost, except briefly when unable to see his way out of the forests of Abkhasia. He only had to set foot on a summit to recognize every surrounding peak and range; every gorge and valley, glacier and snowfield. Whilst summits, as challenges to be met and conquered, still fascinated him, it was the whole topography of mountain landscape, and the desire to understand every hidden feature that was starting to take the upper hand. He developed the skill to 'read' the confusing jumble of ranges above and below, and thus deduce what must lie, even unseen, ahead. This skill would one day save the lives of himself and his whole party in the Himalayas

His appreciation of topography and his ability to convey this to others was very well illustrated in the year following the climbing of Presanella when he revisited the area and climbed to the summit of Adamello, which itself had been climbed for the first time ever the previous year by Von Sonklar. A collection of Freshfield's writings about his climbs and early walks in the Dolomites was published by Blackwood in their Mountaineering Library in 1937, three years after Freshfield's death in 1934 and consisted of his final and well polished versions of previous writings about the same, to him, much favoured region. For the armchair traveller it is naturally hard to appreciate the extent and quality of the view from Adamello without the aid of a map, but all the same the sweep and real visible distance on a good day are made vivid by his words: 'far away in the east we could trace the line of our wanderings from their very commencement. There were the dolomite peaks of Prinero, a little further the marmolata, pelmo, and the pyramidal Antelao; then the eye had only to leap the broad gap of the Pusteral to run over the Tauern from the Ankogel (above Gastein) to the Brenner. The Glockner was well defined as from Heiligenblut, only that its snows were tinted an exquisite rose colour, as if they had been made prisoner of a sunset. The Ortler and Berina, from which we were nearly equidistant, made a fine

The route across the Caucasus.

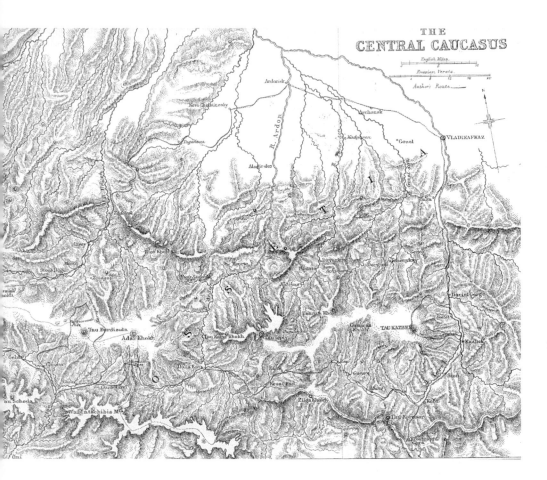

show of snow and ice; still closer at hand we surveyed the great snowfields of our own group, overlooked by our two rivals, the Presanella and Care Alto. To the south lay a labyrinth of granite peaks and ridges, separating the many glens which ran up from Val Camonica. This great valley was visible for miles, and the eye rested with pleasure on its fields of Indian corn and chestnut woods, until led on by the white thread of road to the blue waters of Lago d'Iseo basking between bright green hills. When tired of this prospect we could take a bird's-eye view of the Valtelline, a long green trench of cultivation, heat, and fertility, closed at its lower end by the mountains round the head of Lago di Como. These were crowned by a coronet of snowy peaks, which, so clear was the air, almost seemed part of them, but which were in reality the Pennine giants encircling Zermatt. Most notable of all was the splendid pyramid of the Matterhorn, seen in its sharpest aspect, towering immediately over the Weisstor. In another direction far away across the shoulders of lower hills the wide waters of Lago di Garda glowed like burnished metal beneath the cloudless sunshine, while further still the mounds of Solferino were faintly seen through the haze of heat.

'At such moments the climbers toil is richly paid. Over his head stretches the pure vault of the sky, below lies a vast expanse of earth; the mountain top seems poised between the two, a point in the centre of a hollow globe. From the refulgent snows of the neighbouring peak, glittering with such excess of light as to be scarcely endurable, the eye turns for relief to gaze up into the intense colour of the zenith, or wanders over miles of green and countless changes of blue distances to the saffron of the extreme chain which forms the link between earth and heaven. ... At such moments even the dullest soul shares with inarticulate emotion the feelings which poets have put into words for all ages.'

Such descriptions were echoed at a later date in a poem 'View and Vision' composed after a night sleeping on a mountain side in the Caucasus. While somewhat spoiled for modern taste by numerous classical illusions as was fashionable at the time, there are flashes of genuine intensity of feeling which these cold and remote heights inspired in such an otherwise reserved and generally unresponsive man.

By the middle sixties members of the Alpine Club were rapidly reducing the numbers of maiden peaks and passes that were left to be climbed. In many cases they were searching out new routes to otherwise conquered peaks; and often too there was argument as to who had actually climbed a 'first'. This being the case, imagine the consternation when two guides, Jenni and Fluri, made three first ascents on their own, snaffling these endangered species for themselves! Young Freshfield was a newly elected member of the Alpine Club and decided to fire off his salvo. 'The Gamekeeper', he wrote, 'who should choose the moment when his employer's game was nearly exhausted, to go out by himself and shoot the few remaining pheasants, would, it seems to me, be guilty of an offence venial in comparison to that of these guides.' A ludicrous statement today, but at the time to his readers the analogy was a good one.

There was another aspect to the roamings that took place during his years at University, apart from the fact that he was gaining mountain experience. He had developed a strong bond with François Devouassoud. They generally climbed alone now, roped together, sometimes the magnificent François cleaving the way, at others the tall wiry Freshfield. They forged the link between them that can only grow between two people when each often holds the life of the other in his hands. The pair had begun to acquire something of a reputation among the younger climbers in the Alps and Dolomites, the latter area being one which Freshfield was making very much his own. François, for his part, became devoted to the young man who liked to write poetry in the inn at night. He came to appreciate this strange obsession with summit views which had become so marked that on one occasion, while Douglas sat in the shelter of a rock staring happily and silently over the panorama below, a guide of another party pointed him out as a *'pauvre monsieur, bien fatigué!*

In 1866 Douglas and François had their revenge on the two renegade guides Jenni and Fluri. The two young men had crossed the Eschia pass from Engadine to Bergun. There they cast speculative looks at a number of surrounding peaks, including the Tinzenhorn, then a maiden peak enjoying a considerable reputation. They were undecided what to do when Jenni and Fluri suddenly appeared leading a distinguished member of the Swiss Alpine Club, who had engaged them to take him up the Tinzenhorn. Freshfield and

François at once decided that they could not stand back and watch such a prize carried off under their noses, and therefore also announced their intention of making an attempt on the morrow.

As luck would have it the Swiss and his party got away first, Douglas having had difficulty in obtaining their hotel bill. But being a very rapid walker, he and François, and a local they had engaged to guide them as far as the foot of the mountain, caught the other party in half an hour. François was all for racing ahead at once, but he was restrained while they watched the opposition survey the mountain in a leisurely manner through a telescope. From this angle the Tinzenhorn appeared as an enormous irregular pyramid, 'the final peak looked almost vertical and exceedingly difficult'.

They all ate breakfast as one party at the foot of the mountain, and then, François and Douglas in the lead, started to ascend by means of sloping ledges that led towards the ridge of a buttress on the eastern side. Wild chamois, a mother and kid, were on the path ahead of them and were evidently unable to find any other way of getting away from the humans, for they were eventually to go right over the summit. François used them as an excuse to tease the Swiss, who was already falling behind, exhorting him to *'venire seulement!'* At the point where the ridge of the buttress joined the face of the mountain they were forced to have recourse to a series of ledges of about two feet wide over a precipice at least 1,500 feet deep. On this face they halted, roped, drank a glass of wine, and allowed the other party to catch them. From then on it became very hard work.

'First we wriggled up two very steep chimneys, where hands and knees were both useful, then came the *mauvais pas* of the day, where, instead of working up a gully with rocks on both sides, we went slantingly up and round a projecting crag with nothing but air on the outside. We were enabled to point out to the Swiss a way of avoiding this difficulty.' One feels that this was round one to François and Douglas. 'More chimneys followed separated by sloping ledges, the general inclination of this side of the mountain being certainly a good deal steeper than the rocks leading to the saddle of the Shreckhorn. Once and again we came to absolute walls and there was a momentary embarrassment as to where François might find any support by which to upheaval his considerable bulk.'

Some three hours from their last resting place Douglas and François scrambled along the cockscomb crest to the summit. There Douglas persuaded François not to mount the boulder that was the actual highest point, or to build the customary stone man. Instead they occupied the time reconnoitring a route down, and eating the remainder of their food. Presently, however, they grew anxious about the other party, and François went to see if he could make out what had happened to them; eventually they appeared in good order though somewhat crestfallen, though when Douglas pointed to the still unsurmounted rock saying 'See, Sir, there is the *"Allerhochste Spitze"*; it is still unclimbed' they rushed to it and straddled it in the traditional tableau of victory. This performance one feels definitely leaves the honours with Douglas and François.

For three summers the two roamed the mountains of central Europe, in particular those of Northern Italy, then far less well known than those of France and Switzerland; planning routes and testing ways, making and recording paths for others to follow: sometimes alone, sometimes in company with other older and more illustrious climbers. They met Mr Tucker in 1864 just before they climbed on several expeditions. Ten years later Douglas published his *Italian Alps* in which many of their more notable climbs and exploits are described; and he dedicated it to François Devouassoud, whom he described as 'My old friend [who] had a great deal too much imagination to be merely animally brave ...'

A popular book was to be one eventual fruit of all these wanderings, but it might well be asked why a wealthy young man with good brains should devote himself with such passion to this almost solitary sport. But things have not changed in modern times. The sport of mountain and rock climbing still thrives and is now the prerogative of all classes. But all the same Douglas was already looking for more meaningful reasons to indulge his great passion.

In appearance Douglas and François presented quite a contrast at this time. François the swashbuckler, broad, swarthy and extrovert looked and was as strong as an ox: Douglas, somewhat pale, had grown a moustache which failed to disguise but rather enhanced his receding chin. At first sight he looked deceptively unathletic, but he would quickly demonstrate that he was unusually fit and strong, and he remained so for the whole of his long life. The speed at which he walked was proverbial, and he was capable of great endurance and stoical indifference to discomfort.

At this point he was about to establish himself as something more than a wealthy young man who was able to carry his chosen hobby to extremes of self-indulgence.

Pigmy chalets in the Fellaria Alp.

CHAPTER 3

THE MOUNTAINS OF THE CAUCASUS – IN EGYPT – DEPARTURE FOR JAFFA – VIOLENT STORM CAUSES DIVERSION TO BEYRUIT – INLAND TO JERUSALEM – CONTACT WITH NOMADIC ARABS – THE RUINS OF JERASH – THE SHEIKH OF SUF – REIYEH NOT A CITY ONCE INHABITED BY GIANTS – AT DAMASCUS – FROM SYRIA TO THE TIFLIS – BY RICKETY CART TO PERSIA – THE ABORTIVE ATTEMPT TO CLIMB ARARAT – CROSSING THE CENTRAL RIDGE OF THE CAUCASUS – ALLSOP'S PALE ALE IN THE VALLEY OF THE EREK

Kasbek is a mountain of romance and legend; perhaps one of the most fascinating of all the mountains in the world. It towers magnificently over the valley along which runs that most ancient of routes, the road under the wild, barbarous and then almost unknown Caucasus, out of Europe and into Asia. Sometimes it was known locally as 'Christ's Mountain' because of the legend that amongst its crags the elect may find a rope which leads to a holy cave where are preserved the cradle of Christ, the tent of Abraham, and other sacred relics – but it is more often remembered as the scene of the torture of Prometheus. It was certainly better known than its higher, though less dramatic neighbour, Elbruz.

These two great mountains, and the whole range of which they formed a part, offered a tremendous challenge to the young man who was now ready to turn his erstwhile sport to something of serious account; for often as these mountains might occur in the writings of the ancient world, of their form and extent, heights and inhabitants, practically nothing was known. Before Douglas Freshfield made his first visit, well known authorities were declaring the Caucasus as a single ridge of mountain; that its peaks were flat topped; that there were no glaciers, and so on. When after the publication of his book *The Central Caucasus and the Bashan* and his lecture to the Royal Geographical Society, there were those, as is the habit of armchair explorers, who were unwilling to surrender their theories.

Shelley was nearer the truth when his Prometheus cries:

> The crawling glaciers pierce me with the spears
> Of their moon-freezing crystals, the bright chains
> Eat with burning cold into my bones.

Douglas came down from University College, Oxford, having taken Honours in Law and History, and without delay sought permission from his parents to be allowed to take the best part of a year off during which to undertake an expedition to this remote range. As his plan was to start in January, too early in the season to commence journeying into the mountains, he decided to spend the intervening months in Egypt and the Holy Land. At this time, ten years before Gordon was to be besieged at Khartoum, it was fashionable for the discerning European and American in search of education, to explore the lower reaches of the Nile and its famous tombs and temples. The tourist trade was catered for and it was possible, without undue discomfort or danger, to hire craft on the river as well as make short excursions into the fringes of the desert.

In the meantime there were plans to be made, companions to be chosen and equipment purchased. He early arranged that François should accompany him, initially as personal servant, and later in his natural role as mountain guide, thus making François the first ever alpine guide to wield his axe beyond his native peaks. His other companions were to be his friend C. C. Tucker; and when they reached the mountains they were to be joined at Tiflis by A. W. Moor. Freshfield had been drawn into the company of both Moor and Tucker whilst they were all at Oxford. They were the first independent friends of his own and Moor especially was to share with him the same interests for the remainder of his life. By the time Moor was able to join the expedition Douglas was to be very glad of the extra company, as he declared that he had quite exhausted Tucker's powers of conversation. Actually relations between the two men were to become somewhat strained during the expedition. Tucker was preparing to study for the Bar, and during the course of their travels he had received a letter from his parents saying that arrangements for his being articled had been completed sooner than expected, and that he had better come home. No young man would want to leave an expedition with such exciting prospects before it had hardly begun, and anyway home and work seemed remote enough for him to say nothing to Freshfield and to write a letter to his parents saying that his companion forbade him to leave. At home there was consternation as the result: Tucker's parents called on Freshfield's and demanded that their son be released and sent home. Henry Ray wrote to his son demanding the reason for such high handed action, and poor Tucker's duplicity was revealed. However in the end all was well, extended leave was granted to Tucker, and Freshfield remained faithful to his chosen friend – even if he did find it necessary to tell him off at times. Tucker was at least a reliable and safe man on a mountain, nor was he likely to burst forth in prose and argument on return to England as others were prone to do; all of which was sufficient recommendation, even if he did in later years become the arch bore of Douglas's wife, children and entire social circle.

There was a busy fortnight, spent getting together the necessaries for the journey – which included a tent, waterproof saddlebags, a portable kitchen, and large quantities of Liebig's soup – and they left England on 4 January 1868. It was a very cold winter, even as far south as Marseilles the Rhone was frozen from bank to bank, and the fountains were festooned with icicles. From here they sailed in high excitement for Egypt, on the steamer *Port Said* 'with a miscellaneous batch of passengers, including two French officers who were going to Abyssinia, two directors of the Suez Canal, Gerome the painter, the Viceroy of Egypt's dentist, two missionary ladies bound for Jerusalem, and a party of Algerine Arabs bound for Mecca, who lay all day and night on deck, huddled in their cloaks'.

And then at last there was the Nile – and romance! Tropical nights under a great moon, and a lovely girl with a delightful singing voice; burning desert with lines of camels against the vast horizon, and the girl sitting on the knee of a sphinx laughing down at him. No wonder, so far from Jane Q, he lost his heart a little. Now we get the first sight of Douglas with a girl of his own age and he proved himself susceptible. These were the days when the code of Dr Arnold had been instilled in the hearts of every public schoolboy. Although it is easy to prove that there was hypocrisy in much of the male attitude towards women, still a young man who treated a young woman of his own class as anything other than the fair and weaker sex, was a bounder, a cad, or, in India, a poodle-faker. The majority of young men of Freshfield's background would abide by the rules, though there was naturally the occasional 'Steerforth', which Douglas certainly was not, especially with Jane Q looking over his shoulder. Thus when they joined accidentally with an American family, which included two pretty daughters, who, Douglas admits in a letter to his mother, made a very pleasant foreground to the tombs and temples, her stern concern exercised its influence on him even at such a distance. He was at pains to tell her that only a very mild and harmless flirtation was intended, and should any member of the party arrive home before him, she was not to believe all that she might hear. We must hope that we read correctly between the lines that the romance of Egypt by moonlight was all that it should have been. It is interesting that Douglas thought it politic to tone down some of his adventures for fear that his mother might think the whole project too dangerous. After one of his brushes with bandits in the Bashan he wrote: 'I am glad to think Tucker will not come [home] before me as I shall be spared the pain of contradicting the magnificent fictions he has been carefully elaborating about Persia, Bashan, etc. The amount of Bedouins he has slain with his own hands increases daily.'

But prosaic as his own descriptions of those same events when writing home might be, it is plain that they faced other dangers than that they might tumble from some mountain. At least as far as the Nile was concerned they fared no worse than to get lost by night when ashore, and stand, with their young lady companions, in danger of missing the boat. On another occasion, wishing to witness the dawn, they spent a nervous night among the sinister chambers and columns of a ruined temple; but they were disturbed by nothing worse than dogs and were rewarded by a glorious desert sunrise, and an exchange of courtesies in the tent of a shepherd.

Alas and all too soon it was time to bid farewell to soft nights and romances, and, requested to write something in the book of his special friend, Freshfield wrote a touching poem, which, while it early states that 'saints we leave at home' must have unfaltering devotion – presumably the iron conscience of Jane Q – nevertheless the relaxed feeling of a special gaiety in the relationship comes across. Here are some of the lines:

No more in Pharaoh's porches
   We'll wander where you please,
Or grope through tombs with torches,
   Or climb on Sphinx's knees;
No more time's flight forgetting,
Watch the sun's slow setting
And the first moonbeams fretting
   The old Pyramides.

Tomorrow's dawn will scatter
   The crew that's here today;
Some lives will seem much flatter;
   But you! – I hear you say,
'The time we had was splendid;
I'm sorry that it's ended;
Don't break what can't be mended,
   When I am far away.

It would seem that the young lady had enjoyed, but had firmly controlled, his ardour. What the feelings were of the other girl, who had to endure the company of the Arch Bore, history does not relate.

They were to have a rude awakening from the balmy moonlit nights and calm hot days of the Nile, for after they had left their friends and sailed for Jaffa in the middle of February they ran into a very violent storm, in the course of which the foremast was struck by lightning, and it was so rough they were prevented from landing and had to continue up the coast to Beyruit. It was from here that they had to make their way inland to Jerusalem.

In Port Said Douglas had engaged the services of one Alias Abbas, a Marionaite of the Lebanon, as a dragoman. They met up with him here as arranged, and at the same time also agreed to allow an American, Mr Williams, to accompany them through Syria. Apart from these two the remainder of the party consisted of a staff of muleteers, cook, etc., and they also engaged a magnificent Bashi-Bazouk sergeant when they reached Jerusalem, who, with a soldier, was to provide them with an escort. The journey from Beyruit to Jerusalem was a great disappointment, rain and storms all the way; the rivers swollen, making fording unpleasant and even dangerous, and on one occasion their tents were blown down and torn to shreds. However a short stay at the Damascus Hotel in Jerusalem restored their enthusiasm, which even the gloomy tales of how robber sheikhs were even then plotting against them, failed to dampen.

Here they were unexpectedly joined by an undergraduate friend of Douglas's called Cross, who was ready to share their fortunes as far as Damascas. They had decided that they wanted to see as much as possible of the country, and to get away from the regular routes. Freshfield's plan that they should make a detour to see the so called 'Giant Cities' of Bashan, was agreed. A sensational account of these ruins had recently appeared in England, but the deserted towns of the Hauran had not yet been examined by anyone competent. The account in question was written by a recent traveller, S. L. Porter, and tried to link the ruins with a legendary race of giants; with the fulfilment of a prophecy of terrible destruction and the laying waste of fertile land. He had described great stone doorways with their massive portals still in position, houses and other objects evidently designed for the use of men of great stature, which, he said, had been adapted at a much later date for their own use by the Romans.

'On Thursday March the 12th.' writes Freshfield, 'we defiled, an imposing train, through the narrow streets of Jerusalem – Cross, Williams and the dragoman armed with double barrelled guns, Tucker and I with revolvers, and the two Turkish irregulars bristling with a whole armoury of guns, swords, and pistols.' A most necessary show of strength, for only a day or two later they received a warning from an English sergeant to 'beware the Sheikh of Suf and his men.'

Their first contact with nomadic Arabs was with members of the Beni-Hussan tribe. They came upon them unexpectedly, encamped upon the only suitable site so they were forced to throw themselves upon the hospitality of this singularly poor and covetous lot. But as guests they were protected by the desert code and their property came to no harm. In fact some good came of the meeting for Elias secured the services of the most notorious robber in the tribe as their guide to Jerash, on the principle that he would best know all the paths and roads through the villages.

The lonely ruins of the once splendid Jerash made a great impression. 'Before us were the remains of a noble Roman town, its ruined walls four miles in circumference, not only traceable, but in places almost intact; its public buildings so perfect that, looking round one could say, "Here is the theatre, there the circus, there the baths, there the colonnaded high street, there the later Christian Cathedral."' They made camp beneath the vaulted roof of a bath house, and set out to explore the city; free of guides and touts, peddlers and beggars that infest popular Roman ruins; able to wander in silence and at will through forum and temple. It must have been an eerie experience. After their wet, weary ride to Jerusalem, and the continuing rain and drizzle, Douglas had written to his mother, 'I am no more enthusiastic about modern Palestine than a man could be over the skeleton of a celebrated beauty.' But the next day had dawned fine and now at least Jerash made full amends. Perhaps they were amongst the last travellers to have the city to themselves, for they carried with them Murray's *Handbook to Syria*, fully describing the ruins, and warning visitors against the very infamous character who now paid them an unwelcome call. The Sheikh of Suf had a reputation which spread far beyond the border of the area of his operations, and when, one evening, he appeared before the bath house, they were quick to bar the entrance. However they agreed to examine a packet of testimonials that was handed to them; a unique collection extending over the past thirty years and every one advising travellers to have nothing to do with the fellow. Having studied the documents, and further having extracted a good deal of amusement from them they returned them with a message saying that the Sheikh's reputation was already well known amongst Englishmen and at any rate they were amply provided with their own guard and needed no further protection. This enraged the Sheikh, who first tried to break into the camp, and having failed, laid siege for the night. In the morning they double-crossed him as to their plans with a carefully laid 'red herring' which led to their being able to leave unmolested with the Sheikh possibly laying a fruitless ambush for them on the wrong track.

They pushed on for two days, following the line of the old Roman road to Bozrah, exploring ruined villages and expressing surprise, after all they had been told, at the passiveness of the inhabitants. However they had a further skirmish with a marauding band of Arab horsemen. There were ten of them, fully armed, and obviously meaning business as they galloped down and wheeled dramatically to halt some distance off. Douglas made his party form a square round the baggage train, while Kassim went forward to parlay with their chief.

The gist of the conversation was a request from the chief that Khasim and his assistant should stand to one side while the Europeans were plundered, and in exchange get a share in the spoil. But Khasim managed his horse with great skill, causing it to dance round the Arab, all the time keeping his gun trained directly between the robber's eyes, ready to blow his brains out if any of the party should make a false move. At length, convinced of their determination and their obvious heavy armament, the robbers thought discretion the better course and made off.

They spent a night in Bozrah, being well treated by the Turkish Commandant there, before setting off with high excitement into the area that had been so dramatically described by Dr Porter. 'A perusal of his pages', said Douglas, 'had set before us the exciting prospect of seeing whole towns, deserted indeed, but so little ruined that they might be inhabited again at a moments notice, although said to be of an age compared to which Pompeii may be considered a modern city.'

But their excitement was short lived. There were no cities that could have been inhabited by a race of giants and the remains at Reiyeh proved to be almost completely Roman with the exception of those modern hovels that had been constructed out of the ruins. For the present they concealed their disappointment, hoping to find evidence to support Porter's theories elsewhere. But everywhere they were confronted by the same evidence of Roman occupation. Roman roads, temples, tombs, and baths; at Atil they even found a carved winged figure of Victory and a head of Apollo. Soon they were able to forget the giants and become lost in the wonders of reality.

There was a sequel to Douglas's eventual publication of what has long since become the established truth about the cities in question. Porter thought fit to launch a personal attack in the preface of a book he wrote subsequent to the publication of Freshfield's *Central Caucasus and the Bashan*. It is true to say that Douglas was more often right than wrong when he put forward theories and suppositions concerning what he had seen and heard on his travels. On matters geographical he was most certainly always right, but on matters archaeological and historical not always so. In this case, at the age of twenty-three, in spite of natural shyness, he was ready to take on and defeat entrenched opinion. Later he would develop a quick, epigrammatic advocate's wit which would make such exchanges highly entertaining. Such style was still some years off, but his letter to Dr Porter is worth quoting as it demonstrates the confident manner in which he was prepared to cross swords with a well known and established traveller.

6. Sussex Square.
Hyde Park. W.
April 14.1870

Sir,

I do not wish to enter into a discussion in which I fear we should neither of us succeed in convincing the other. But having read with some regret the personal attack which you have made on me in the preface of your new volume I feel it necessary to trouble you with certain facts relative to the view I have taken of the ruins in the Hauran and the remarks I made on your book 'The Giant Cities'. You are probably aware – though you do not mention the fact in your new preface – that I am not alone in my opinions. Mr Fergusson, 'History of Architecture' Vol. II, page 301 is sufficiently explicit ... [Here follow a number of quotations from books, and letters he had received which support his views] Moreover others well qualified as architects or biblical students have expressed their concurrence in the view which was formed by our party – consisting of Mr C. C. Tucker, fellow of University College, Oxford, the Rev J. Cross, Mr Williams of Boston U.S. and myself.

In the lately published preface you express surprise at having admitted the existence in the Hauran of buildings of massive and peculiar architecture, I do not acknowledge them to be the work of the gigantic Raphaim. My conception of giants is not formed on certain Irish fairy tales nor did I look for buildings as big as the pyramids. What I did look for in vain was any building in the Hauran which bore traces in its size of having been built by men of unusual stature. I am ready to admit, and have often stated, not reluctantly but at every opportunity, that some few edifices, co-aeval with the Israelite conquest, may still exist in Bashan. But it appears to me out of place to talk of the building now found in the Hauran as cities of

Raphaim as it would be to talk of the ruins of Rome as Etruscan. No new fact or arguments have been brought forward to prove the alleged antiquity of the Hauran ruins and I therefore regard the general use of the arch, the frequent occurrence of Greek or Roman ornaments and inscriptions in the most massive houses, and that of many of the ruder, and at first sight more primitive, buildings are constructed of fragments of Roman temples as conclusive evidence against the theory you desire to establish.'

And he goes on, bit by bit, to demolish each argument put up by Porter, and to end victor in the field.

Porter, born in 1829, was an Irishman, who after a distinguished academic career spent some years in Damascas as a missionary among the Jews. He travelled extensively throughout the then little-known area of ancient Bashan, producing accurate maps, and, apart from the *Giant Cities of Bashan*, several useful guide books. But it does seem that in this case he allowed himself to be misled by several unusual features of the ruins of the Hauran. Modern discovery has failed to find evidence of any significant buildings that were constructed before Roman rule. After the conquest of the area by Augustus it formed part of the Kingdom of the Herods, and citizens were encouraged by tax concessions to settle and develop it. At the break-up of Roman rule the cities that had grown where only villages had existed before, soon became untenable and deserted.

They reached Damascas after a leisurely ramble through those ghost towns of gleaming marble and black basalt, finding here a mill that was still working, intricate systems of reservoirs; and there, fantastic stone portals that still moved in their sockets, covered with carvings of vines.

Douglas had fallen from his horse through a leather breaking as they approached the city, so their triumph at entering was damp-ened. During their week's stay the weather turned very cold, and they had to have fires in their rooms, and when they finally moved on to Baalbec a fall of snow forced them to seek shelter under a roof instead of relying on their tents. Tucker and Freshfield did not let this prevent them from climbing to see the cedars of Lebanon, and, with François, separated from Cross and Williams, repaired to more familiar ground. In actual fact the simple climb to the grove proved very hard work, the soft snow being above their knees, but they felt that the great trees repaid their efforts. At that time the trees were both more isolated and more numerous than the remnant of the forest that exists today.

But the time was coming for Freshfield, Tucker and François to leave Syria and approach the real objectives of their journey. They sailed on 12 April, breaking for a few days in Cyprus where they stayed with the archaeologist, Wood, who was excavating Ephesus, before boarding ship in earnest for Constantinople.

Almost a month after leaving Syria, on Saturday 9 May, Douglas wrote to his mother: 'We are now fairly arrived at the foot of the "Mystic Mountain Range" and in the interior of the terrible barbarous Caucasus – I am sitting in a comfortable room in a French hotel, with a stand of carriages waiting for hire below.'

After all they had been told, to arrive in such apparently normal and civilized surroundings might well have been a disappointment, but in fact Russian colonization of the Caucasus provinces was at that time far from complete; the people of Suanetia, for example, and many others, still maintained a wild and effective independence, as Douglas and his party were later to discover, very nearly to their cost. But in general it could be said that effective government, with all its attendant conveniences and inconveniences, extended over the basin of the Kur to Tiflis (the modern Tbilisi), over the watershed to Imeritia and the Black Sea coast. But partly through the creaking officialdom of the mighty Imperial Russia, and partly because the whole area was surrounded by often ineffectively administered parts of Turkish Armenia, Persia, and the almost unknown wild areas of the main Caucasian range to the north, they soon found that it was very difficult to get anything done. They reached Tiflis on 13 May, over a month before Moor was due to join them, and set about making arrangements to fill the intervening time in an expedition to Persia and a visit to Ararat.

This would entail a round trip through difficult and sparsely inhabited country of nearly 600 miles, and they had to make up their minds that they would tackle it without their tents and other camping equipment, none of which had yet caught up with them. Furthermore, should they have the chance to attempt to climb Ararat, they would have to do so without boots. Before they could start, the tedious formalities had to be complied with, permits to leave and re-enter Russia, papers entitling them to Cossack escort should it prove necessary, and so on. Travel, even on the main routes of the area, was a singularly uncomfortable business. Tiflis was the principal town of the Caucasus, having 80,000 inhabitants, yet with no roads at all to connect it with the Caspian, the Black Sea, or the Persian frontier. The best that could be managed was a vile rickety cart, lacking springs or seats; the usual thing being to rig a cat's cradle of rope from side to side over which rugs were spread to provide some cushioning. Even then there was no protection against wet or dust. 'It would fill a volume' wrote Douglas 'to narrate all our experiences, and the stories we heard from other, and partly Russian sources, both of the badness of the roads and of the insolence, ignorance of truth, and rapacity of the postal officials.

Nevertheless with the bland self-confidence that was the hallmark of the travelling Englishman of the time, they departed from Tiflis on 20 May. Soon they were crossing the wild thinly populated part of Georgia that comprises the steppe country basin of the Kur with its underground villages; every post-halt meant a considerable delay while the relay was rounded up off the steppe or brought from their underground stable. Their first night on the march was a pretty miserable affair, having grudgingly been given permission to sleep on the floor of an official's house along with his dog and hungry fleas. But this was to prove a luxury compared with the treatment they received later from other officials. Eventually they crossed the pass over the watershed between the Kur and the Araxes on horseback. They were now in miserable wet and muddy country on the edge of the Gokcha Lake. 'Fancy the wildest, ugliest part of Wales in bad weather, with mountains, swamps and rainstorms all on an enlarged scale, and some feeble idea may be formed of this part of Armenia, as we saw it.' However on the 23rd they were rewarded by a parting of the clouds and a magnificent view of Ararat. They decided to wait until their return from Persia before making an attempt on the mountain, in the hope that by then the weather would be improved. François contented himself with speculation as to how the elephant had climbed down after leaving the Ark, and on how many years it had taken the tortoise to reach the bottom – there was a thought that it might have turned on its back and made a long glissade of it. Douglas speculated as to the final resting place of the Ark, and later even introduced some thoughts on the matter in an article for the *Geographical Journal*. But he got cold feet and changed his mind. In a letter to the Secretary he said 'I have erased one passage because I should not care to be recorded as having seriously discussed at a meeting of a scientific body, any possible connection between Noah's Ark and Ararat.' Had he known that the same subject still surfaces from time to time to this day, both taken seriously and dismissed out of hand, he might not have been so timid.

Between Erivan and Nakhitchevan they had to cross three arms of the river, one of them at least a hundred yards wide, a thick, brown, swift-flowing mass that proved difficult to ford. The cart on which Douglas was riding was dragged across, assisted by some locals who were anxious to earn themselves some honest copecks, and on looking back from the far bank he was surprised to see the cart on which François was riding virtually out of sight beneath the brown lumpy water while the mountaineer stood upright, his magnificent burly form like 'Pharaoh in the Red Sea'. Crossing rivers was not his strong point apparently, and he had argued forcefully that they should wait for the floods to drop before attempting the crossing. As the result of all this, their driver, so pleased with his efforts on their behalf, granted himself the prize of a drink of Vodka and a pipe. His employers had to wait miserably in the rain until this was over.

Nakhitcheven proved to be a decayed town that boasted a ruined mosque, a passport bureau, a custom house and a magnificent Governor: 'a stout man, whose final cause, as far as we could make out, was to serve as a receptacle for Russian decorations'. From here to the frontier, though still trundling in the usual terrible carts, they were provided with a magnificent Cossack escort, so that in spite of the dilapidated state of their conveyance they felt like royalty.

The Russian ferry boat that was to take travellers over the flooded river on to Persian soil was out of action when they reached the miserable hamlet of Djulfa, and they found that they would have to wait until the next morning for the Persian boat to make a crossing. To their disgust the Russian official was so busy proving that he had earned the Persian decoration of which he was the proud possessor, in entertaining a senior official, that the English and their followers were forced to spend the night in an unfurnished hovel that had neither doors nor windows and the floor of which was several inches deep in mud. It made matters worse when, in the evening, they took a walk in the direction of the official's house and distinctly heard the sound of popping corks. Later that evening Tucker was taken ill, and a request was sent to the official for the loan of a saucepan to make some soup for him. This was refused, much to their fury, on the grounds that they did not keep things to lend. Luckily Tucker's predicament turned out to be not serious, otherwise they might have had trouble. As it was, on their return to Tiflis, the incident had generated sufficient feelings for Douglas to lodge a complaint against the official, and was given to understand that the man would be dealt with.

Tabriz displayed many of the more attractive features of an eastern city, not yet given over to Cook's tours. The bazaars were filled with goods from all parts of the world, some of fine quality, but they soon discovered there was little chance of finding a real bargain, the traders being very astute. They found clean lodgings with flower-painted paper windows that looked out on a garden – altogether a very pleasant interlude. In a day or two Douglas wrote to a friend: 'Tabriz is very charming as a resting place to a European traveller, it gave me far more of an Arabian Nights sort of city than anything else I have seen – not that there are splendid buildings but that the modes of life and government are strictly eastern – Capital punishment is merrily inflicted, twelve people beheaded a week is considered nothing.'

But 3 June once again found them approaching Djufla of evil memory. This time, as they came towards the bank of the river, and the Persian post, they were enveloped in a furious dust storm and had to gallop through almost nil visibility to reach shelter. The crossing was made without difficulty, and they were even able to obtain saddle horses instead of the usual cart, which they had come to blame for Tucker's bout of sickness. By the 6th they were approaching Ararat, after sharing a further ferry over the Araxes with a tribe of nomad Kurds, a picturesque and happy party, accompanied by their camels and flocks.

Later in the year, and very much to the annoyance of the Russians, Freshfield was to lead his little party triumphantly to the untrodden summits of some of the mightiest peaks of the Caucasus, but Ararat, already twice climbed, was the scene of their failure. Douglas left two accounts of the ascent, one written on thin blue paper and posted home as soon as they reached Tiflis; the other, substantially the same in content, was written when he got back to England and later published.

Ararat, a beautiful almost perfect cone, rises 16,946 feet above sea level, its true base being less than 3,000 feet above the sea. The first successful attempt had been made by Herr Parrot in 1829; the second, a regular military operation, by General Chodzko, the latter remaining camped a few hundred feet below the summit for a whole week.

On the morning of 7 June Douglas and his party, consisting of a Kurd chief and his servant, four Persians, the owners of the horses they were riding, and three Kurds who were willing to act as porters, plus Tucker, François, and the interpreter, who for convenience they had christened Paul and who had been with them throughout their stay, set off up the bare, stony slopes leading towards the mountain. They climbed to the green plain that fills the space between the foot of Ararat proper, and its 4,000 foot neighbour, little Ararat. There they looked for a collection of underground huts which they had been informed were inhabited and from which they could get bread. They found the huts on a knoll above the plain, but they proved deserted. A door of twisted sticks led them into an evil, earthy, tomb-like dwelling linked by dark passages to other chambers. Holes in the roof, which did service for both light and chimney, proved most treacherous to the horses above, one of whom fell through and with great difficulty had to be extricated. Because of the lack of supplies a party had to be sent back to fetch both food and a tent, which, when it arrived, proved far too heavy to be of any use on the mountain. However the porters were ready to go with the climbers even without a tent, and the party, leaving the owners of the horses, set off to camp as high as possible before night. They established a bivouac just below the snow-line at about 8,500 feet, rolling themselves in their rugs by the fire, prepared to start again when the moon rose at midnight.

They started just after midnight, climbing two snow slopes to the ridge above their bivouac which looked down on a deep semicircular hollow between them and the main mass of the mountain. They followed along this ridge in brilliant moonlight, making a circuit of the hollow, and by daylight they were not far from the face of the cone. As they had advanced along the ridge, making excellent time,

Douglas remarked to his two companions how fit he felt, although they had none of them been able to get any training that season. But he spoke too soon. Before the sun had risen he began to feel pains akin to violent indigestion, brought on, he thought at the time, by the warmed wine they had drunk before starting. He struggled on for three hours after the attack had started, hoping it would wear off, but it grew much worse and he became so sick and giddy that he was forced to stop in a sunny patch among the rocks, leaving the others to try the summit. After dozing for a while he made an attempt to follow them, but soon had to give it up as hopeless.

But the others, François and Tucker, fared little better. They had a difficult climb through crags of lava and presently the snow took the form of hard névé, and François went ahead to cut steps. But even he was defeated and had to give up through exhaustion. Tucker made a further brave effort on his own. For nearly four hours he worked his way painfully upward, with throbbing head and severe breathlessness, till at last he too was forced to turn back, some 800 feet below the top. The whole party reunited at the huts at 6.30 p.m., having been eighteen hours out on the mountain. The three were disgusted at their failure, but had to give up any thoughts of a further attempt because time was pressing if they were to meet Moor and explore the Caucasus, the object of the whole expedition.

Having taken the more attractive route through Georgian hill-country they arrived back in Tiflis on 19 June to find letters from home, the rest of their baggage, and Moor waiting for them.[1] The return journey was unhappy for Douglas as on the first day down from the mountain he was attacked by a violent pain at the back of the head. The next morning they were able to get hold of a Russian doctor, who said there was nothing the matter with him and 'prescribed a mild solution of peppermint, which was neither nice nor useful; in the evening he came again and ordered leeches and a mustard plaster. This vigorous treatment was effectual.'

The city was in a great state of excitement, owing to an expected visit from the Emperor's son, the Grand Duke Alexis, and it was very difficult for a foreigner who was not covered with decorations and epaulettes to get anywhere with officials. However in spite of this

[1] Refer picture bottom p. 217 of party in Tiblisi after having been joined by Moor.

they were able to hire a carriage of sorts to take them on their journey north to the post station at Kasbek. As they left the city the roads were being covered in earth to spare the royal bones discomfort: 'a proceeding which, if the weather held fine for a few days, would be certain to throw dust even in Imperial eyes.'

In this direction the roads were better, and the post houses quite substantial affairs, though the officials were as surly as ever. They had left Tiflis on the 26th and by the 28th they were crossing the great pass over the central Ridge of the Caucasus in the midst of magnificent mountain scenery, greeting again the familiar mountain flora, especially luxuriant because of the springs that burst forth everywhere. Beyond the pass they descended into the rugged treeless valley of the Erek; a more forbidding land of bare crags and scattered clusters of stone hovels. At the first post house they found the postmaster tipsy. 'As an English traveller mentions the same fact in 1837' writes Freshfield 'and as he was in a similar happy condition upon our two subsequent visits, it is fair to suppose the complaint is chronic.' Luckily for them this was not the post house nearest to the mountain or they might have had a difficult time. As it was they found a host who was unusually civil, and, though his charges were high, they were given good food and fair wine. There was even a bottle of English beer – Allsop's Pale Ale, at one rouble fifteen copecks a bottle. Just before they arrived the clouds lifted and they were vouchsafed an awe-inspiring view of their goal, towering many thousands of feet above all its neighbours.

A Georgian church.

CHAPTER 4

FRESHFIELD'S CONTRIBUTION TO MOUNTAIN EXPLORATION – HIS SUBSEQUENT ACCOUNT, THE EXPLORATION OF THE CAUCASUS – TRAINING FOR THE ATTEMPT ON KASBEK – THE ASCENT – 'SCARCELY ONE EASY STEP' – ON THE CREST OF THE HOME OF THE LEGENDARY ROC – THE DESCENT JUST AS HAZARDOUS – THEIR SUCCESS NOT CALCULATED TO PLEASE – WHEN PROVEN THEY BECOME LOCAL HEROES – IMPERIAL REGIME BRANDS THEM LIARS – THROUGH OSSETIA TO SUANETIA – TORMENTED BY THE VILLAGERS – CLIMBING THE KARAGOM GLACIER – THE MAGNIFICENT PEAK OF USCHBA – CONQUEST OF ELBRUZ, THE HIGHEST MOUNTAIN IN EUROPE – CLAIM THAT ELBRUZ IS IN ASIA – HOME VIA SEVASTAPOL – THOUGHTS ON THE CRIMEAN WAR

Until now the journeyings of Douglas and his companions had been nothing more than an adventure trip. They had gone further and been more adventurous than perhaps most of their contemporaries, but they had been nowhere unknown to some of their countrymen at least. But now they were on the edge of mountain country that was virtually unknown except to its inhabitants, who themselves still had a few more years to go before their medieval and feuding inter-village warfare was to be disturbed by the incursion of Russian officialdom. For Douglas it was to be the start of his important contribution to mountain literature and mountain exploration, and because of the great political upheavals that followed during the next one hundred years, a unique record of a vanished and extraordinarily interesting world; a world at the very edge of, and largely unsuspected by, civilized Europe. His final complete work, and the summation of the opening of the whole area, *The Exploration of the Caucasus*, is a model of its kind,[1] and would have earned fame had it been the only work of his life. To read it now is fascinating for many reasons, not least for the light it throws on the background that formed the persona of the most terrible Georgian of the all – Joseph Stalin. But for the present Douglas and his companions were looking

[1] Published in two editions, the second in 1902, by Edward Arnold with photographs by V. Sella and others.

to open up a new Switzerland where others of like mind could follow, just as they themselves had followed the great names of Alpine Exploration.

With the fiasco of Ararat still very much in mind Douglas was determined that his party should not attempt Kasbek without a day of training, a somewhat modest program considering what lay before them. Plans were made to utilize the time climbing surrounding slopes in an attempt to pick out the best route to the summit. They enquired if there was a native of the village who knew the way up a nearby peak which would give them a clear view, and presently a rather feeble looking fellow appeared, and, through lack of any alternative, was duly engaged.

They started at five the next morning to find this vantage point from which to examine this great and frightening mountain of such beauty and mystery. Many of the stories they were told, and which had been handed on by other travellers, including a lady who had published her letters from the area in 1811, Freshfield tells us, concerned the venal wickedness of some, and the gullibility of others of the mountain people. Deserted monkish cells at 11,000 feet bore witness not apparently to the great holiness of their erstwhile occupants, but their slothful ability to persuade the less fortunate to keep them in their state of idleness; 'vast pretenders to piety' the lady called them. The mountain gets its name, Freshfield also tells us, from Prince Kasbek, or Kasibeg, who was 'the first of the mountaineers to perceive that his best policy was to recognize a *fait accompli*, and to embrace Christianity and acquiesce in Russian supremacy'. The next two generations may well have had cause to regret the Prince's decision.

The party were able to enjoy a glorious sunrise from a vantage point some 1,500 feet above the village, close by an ancient Christian church, which, in spite of the fact that it was in a shocking state of repair, was held in considerable reverence by the natives. From here they picked out a snow peak they thought they could climb during the course of the day, and which would afford them the view they sought. As they had rather expected, the guide declined to go any further than the snow line, which they reached after a comparatively easy walk up a broad grassy ridge covered with flowering rhododendrons and several kinds of gentians. From the summit they

Kasbek from the south.

were able to form their plans for the morrow, though it was impossible to tell which of the twin peaks would offer the best chance of final success. For an hour they studied the mountain, planning how best to capture the crystal castle with its neighbouring temple of the golden dove, both of which tradition said, would be found at the topmost summit, 'and then by a rapid act of what might be called "snowmanship", rejoined Paul and Alexis [their interpreter and guide respectively]. The snow being in excellent order we sat down one behind the other, at the foot of the rocks, and letting go, slid with great velocity to the base of the peak'. Much to the consternation of the pair who were watching!

On their return to the village they found the Governor had arrived, having come this far in order to meet the expected Grand Duke. He took considerable interest in the Englishmen's plans and helped them to select and come to terms with four porters who agreed to carry their gear as far as the first bivouac. That evening too, the Governor arranged, for their benefit, a display of local sword dancing. Such generosity was mainly prompted by the fact that secretly the Russians thought that the party had no hope of attaining their goal.

The next day proved on the whole an enjoyable start to their venture. Most of the morning was occupied in a long steep climb, which was made a pleasure by the profusion of many different kinds of flowers. Presently they crossed some wide upward sloping alpine meadows to the snout of the Ortzviri glacier which sweeps round the southern flank of the mountain. They continued to climb steeply up its left flank, until, at a height of about 11,000 feet, they found a mossy hollow under the southern spur of Kasbek that would make a suitable place to bivouac. But after such a good start they had rather a depressing evening – wind and rain made it seem unlikely that they would be able to carry on in the morning.

The various hermits and holy men, spurious or otherwise, that had made their homes in cells cut in the rock face of the sacred mountain, had evidently provided shelter for the porters in the now deserted hide-outs, for there was no sign of them when, at 2.45 a.m., Freshfield, François, Moor and Tucker made a start, in spite of the fact that they fired off a pistol to attract their attention. But the climbers (and probably the porters) were rather more pleased than sorry that they would not have to cope with anyone so inexpert on whatever hazards might lie above.

Of their start Douglas writes: 'The morning was calm and lovely and we fully enjoyed the moonlight view of the great glacier and the ice-mailed peaks around, and the glorious sunrise flush that soon succeeded it.' By 6.30 they had reached 15,000 feet and were on the actual face of the mountain, and it was from here that their real difficulties began. They found themselves having to cut steps up a steep slope of blue ice that was covered with a layer of new snow and split by giant crevasses. François was in the lead followed by Douglas when they came to a crack about four feet wide, its lips fringed with great icicles and its further edge about five feet above them. They had all crossed over without too much difficulty, although obviously extreme care was needed, when it was found that the rope had got hitched round one of the icicles. Tucker, who was last man, had to work backwards cutting steps below and behind him, never an easy task. Suddenly he slipped and shot downwards into the chasm. Freshfield and Moor took the full force of the jerk, and by great good fortune their ice axes and footholds remained secure; but it was quite a strain, as Tucker now found himself head down, and they had to hold him while he worked himself upright and regained his foothold. Although, Freshfield tells us, nothing was said at the time, obviously the incident had its effect on all of them; but for the next four hours they were forced to give all their attention to the climb, on which even the naturally prosaic Freshfield was forced to admit, 'there was scarcely one easy step'. For much of the time it proved impossible to cut steps because of the snow that lay on top of the steep ice, and they were forced to climb on their hands and knees clinging with their ice axes. To add to their troubles there was a bitter wind that blew ice particles blindingly into their faces and numbed their hands so that they could hardly hold on. At last, at 11 a.m., they reached the saddle between the two peaks and paused to take breath. It was François who had suffered most, having lead for the greater part of the climb, and they left him to recover while they started up the eastern peak, which was now shown to be obviously the higher as well as the easier of the two. The last part was not so bad, snow alternating with rock, until, just after François had rejoined them, they stepped onto the crest, the first men to dare the home of the legendary Roc.

In Tiflis Freshfield and his little party had been the objects of pity and amusement in ruling quarters. How could this slight, haughty, shabby young Englishman succeed, where high-ranking Russian officers had failed? News of their success, when it came, was hardly calculated to please. An informant later told Freshfield that when the Grand Duke read a despatch reporting the success of the climb he complained that the Russians, brought up in the country 'have sent expedition after expedition, all returned and said impossible – and now three Englishmen come out and walk up the mountain as soon as they see it'.

Unfortunately the colonels and generals of the Russian army took it as a personal and national slight that a non-military English party should succeed, and did all they could to cast slurs on the achievement. However the genuineness of their claim could not in fact be disputed because of the manner of their return from the summit.

After ten minutes on the snow dome of Kasbek, because of the cold wind, they were forced to return from the saddle. They were now faced with a dilemma. The steep ice and snow slope, such as the one they had ascended, presents an almost impossible return journey. They decided that in these circumstances it would be far too dangerous to make the attempt, for should one of them start to slide there would be nothing to prevent the whole of their little party being swept to certain death. The northern flank of the mountain however, presented, as far as the eye could see, an easy snow slope. They had a hundred or so feet of axe work, and from then a steady downwards trudge through snow on to the extensive snowfields that feed the great glaciers that flow into the Terek valley. However their difficulties were not yet over.

They were in an entirely unknown area, separated from their camping equipment, 14,000 feet above sea level. As Douglas wrote 'it was most undesirable to hazard our chance of reaching terra cognita ere nightfall by any rash or hasty move'.

First they kept under the rocks at the left side of the northern glacier, then, when it became too broken to negotiate further, they climbed to the crest of the ridge that separated two of the three glaciers and followed it down. After passing the foot of the second glacier they were shrouded in dense fog which made it difficult to find their way out of the savage gorge in which they were enclosed. At last they came to pastures, and at 7.45 p.m. agreed to share the hospitality of some herdsmen, spending the night lying in the open under an overhanging cliff with a stone wall for shelter and stones for pillows.

They arrived back in the village of Kasbek at 9 a.m. the next morning, but their coming created very little excitement, everyone expecting them to say that they had reached the summit, and no one believing that they had. But the return of their porters in the evening changed matters. These men had supposed them lost, and in great excitement told the villagers how the tracks of the climbers were visible on the mountain to a great height. At this the herdsmen told how the party had appeared from the direction of the mountain on the north side, and immediately Freshfield and his companions became heroes. The chief seemed to find it especially amusing that this little party should succeed where generals with whole companies of Cossacks had failed. Perhaps they would have been somewhat hurt to know that their despatch, sent to officials at Tiflis who had expressed a desire to know how they fared, was published in the paper alongside the official view that they were liars; a matter which neither the Imperial regime nor its successor have ever seen fit to correct.

Within a week of their having left Tiflis they had accomplished the first major objective, and now with high hopes they set out to complete the second and perhaps the most important. The direct distance as the crow flies from Kasbek to Elbruz is about 120 miles, and the central range of the Caucasus which runs unbroken from Adai Khokh nowhere falls below 10,000 feet on the whole distance to the source of the Baksari and Elbruz itself. It was Freshfield's plan to explore up the length of the chain on the southern side, following the valley of the Terek, crossing the headwaters of the Ardon, which flows off to the north, and the Rion and the Ingur which run southwards from the watershed. The first part would be through Ossetia, and the latter through Suanetia.

The first few miles were accomplished in grand style, their carriage being hitched to both horses and harness used by the Grand Duke and still decorated with gay ribbons. They were able to proceed in this manner only as far as Res, the highest village in the Terek valley, and from there on it became a question of walking and climbing and hiring porters for the baggage. But they were taking a good deal for granted. The inhabitants of the grim, fortified villages with their numerous defensive towers and ruinous stone hovels were every bit as truculent and excitable as their appearance suggested. The men were certainly picturesque, with their tall, fur hats, flowing frock coats and wide belts stuffed with every imaginable type of weapon. On their very first foot stage which would lead them over the pass into the valley of the Ardon, a great deal of hard bargaining was necessary before they could persuade a large company to carry the very lightest of loads each. Once over the pass and on the descent they became very insolent, pushing and jostling their employers. Finally on arrival at Zacca they had to take refuge in a hut in order to get away from the shouting mob of porters and villagers. They sent Paul, the interpreter, outside with the money to pay off the men, hoping that this would get rid of them and that they would return to their own side of the pass. But after taking the money they started goading and shouting, till Moor, Tucker, Devouassoud and Freshfield were forced to come out. By this time Paul was very much enraged, while their erstwhile porters, having snatched his sheepskin coat, were shouting abuse from some fifty yards up the path. Douglas, thinking that decided and immediate action on his part would restore order, marched directly up to them and firmly grabbed the coat. This did not have the desired effect. The men surrounded him and commenced beating him about the head, which was well protected by his hard wide-awake hat. The others then decided to come to the rescue, charging down the hill, ice axes levelled, straight into the melee. After a sharp exchange of blows the enemy took flight, but not until they had rolled Tucker into the ditch and finally secured the coat.

The party were able to hire some horses for the next stage, very glad to be able to proceed without the benefit of such doubtful company. They were lucky that night to find a deserted barn in which to camp, and were not forced to approach one of the unattractive villages for hospitality.

But as they penetrated further they were able to revise their opinions of the Ossetes. They were fiery and vengeful, often engaged in long bloody feuds with neighbouring families and villages. But they

Overleaf: The small hamlet of Pari.   © Fondazione Sella and Instituto di Fotografia Alpina Vittorio Sella-Biella.

An Ossete village.

were to find, at the same time, that they were not entirely undeserving of the description that had been applied to them as the 'Gentlemen of the Mountains.'

However the people of Suanetia, upon whom they came next, proved a very much more menacing prospect. An earlier traveller in the region had reported; 'In the expression of their countenances insolence and rudeness are prominent. Hoary headed obstinacy is there often united to the stupidity of savage animal life. These people have often committed ten or more murders, which they generally consider not only allowable but necessary.'

In his lecture to the Royal Geographical Society the following year Douglas described the area inhabited by these truly savage people, through which he and his party had passed. 'A large basin forty miles long by fifteen broad is encircled by glacier crowned ridges, and divided into numerous wooded gorges and meadow basins by lower spurs. It is accessible to the outer world only by a narrow, and, at times impassable ravine, or by as a people apart, the upper glens

having been renowned as harbouring the most savage and untame-
able of the Caucasian races.'

They had little idea what to expect when they entered the area and
came in sight of the extraordinary cluster of villages ahead. They
estimated that there could not be less than fifty of those queer defensive towers, looking like armless windmills, in a variety of states of
preservation and all surrounded by low barn-like structures of stone.
The Gebi porters, whom they had with them, had to be paid off and
dismissed at the first of these villages, and Douglas's party was left to
the tender mercies of the inhabitants. They found a barn in which it
was intimated they could set up quarters; a gloomy ill-lit affair with
small loopholes for windows. They were soon the centre of a silent
hostile crowd that watched their every move and at first refused to
sell them any food – though they later relented far enough to sell
fowls and eggs. Paul set about preparing a meal in a nearby open-
fronted shed, there being no chimney in their barn, but the lounging
watchers made movement almost impossible and they were eventually forced to retreat to their own quarters for privacy, and barred
themselves in for the night by pulling a bench across the door. They
slept with their revolvers close at hand.[1]

In the morning they decided that they must have a day for cleaning
and mending their equipment, and restocking with food. Somewhat
heartlessly they left François and Paul to cope with this while the rest
of the party climbed a ridge to enjoy the wonderful, wild Caucasian
scenery without being pestered by staring villagers. They returned to
find that the others had made good progress, François with the laun-
dry, and Paul had found a man willing to provide two horses to carry
the luggage. But there was also bad news. As the result of a severe
wetting of a few days before, tents, mattresses and so on had been
left in the sun to dry. It was now found that various small articles
were missing, including a tent pole, which was of a certain type and
impossible to replace in the circumstances. They spent an unpleasant evening. Evidently encouraged by the success of their petty
pilfering, and becoming openly contemptuous of the strangers, the
villagers now grew unbearable; jeering, pointing, jostling or just
staring stupidly, impeding every action. In the end trying to eat

---

[1] The village in question was Ushkul (see picture p. 245).

supper under these circumstances became impossible, and they force marched the whole lot out of the barn. The doors were immediately kicked open again and the invasion repeated, and it was not until Douglas collared one of their tormentors and openly made an example of him that they were able to shut the doors and maintain comparative peace, though the jeering crowd remained outside for a long time. Before they retired for the night Moor fired five shots in rapid succession into the air as a display of strength, and this had its effect for they were left alone until the morning.

During the night they worried that there might well be an ugly scene when they came to leave, and so it proved. After they had paid all the just demands for money, they were still surrounded by a clamouring crowd all making exorbitant demands for this or that. The horseman had arrived with only one animal instead of the promised two; but they resolved to carry the remaining packs themselves rather than to try to hire porters from such a hostile crowd. At last they were ready to start. Lifting their packs they prepared to leave the barn in a body, but François and Paul paused for an instant and looked back to make sure that nothing had been left behind. The villagers immediately took advantage of this tactical blunder, separating the two parties and shutting François and the unfortunate Paul in the barn. Immediately the others turned round and charged the doors with their ice axes and in a moment released the pair. One of the ringleaders among the villagers intervened to prevent their getting away, but Douglas thrust his revolver against the ruffian's cheek, and forced past him. Once again they formed a square round their baggage, and, revolvers levelled, marched through the yelling screaming mob. Several of the opposition drew their swords, while others ran off and came back with guns. The situation began to look really ugly when one of the villagers, evidently wanting to avoid bloodshed, shouted a suggestion. As soon as this had been interpreted to the explorers they followed the advice and scattered a few small coins amidst the crowd. Immediately there was a scramble, and taking advantage of the momentary distraction the party managed to escape. There was little doubt that it was their revolvers that had saved them, and that they were furthermore very lucky to have got away without having to use them – for had they done so they would certainly have had to flee the country.

The journey from Kasbek to Pari, through all the wide variety of

Caucasian scenery, took them a month. In very little time they realized that all the earlier descriptions of the mountains were far from
the truth, and their own preconceived ideas utterly unfounded. Here
was no second rate mountain range, lacking in interest for Alpinist
and geographer alike; but a continuous chain of mighty ridges and
peaks, that for height, grandeur, mighty snowfields and glaciers,
chasms, gorges, forests and crags, far surpassed anything their
beloved Alps could show. Here they realized was work and sport for
the most insatiable member of the Alpine Club. As they pushed their
way westwards, sometimes in dense forests, or glens choked with
fantastic vegetation, or meadows where ordinary little weeds, so
tame and familiar at home, towered sometimes even higher than a
man and presented a tangled thicket in their path, their excitement
and pleasure mounted. It was many years before Freshfield could
return, or before da Sella, the greatest mountain photographer of all
time, could record for all to see the peaks and glaciers with which
they were faced. It was hard enough to brave the hurdles erected by
officialdom to make the journey to this remote corner, and nearly
twenty years before Freshfield's death the Revolution was to seal
completely the area from outsiders until more recent years, when
organized climbing parties from the west became a more regular
feature. Perhaps the new regime in Russia will allow the mountaineering community and skiers of the world the access that Freshfield dreamed of, but not, hopefully, to be festooned with the ski lifts
and cable cars that have ensnared the peaks of central Europe.

Having no other method, Douglas recorded each new angle of
mountain scenery with dozens of careful outline sketches and neat
diagrams of every important feature. In spite of the difficulties of
supply and porters they did not remain at valley level, but at one
point actually crossed the main range by climbing the stupendous
icefall of the Karagom glacier. Nineteen years later he was to revisit
the spot where they had lit their fire and spread their capes to rest
before braving the inhospitable icy wastes above, and called to mind
that first occasion. 'Looking northwards over the great frozen billows, we could see beyond the point where they plunged out of sight,
the fir forests and corn land of the Urukh. In the opposite direction
the great icefall closed the view and gave no hint of the mysterious
region from which it flowed. Next morning at daybreak we set out on

our adventure. For two hours a shepherd's track helped us as far as the highest grass on the west bank of the ice. Here we were close to the foot of the last and the loftiest of the frozen cascades, and the work of the day began. At first all went smoothly; we found corridors between the great blocks and were able to avoid the chasms that seamed the slope. But when these chasms became more and more continuous and, running across the snowy dells, forced us right or left into the intricate labyrinth and among the crystal towers, the prospects of our success began to look very questionable. We had to encounter in aggravated form all the familiar difficulties and perils of an alpine icefall. The aggravation consisted chiefly in the constant repetition. No sooner had one turret staircase been hewn out of a crack in some imposing barrier, than another castle appeared behind it. The glacier was something more than a mountain dragon; it was a very hydra. But our motives for perseverance were strong. To retreat meant a long tramp down to a distant village where we should have to trust to signs to get provisions, and run the risk of being arrested as suspicious characters, and be sent down, some two days journey, to a Cossack outpost on the northern steppe.'

There was one particular moment of this struggle that stood out in his memory; on a long narrow rotten snow bridge that ended in nothing. 'The leader had to lean across to cut a precarious foothold in the opposite bank of ice, and then make a bold leap into his pigeonholes. Devouassoud leapt, and we followed. The rest was not quite so bad, but there was a great deal of it. We wearied of the exquisite beauty of the icicle fringes and the blue ravines, of the fantastic form of the sun smitten towers and pinnacles. There was not a moment's pause in the battle; we halted for neither food nor rest ... It was half past one, and we had been six hours in the fall, and nine hours from our bivouac, before we sat down on the level snows to consider our further course through undiscovered country no human eye had ever before seen.'

But the rest of their difficulties on the crossing were mainly those caused by their unfamiliarity with the terrain, and by nightfall they were safely at the level of the first stunted birches on the far side. They 'lay down beneath the highest birches with ice axes driven in below us to prevent our rolling down the slope, as heedless as any Caucasian shepherd of the absence of supper or the showers that passed over us. We were conscious of having lived a day that would never fade from our memories.'

They returned to the south side of the range and joined the rest of their party and baggage by a more westerly pass on the following two days, and continued their westward exploration along the line of the range. To reach Suanetia they crossed four passes over the spurs that separated the sources of the rivers, their rapid changes of height giving them a wide variety of scenery and vegetation.

Apart from the various excitements and uncertainties that their porters and the people of Suanetia could be relied upon to provide, they had, as mountain explorers, one moment of very special astonishment mingled with awe. After a hot, severe climb near a group of villages known as Latal in Suenetia they reached the crest of a spur that separates Latal from Betscho. Moor and François were ahead of Freshfield, who had stopped to examine the mountain faces revealed to the north. But something had evidently excited the other two, so he hurried to join them. Freshfield is always at his best when describing some great peak which has aroused his interest, and something of the excitement he feels is communicated even through his stately prose. 'On reaching my companions I was at no loss to discover the cause of their emotion. Due north, above the low wood of the adjoining hillside, shot up two towers of rock, one slightly in advance of the other, forming, as regards height, steepness, and outline, beyond all comparison the most wonderful mountain mass we ever beheld. Tier above tier of precipices rose straight up from the valley, culminating in two tremendous towers, separated by a deep depression. The twin summits resembled one another in form, and appeared to be long roof-like ridges, falling away in slopes of mingled rock and ice of terrific steepness. The idea of climbing either of them seemed too insane to be so much as suggested, and even the lower spurs of the mountain above the meadows of Betscho are so tremendous that it looked as if a stone dropped from the top of either of the peaks would scarcely stop rolling before it reached the valley. There was no mistake about it, the Caucasian Matterhorn was found at last.'

Later some of Douglas's more literary friends would level the charge at him that he was too impersonal in his writings; that the marvels of nature that his eye witnessed did not call forth from his pen the spiritual outpourings that were popular in some quarters. He followed the established tradition amongst travellers and explorers who took their wanderings seriously. To describe what he saw with colourful accuracy was enough, he never thought to range himself alongside the wonders of nature as an object of interest. But the scenes themselves when they excite him, are vividly described, and the emotion he feels comes through in the prose. Thus it is not to be wondered at that in later years, in all the hundreds of photographs that were taken on his expeditions in the Alps, Caucasus, Himalayas, or elsewhere, in hardly any of them does he appear himself. It comes as something of a surprise to detect a tall, thin rather stooping figure with hanging clothes and faithful wide-awake, furtively in the distance; or poised impatiently, caught unawares, agreeing to stand still for no more than a few seconds.

Often during that day, the last they were to spend on the march before reaching Pari, their eyes returned to this magnificent peak, Uschba, framed at times by the branches of the copper beeches and aspens between which they pass.

Pari was only a small hamlet, but it had acquired significance as having been the residence of a former native Prince who had previously murdered the Governor of Mingrelia, and since then, and the confiscation of the Prince's property, there had been a small company of Cossacks stationed there. The latter proved of great assistance to the explorers, providing them with dry lodgings, and obtaining for them some of the most amenable looking porters that they had the good fortune to see for a long time. The Cossacks also proved a help in a further matter. From this point, and in order to find the base of Elbruz, they would have somehow to cross the main range of the Caucasus again, the mountain lying like Uschba to the south, separately, to the north. The Cossacks were able to advise them which of the two passes that were possible would be the best, and the route by which to reach it.

They left Pari on 24 July heading north. The porters very soon proved themselves, if not robbers, at least normally lazy and grasping, sitting down to take a rest after every short stage. Finally they stopped altogether and stated they would go no further unless the agreed price for their services was increased at once. This Douglas refused to do, and said they would all return to Pari instead. Seeing he was adamant they gave way and the party continued until they reached a point where the loud roaring of a river made conversation impossible. Here, although it was early in the day, the porters intimated they were about to set up camp. The explorers continued, ignoring all protests, until about 5 p.m. when they agreed to halt. It is impossible not to notice, whatever one thinks of ruling class Englishmen lording it over the natives in their own country, the robust manner which seems to have come naturally to the young explorers as they dealt with these ever recurrent problems. On this occasion Douglas was not to be taken in when the porters here said that they knew a threat had been made by the people of the last village through which they had passed, to follow them and steal their baggage in the night. They said that they thought the best way to deal with this threat was for the explorers to divide all their goods between the porters, and each man would guard his pile during darkness, an obvious precursor to their making off with the whole lot. Needless to say the suggestion was rejected. It was doubtful, as it turned out, if anyone would have been able to stir during the night, for all the party were kept awake by the torments of mosquitoes, and an especially vicious little black fly.

The following night they camped, still on the south side of the range, but in a high valley amongst the peaks. After they had made camp an armed party was seen approaching from the direction of the pass, driving cattle. It turned out that they were a raiding party that had been to one of the villages to the north on a cattle stealing expedition. At once the porters said that they could go no further, otherwise the villagers ahead might hold them responsible for the thieving. Eventually all except one, obviously an old hand at the cattle rustling game, agreed that the company of foreigners was sufficient proof of their innocence, at least on this occasion. The next day Douglas was very unwell, but he managed to keep going until they reached the head of the pass. Here they were disappointed by the weather which turned misty, and later started to snow, so that they were not treated to the fine view of Elbruz to which they had been looking forward. As they descended further down the north side the snow turned to heavy rain, and they were glad to find a rude log hut for shelter. Here, as was becoming almost routine, there was further trouble with the porters who demanded immediate payment and further money if they were to continue. This time Moor dealt with the matter extremely well by totally ignoring the ringleader, and concentrating on the two men that appeared to be the most amenable. All the same patience had been stretched pretty well to the limit by the time they reached a further hut where they decided to stay the night.

The Cossacks had given a good report of the people they would find in the northern villages. In this they were justified – the party were to fare much better at the hands of the Mahommedans than they had in those of the so-called Christians of the south.

They were greeted at the village of Urusbieh by three princes, brothers, who while they had no actual powers, were the leading members of the community, and because of their comparative wealth they were able to exert considerable influence in an apparently benign manner. They had heard of the English, knew of Shakespeare, and the events of the Crimean war. They paid a small tax to their rulers but were otherwise left in peace except for occasional travellers from Patigorsk, whom they always entertained with all the hospitality at their command. Like the Cossacks they were to prove a great help in obtaining food and porters for the intended four day expedition against their mountain; at the same time expressing polite disbelief that they would achieve their goal. They had helped others to attempt the same task, and all had returned defeated.

On the 29th they started out towards the base of the highest mountain in the Caucasus, if not in Europe, whose domed summit they had not seen since they had caught sight of its gleaming silver from the deck of their Black Sea steamer as they approached the shores. Their path led them to retrace their steps from the pass to the head of the Baksan valley where they turned right in order to reach the south-eastern Elbruz glacier. Their first near view was as they climbed up the glen through long, and strangely, snake-infested grass; but apart from its sheer mass and height Elbruz, seen from close range at any rate, did not, in their eyes, have the dramatic appearance of many lesser mountains. It certainly did not do so for Douglas, who, on his return, described Elbruz as a 'bloated and uninteresting monarch'. They pitched their tent for the night close to the bivouac of some mountain shepherds, who provided them with milk and cheese; but their charges evidently did not think much of the alien intruders, and spent the greater part of the night butting the sides of their tent.

The plan for the next day was to reach a position above the 12,000 foot mark, from which to make their assault. In half an hour they reached the end of the glacier and began to ascend the steep hillside on its right. After negotiating a line of crags that barred the way they found themselves amidst snow and rocks on the side of a ridge, the crest of which was some 600 feet above their heads. As this time it was Moor who was feeling unwell, Freshfield with Tucker and François left him with the porters while they climbed the ridge to find a suitable site to bivouac, and to get some idea, what lay ahead for the morrow. At the crest of the ridge they found themselves looking up a vast snowfield, shaped like an 'inverted teacup' with twin rounded summits at its apex. It did not look as though there was going to be any difficulty for experienced mountaineers, and they returned to a spot a little below the ridge that they had selected for their bivouac. They had to dig into the side of the mountain with their ice axes in order to make a bit of ground wide and level enough for their tent. It was worth the trouble, for from this precarious ledge that they had made for themselves, they had the most wonderful view of the range, with the twin spires of dramatic Uschba rearing into view. Freshfield describes the spot as an eyrie. Perhaps it was this place he had in mind when he wrote his poem 'View and Vision' in which he describes, as seen from the heights, the valleys of Suanetia with their bloodthirsty inhabitants, and the wonderful profusion of flowers that grow right to the feet of the great Caucasian glaciers. His descriptive poems like his prose, display exactness when describing the features of the landscape.

They were crowded that night in their little tent, for Paul, their faithful interpreter, had pleaded to be allowed to come with them to the summit of the great mountain in whose locality he had lived all his life; a request to which they had agreed since they had not been able to espy any difficulty ahead that a novice could not negotiate with expert help. The cold was intense, their small supply of drinking water was soon frozen and they were forced to start at 2 a.m. – thirsty.

Before they settled down for the night there had been a not unusual argument with the porters, who had demanded, once again, extra payment, which was, once again, refused. When they came to start there were no porters in evidence, so no attempt was made to rouse them, as the climbers were pretty well certain that they would be able to return to the same place by nightfall.

Paul found the first part of the climb, which consisted of a series of steep snow banks, very difficult, and he required a good deal of assistance, which at least had the effect of keeping the others warm. But by the time that they reached the level of the great snowfield there was little to distract their attention from their discomfort. They could only trudge upwards in gloomy silence, axes under their arms, hands in pockets, their minds concentrated on the misery of their extremities. There was only one momentary diversion which provided them all with some entertainment. Douglas suddenly vanished into a hidden crevasse, which, as they were roped together, was not in the least dangerous; though it proved quite a long task to extricate him, as the sides kept breaking away when he struggled to pull himself out. The slope now became steeper, the wind stronger, and the cold more intense. There was a further distraction when the morning star rose with unnatural brilliance which, with the dramatic effect of a distant thunderstorm over the steppes, emphasized their weird lonely situation. But their pleasure in this was momentary and they soon relapsed into their former state of icy despair. Their morale was to be lowered still further when, without a word, Paul suddenly turned tail and fled down their tracks, unable to bear the torture any further.

Freshfield left several descriptions of their final approach and conquest of the summit. As he implies himself, apart from the intense cold they suffered on this occasion, Elbruz presents almost none of the dangers and difficulties of many a lesser peak. But the first ascent of the highest mountain in the range, perhaps has a certain special interest, and the following is taken from his *Central Caucasus*. 'A sunrise seen from a height equal to that of the top of Mont Blanc is a scene of unearthly splendour, of which words can convey but a feeble impression. A sudden kindling of the eastern ranges first warned us to be on the watch; in a moment the snow on which we were standing, the crags above us, indeed the whole atmosphere, were suffused with rose-pink. The cloud on the summit, which changed from black to grey as daylight dawned, now caught the pervading flush, and suddenly melted away, like a ghost who had outstayed his time. As the hues faded there was no increase of warmth as yet, and, in spite of the improved look of the weather, it became a serious question whether we could go on. By 7.30 a.m. we were at a height of over 16,000 feet, and had now reached the rocks which form the upper portion of the cone. Finding what shelter we could among them, we stood shivering, kicking our feet against the rock, and beating our fingers, to preserve them if possible from frost-bite, while the debate as to whether we should turn back or not was carried on in voices almost inaudible from the chattering of our teeth. On the one hand, the wind did not abate, and the risk of frost-bite was growing serious; Tucker and François had no sensation in their fingers, and my toes were similarly affected. On the other hand, the rocks were less cold to the feet, and gave some shelter from the weather. Looking back, we saw, to our surprise, two of the porters advancing rapidly in our footsteps. We had almost decided to turn when they came up with us, looking fairly comfortable in their big sheepskin cloaks, and quite unaffected by the cold. A third, however, who had started with them, had, like Paul, given in. I said "If a porter goes on, I will go with him." "If one goes all go," added Moor. The decision was accepted, and we again set our faces to the mountain.

'From this time, the cold, though severe, ceased to be painful. A long climb up easy rocks, mostly broken small, with here and there a large knob projecting from the surface, brought us to the foot of a low cliff, to surmount which a few steps were cut in an ice collar, the only approach to a difficulty on the mountain. Arrived on the top of what had for a long time been our skyline, we saw as much more rock above us. Doubts were even now felt, and expressed, as to our success. We persevered, however, making but few and short halts, until the base of some bold crags, we had taken long to reach, was passed. Almost suddenly, at the last, we found ourselves on a level with their tops, and stepped on to a broad crest, running east and west. We turned to the left, and faced the wind, for a final struggle. The ridge was easy, and, led by the porters, we marched along it in procession, with our hands in our pockets, and our ice axes under our arms, until it culminated in a bare patch of rock surrounded by snow. This summit was at one end of a horseshoe ridge, crowned by three distance eminencies, and enclosing a snowy plateau, which, even to our unlearned eyes, irresistibly suggested and old crater. We walked, or rather ran, round the ridge to its extremity, crossing two considerable depressions, and visiting all three tops; under the farthest, a tower of rock, we found shelter and a quite endurable temperature.'

But anything the Monarch lacked in the way of thrills and excitement in the ascent, it certainly made up in the wonderful panorama revealed from the summit. There is little doubt from the descriptions Douglas gave of the mountain as seen from a distance, or of what they saw while actually climbing, Elbruz did not impress him greatly at the time. But as he grew older he came to appreciate other considerations, in assessing the qualities of a mountain, than its ability to make the climber feel like a rock limpet. In referring to this ascent in his later work *The Exploration of the Caucasus* he writes: 'After a lapse of nearly thirty years that view – that vision rather – remains bright in my memory ... And there let me make a confession that may surprise many, and shock some modern climbers – I love summit views.' He was something of a connoisseur after all.

With his companions, Douglas had ascended the eastern summit, which was later discovered to be slightly lower than the other, western mound. Nevertheless it is generally conceded in the Western World that our explorers have pride of place as far as the conquerors of Elbruz are concerned. The Russians, however, neither then, nor since, have conceded that foreigners were the first up their mountain, and instead give honours to an expedition of 1829, led by a General Emmanuel, who, together with an escort of Cossacks and with several cannon, reached the base of the mountain and despatched a party for the summit. The main body of this party bivouacked for the night at about 11,000 feet and the next day made considerable progress, but, by their own admission, were forced to turn back by the lack of time and the softness of the snow. However, the gallant General, observing the operation from the bottom with the aid of a telescope, said that he had observed a figure, dressed as a Tcherkess, far ahead of the others, climb round the base of the highest rocks that could be seen and vanish into the mist. When the whole party had returned the General declared that there would be a valuable bounty for the Tcherkess who had, alone, reached the summit. That evening, sure enough, a Tcherkess named Killar presented himself and claimed the money. None of the other climbers that were on the mountain at the time mentioned any knowledge of him, and the only confirmation of his story was what the General claimed to have seen through his telescope. One thing is certain – hardly anyone at the time believed the claim, as Douglas discovered later when he inspected a tablet commemorating the event. But this cynical deception has become the official record as far as Russia is concerned.

Curiously enough, throughout the rest of their stay, Freshfield and the others were treated with a great deal more consideration and respect as the result of their success. The event too caused a stir of excitement in England where it was reported in a number of papers. In fact a lengthy correspondence – faithfully cut out and retained by Jane Q – was to ensue in *The Times* as a result of the claim that the highest mountain in Europe had been climbed. It was not Freshfield's claim to a first ascent that was put in doubt – it was left to a German paper to do that – but the claim of Elbruz to be in Europe. For so long had Mont Blanc been the Monarch of our own continent, many were loth to see it deposed in favour of one which, if it was in Europe at all, had only crept in by the back door by a matter of a few miles. Freshfield ended his lecture on the Caucasus to the Royal Geographical Society with an appeal to them to end the discussion on the matter by giving a final decision as to where the boundary between Europe and Asia lay. He and others of similar conviction argued that it was convenient that the dividing line was the summit of a mountain range. Furthermore, as Elbruz was quite firmly to the north of the main watershed, then there was every reason for saying that it was in Europe – for so situated it could not possibly be in Asia. This contention would not have excited much attention outside geographical circles, had it not been for the fact the Elbruz is higher than Mont Blanc, and its claim to be in Europe would reduce the Alpine Monarch to second place in the continental hierarchy. It is true to say that the question was only finally settled in the late fifties of this century, when the Russians defined their frontiers and the frontiers of Europe in such a way as to place the matter beyond doubt, and putting the whole of the Caucasus ranges quite firmly in Asia – thus finally leaving Mont Blanc to reign supreme and unchallenged. Freshfield's claim that he and his party had climbed the highest

Elbruz from Pattigorsk.

The Nile Boating Party: standing – far right, Tucker (with pipe) and D.W.F., centre left, Devouassoud.

mountain in Europe, at the time it was made, was a reasonable one. He was concerned with geographical accuracy; he was the last person to make such a claim from delusions of grandeur or self-advertisement.[1]

Their return to the world of men below was uneventful and they arrived at the village of the three Princes the following day, to be quickly surrounded by excited inhabitants, who, on hearing the stories of the porters who had reached the summit were perfectly ready to believe in their claim to success.

There was one disappointment for the villagers; close questioning of the climbers failed to produce any stories of the giant cock that they believed guarded a treasure from the approach of men, or even of any of the lesser spirits and genie that they supposed lived in the recesses of the mountain. However, in spite of this everyone was delighted and impressed with their achievement, including the Princes, and showed their feelings in the characteristic manner of the region – hugging and kissing! One gathers from the accounts that the three Englishmen submitted to these peculiarly foreign gestures with good grace.

Douglas wrote to his mother: 'we went to bed with a weight off our minds, feeling that, come now what might, the three great objects of our journey – the ascents of Kasbek and Elbruz, and the establishment of a high level route between them – were fully accomplished'.

By 5 August, still in sight of the twin domes of the vanquished Elbruz, they travelled north and were enjoying the civilized delights of the small fashionable watering-place, Patigorsk. While they stayed there, resting and discussing their future plans, they heard that General Loris-Melikov the Governor of Cis-Corcasia was staying nearby. Douglas obtained an interview with him and put forward his plan to head south and inspect the northern side of the central range. Possibly because of their recent success, and the now obvious fact that they were quite capable of carrying out their intended explorations, official cooperation and assistance was very much more willing and extensive than previously. The General promised to write to the military posts at Naltschik telling them to have horses prepared for the party, as he assured them that the route

[1] Once again however, Elbruz has been elevated to its European grand status. Since 1990 it has been acknowledged as being in Europe.

The Georgian Castle, Tiflis.

they proposed was practicable for animals and they would not have
to hire porters.

Five days later they experienced the tangible results of this new
attitude, for on their arrival at the little fortified town of Naltschik
they were taken at once to rooms that had been prepared for them,
and which were, by the standards of remoter Russia, quite comfortable. After breakfast the following day they called on the Commandant, who informed that he had arranged the hire of horses and
attendants from upper Tcherek. Then, in the course of conversation,
he casually mentioned the price they would have to pay. This proved
quite unacceptable.

They postponed any further arrangements until the arrival of the
horses and their owners the following morning, when they entered
into a long bargaining session. The result was that eventually they
were able to arrange for the hire at 130 roubles instead of the 400

demanded. Douglas remarks wryly that it is unsafe for foreign travellers to leave money arrangements in the hands of Russian officials.

Their return journey completed as it were, the full circle; from Kasbek to Elbruz on the south side of the range, from Elbruz back to Kasbek on the north. On the return trip they made no spectacular climbs nor attempted unknown passes, but were content to admire the tremendous cliffs and gorges, forests and tumbling waters; while over all towered aloof and jagged silver peaks. The people were generally friendly on this side of the range, though they displayed the usual aptitude for driving a bargain. But none of the party could fail to remark on the difference between the generally hard working, friendly, industrious Mohammedan tribes in the north, with the murderous Christians of the south, who considered lying and thieving, raiding their neighbours and the odd murder worthy employment.

They arrived back in Tiflis early on 26 August and were almost at once made aware of the fact that not a single Russian was going to believe their claims. Of their ascent of Kasbek it was remarked in their presence by one Russian officer that it would have been just as easy for a Russian party to say that they had been to the top. The two ascents apart, the general published accounts of the conformation, people and flora of the Caucasus were so much at variance with what Freshfield found to be the case, that they made a considerable first contribution to the geographical knowledge of the time. What is interesting to note is the length of time that it took for the old traditional beliefs to die. For a long time after the publication of the story of Freshfield's journey the old theories were still being repeated in many publications, and it was this fact that was to send Freshfield again to the Caucasus, stimulated by the first photographs to appear of the region, and lead him to the writing of his major work on the area.

The return to Tiflis saw the close of the major part of the expedition. François was to return to his native Alps, Moor and Tucker were soon to leave for home and other commitments; only Douglas was to continue his wanderings a little longer.

While at Tiflis there was a sudden less agreeable reminder of those idyllic days on the Nile. A letter from his mother awaited his arrival. A certain young American lady had been in touch with her through a mutual acquaintance, claiming that her affections had been trifled with. To his mother, Douglas wrote from Tiflis, with an air of somewhat over-studied aplomb: 'Really the only partially amusing part of the Home News is T. . . .'s report of Miss B. . . .'s expectations. As the charges made are so definite it is worth while explaining to you their grounds – though I should not dream of taking the trouble of doing so to anyone else. While we were in Egypt I had no reason for suspecting Miss B. . . . of being on a sporting tour; nor do I know why I was pitched on instead of Tucker as the game. As for the correspondence – 'Mr B. . . . having been very civil in Egypt I promised to write from Jaffa to put him up to any trips. From Beyruit accordingly I wrote him a line. At Damascus I received via Wilson a note from Miss B. . . . saying that her father being unwell she was acting as his secretary, acknowledging my letter and hoping to hear we had emerged alive from Bashan. I debated what to do, but concluded that politeness required a reply, and wrote a careful geographic note, seen by Tucker. Since then I have heard no more of the family.' As for the photograph – ...'[1]

He goes on in his letter to tell how the usual ship-board photograph came to be taken – 'This explanation is solely for your benefit, if the females of the family like to babble – let them, and I'll pitch into them when I come home. Of course one would be uneasy at being supposed to have trifled with the young lady, but as my mind is quite easy on that score I cannot grieve over her possible disappointments ... The only safe thing these days is to set one's affections on things above an elevation of 11,000 feet. We have been so high lately you need not fear a fall to any contemptible maiden under 5ft. 10ins.'

So much for the romance of the Nile and fond memories. It seems that the lady had made enquiries as to the extent of the Freshfield fortune, and decided that after all she might have reason to regret the lines that Douglas had put in her mouth 'The time we've had was splendid;/ I'm sorry that it's ended.' Perhaps it was the story of this soured romance that dogged him all his life, for it was repeated by his mother who felt that from now on that he was vulnerable to the wiles of scheming young women, to her daughter-in-law, and eventually she too did so to her married daughters, who, when Douglas was a distinguished old gentleman in his eighties, expressed grave concern as to his relationship with a well known author staying at the same hotel in Venice!

[1] See photograph p. 84.

They had been warned that as soon as they were safely out of the country it was likely that the government in Tiflis would officially deny that their party had climbed Elbruz and belittle the remainder of their achievements. Because of this warning they were careful to leave a full written description of the whole of their tour in official hands. Having done this, and completed the remainder of their arrangements, the party set out on their return journey to the Black Sea port of Poti. They varied their route slightly from that by which they had arrived in the region, by going south of Achaltzich; this gave them the opportunity of traversing some of the beautiful forest and hill area round Abastuman, and of admiring the tremendous panorama of the whole range they had lately explored, from the height of the Sikar pass.

There is perhaps one further section of this long tour which is worth a more detailed mention. Douglas said goodbye to the burly dependable François on 6 September, and on the 7th he was himself bidding farewell to the frosty heights of the Caucasus from the deck of his steamer as he sailed away to Sevastopol.

Almost exactly fourteen years earlier, the battle of Balaclava had been fought. Its story, with that of the whole campaign, was still fresh in the minds of Englishmen, and the battlefields still bore the scars of that harsh and futile war. 'On the afternoon of September 10th ... we entered the harbour of Sevastopol, at the mouth of which stands Fort Constantine, looking as strong as ever, though its southern brother is utterly destroyed. The interior of the town presents a scene of destruction for which we were quite unprepared. Not only are the dockyards and government buildings blown to pieces, but the main street is deserted and grass-grown, and the houses that line it, built of white stone, stand roofless and shattered wrecks. Nowhere but at Pompeii have I seen such desolation. The population has fallen from 80,000 before the war to 8,000; it is now rising again, owing to the recent establishment of the ship-building yards of the Black Sea Steam Navigation Company in the Admiralty Creek. Their new machinery sheds are the only signs of life about the place. 'We were surprised to find the lines of the Russian defences so perfect; the lower story of the Malakhoff tower still stands, surrounded by the big ditch and high mound; the salient angle of the Redan looks fresh and sharp, and a dismounted cannon lies in one of the embrasures. On the heights outside the town, the trenches are easily traceable, and at a greater distance, where the huts stood, the ground is strewn with fragments of broken bottles and old shoe leathers. The French dead have been, as far as possible, collected in one cemetery, which is planted with trees, and placed under the charge of a resident guardian; but the bodies of our countrymen lie scattered over the downs, in more than fifty small enclosures, each surrounded by a low wall. At the time of our visit these graveyards were covered with a dense growth of weeds, many of the tombstones were broken and the inscriptions erased, and we saw everywhere proofs of a carelessness and neglect which are discreditable to the English nation.'

It seems that the government that had so futilely squandered the lives of their countrymen, were anxious to forget their squalid end. Bowed down from fever and ill from exposure, they had fought the most unnecessarily prolonged battle in history. Perhaps the greatest victory of the men that lay in these pitiful lonely little compounds was that their successors in the British army never again had to suffer the terrible effects of an organization totally unable to provide food and clothing, let alone any form of medical support, whatever else may have been their fearful lot.

Of the most famous sites Douglas says: 'The battlefields of Bala-clava and Inkerman are marked by simple stone obelisks. It is diffi-cult to recognize the "Valley of Death" in a slight depression between two grassy knolls; the heights of Inkerman are more like what fancy pictures them, and the ravine up which the Russians came to the assault is striking, apart from its associations.'

Once set out for St Petersburg (Leningrad) and Moscow, he wrote to his parents that he was 'fairly on his way home'; for now he was on a railway system that stretches all the way to the English Channel. He stopped briefly for a tour of sightseeing in both the major cities of Imperial Russia; was unable to obey a royal command to be presented to the Emperor – for the simple reason that the command was delivered after the time that the interview was to have taken place – had dinner with Tolstoy; and went to the ballet. At St Petersburg the newspaper cuttings that had been sent on by his mother, concerning the reports of their triumphs, arrived. Messrs Vaux and Rivington carried on an open correspondence in the columns of *The Times* with a distinguished member of the Royal Geographical Society as to the true locality of Elbruz and Kasbek; while the editor of *Pall Mall* repeated the assertion of the German paper that the Englishmen could not have been up Elbruz as they claimed, as the two mountains in question were actually situated at the eastern end of the Caucasus and not in the region explored by Freshfield at all. Douglas was later somewhat annoyed that this paper, which had been so ready to publish the German report, should nevertheless refuse to publish the truth when it was demonstrated to the editor. Not much has changed it seems.

The explorers and mountaineers of the last century were a notoriously cantankerous lot. What rows there were, and to be, over such great matters as the true source of the Nile, within the R.G.S. or 'Almer's leap', within the Alpine Club. That there should be dissent over this young man's confident claims was only to be expected.

But in spite of public argument, there was no gainsaying one thing; that for English mountaineers the Caucasus had been 'discovered'.

Uschba from above Latal.

CHAPTER 5

Looking lean, fit, and full of bounding confidence and with a new found sense of authority, Douglas burst in upon his parents who were staying at Tunbridge Wells. They were naturally full of pride at his fame, his success, and relieved at his safe return. Douglas was full of his plans for the book he would write to cement his triumph and establish his experience of the Caucasus as the correct and acceptable truth. But his return was to see the start of a running battle that was to continue almost throughout the first half of his active life. Neither Henry Ray nor Jane Q considered his hobby, however earnestly followed and however important his discoveries, a proper field to occupy the whole time of someone with his talents and opportunities. His father was certainly not prepared at this early stage to surrender his dream of a son who would one day be one of the great names at the Bar, and there was no obvious reason why he should not realize this ambition. If great influence in legal circles was what was required, then Henry Freshfield was one of the most influential; if powers of patient research coupled with clear and eloquent argument were needed, then it looked as though Douglas was well on the way to acquiring them. The stumbling block was the inclination of the young man himself, whose mind and ambitions for the present, at least, were fixed on horizons further removed than the law courts, and summits higher than the Woolsack. The whole idea of applying himself to this mode of life depressed him considerably, but no son of Jane Q stood much chance of being anything other than dutiful and responsible, and he agreed to fall in with his father's plans.

Encouraged by the praise he had received for his first, privately printed, book of travel, and to some extent spurred on by the energy and faith of his mother, he soon embarked on a full account of the journey. At the same time some of the claims of his party, and the resultant public debate in the press, had not gone unremarked in more sober quarters. Before long Douglas received a letter from the Secretary of the Royal Geographical Society inviting him to submit a paper, or rather an account of the journey, to the Society. Honoured by the invitation, and also anxious that the truth of their exploits and the results of their exploration should be appreciated in the right quarters, he at once set to work, and in due course sent in his paper. The immediate result was an invitation to call on the President of the Society, Sir Roderick Murchison,[1] at his home in Belgrave Square. Almost half a century later Douglas wrote of this meeting: 'I found a formidable but friendly veteran sitting at his library table. He approved the paper except as to its length. I suggested that incidents of travel could easily be shortened. But Sir Roderick was decisive: "Keep the narrative: in reading leave out the geography – you can print it in afterwards." The President than went on to question Douglas about another matter, his theories about which were creating a certain amount of interest. One of the most dramatic features about Kasbek, which had acquired for the mountain considerable fame both outside as well as inside Russia, was the disastrous series of avalanches that were supposed to occur at periodic intervals. When Freshfield and his companions had first arrived in Tiflis they were told that they would be just in time to witness the next of these dramatic events which regularly carried away the Darial road. That this had happened several times, caused by flash floods issuing from the Devdorak glen, was certainly true; but that it happened with any degree of regularity or that it was caused by avalanches, proved mistaken. Freshfield maintained to Sir Roderick that the harm was done by sub-glacial water which, held in pockets, was unable to break out until sufficient pressure built up to burst away huge sections of the glacier and surrounding rock and mud. Under these circumstances, with the aid of the rush of pent-up waters, he thought it possible that the whole mass would be capable of crossing the almost level miles to the Terek valley.

[1] Sir Roderick Murchison (1792–1871). As a geologist he travelled extensively in Russia and Scandinavia.

   The lecture was subsequently delivered to the Royal Geographical Society on the 11 January 1869 and was the first of many that he was to give to this body, and many other bodies, during his life. He had a clear, resonant, slightly sibilant voice and an authoritative manner; he regarded lectures as a method of imparting serious geographical information, theories or argument, and not as an evening's entertainment for the members. He distrusted flamboyant delivery and did not look with much favour on a later generation of speakers that sometimes resorted to flippancy in an endeavour to make a favourable impression. This did not mean that he was averse to the use of more modern methods to lend weight to argument when they became available; he regarded the lantern slide and other photographic methods as perfectly legitimate adjuncts to the lecturer's art. Before a talk of this kind he liked to make detailed preparation, and did not depart to any great extent from his notes. Speaking in committee or debate, however, was a very different matter. Here he loved to score a quick point, or thrust sharply, often with wit and sometimes unkindly, at his opponent's weak spots. In those days people cared less for the laws of slander and libel; debate was more robust and personal idiosyncrasies fair game. The lampoon, the caricature and satire were a popular inheritance from Georgian times. He was to carry this tradition forward into the twentieth century, but modern boorishness and loudmouthed brutishness in debate would have been anathema to him. There were several occasions in his last years when he was upset to hear that he had given offence to younger friends who were not used to such spirited methods. He was ruthless with the pretentious. A story is told of one occasion during his time as President of the Alpine Club, when the desirability of allowing a particular application for membership was being discussed. The gentleman in question had a moderately distinguished climbing record behind him, but had, unfortunately in his letter of application given his occupation as 'chemist'. He was in fact a scientist of some distinction, but one member, having visions of coloured bottles in the window of some small premises of trade, suggested that he thought such an applicant hardly suitable. Freshfield, remembering the wording of the members own application, turned on him, and in a note of tender enquiry asked, 'But pray Sir, are you not something in the City too?'

'A love of one's subject is no bad qualification for dealing with it,' he was to write later, and in spite of his new obligations in the field of the law, and the still more pressing concerns that were to surround him by the end of the year, he still managed to give time to satisfy his love for mountains. His first book on the Caucasus, describing their travels in the Bashan and Persia in addition to the more interesting advance into the range itself, did not take a great proportion of his time, because of his method of note taking and then writing letters home while the whole of each episode was still fresh in his mind. Then, once home, it was a question of refreshing his memory – his mother returned his letters to him – and giving the whole literary style and form. Nor would he forego his summer visit to the Alps. It was not to be a season of particular note from the climbing point of view, but a pleasant high level ramble through his favourite scenery and spectacular views. But it was a visit that was to be the cause of great changes in his life. Apart from the climbing parties of some-what prosaic background; the clerics, the lawyers, teachers, profes-sional and businessmen, there were others of a different cast, who had different motives for their passion who numbered amongst their ranks some of the star performers. The central figure in this circle of climbing enthusiasts was undoubtedly the brilliant, moody, intellec-tual volcano – Leslie Stephen. Stephen epitomized the army of intel-lectuals that found release in the Alps, and he was also a typical member of the Alpine Club – disclaiming all desire for competitive climbing upon maiden peaks, but never able to resist a race; striding carefully and calculatingly upwards, making light of danger and physical discomfort. To men of his kind the Alps were an escape from the growing complications of life at home, and a means of absorbing their minds in physical problems as a distraction from the ethical and religious torment that they suffered. Two years previ-ously, in 1867, he had married Minny Thackeray, daughter of William Makepeace Thackeray, and in so doing had drawn into the Alps part at least of the young literary and artistic circle that surrounded them, including their young cousins the Ritchies.

Freshfield and Stephen had not at this stage joined forces in any climbing expeditions. Freshfield was by now a frequent contributor to the *Alpine Journal*, of which Stephen was the editor, and Freshfield was an admirer of Stephen's descriptive writing, and to some extent used it for a model for his own – Freshfield's background was rich, and, on the whole, the intellectual aristocracy of which Stephen was part despised riches; but on the other hand they both shared an approach to the problems of mountain climbing that might be described as scholarly. Neither was rash or foolhardy, risk was something to guard against, and, as far as possible, moves were carefully thought out; if they appeared nonchalant, or spoke of the dangers in a deprecating manner, then it was all part of the established tradition. Perhaps an element of 'gamesmanship' had crept into mountain-craft.

If there was another strand to Victorian upper class society than that of the 'Forsytes' it was the new intelligentsia. A small coterie, they were welcomed into the menage at Little Holland House to meet the artists, musicians and writers of the day, whose wives, models and mistresses wore such singularly unstayed garments and whose soulful poetic feelings were so eloquently displayed in their large eyes and whole demeanour. It is surprising how many of them had connections with India. Already several generations of the new rulers of that great and mysterious continent had rounded the Cape, served their gruelling apprenticeship in the Indian Civil, before marrying one of the latest batch of pretty young hopefuls sent out with the express purpose of finding a suitable match; one who would stay the course, find high promotion, and not die until his visiting wife had reared a new succession back home in England.

The families of Stephen's in-laws, the Thackeray family and their cousins the Ritchies, were many of them involved with the civil administration in India. Then it was not uncommon for the wives and children of Englishmen doing service in India to spend much of their time in Paris. Living was cheaper and the demands of city life and fashion were easier than those of London. This background of easy social comings and goings, the relaxed attitude of the young, was very different to that prevailing in Freshfield circles. Annie Thackeray, 'Aunt Annie' to a whole tribe of Ritchies and their descendants, was a copious letter writer, a devotee and biographer of her father, and a considerable novelist. She also became lynch-pin for the family and their many connections. Her correspondence is a great source of material illuminating almost all of the literary and social circle of her day. The principal recipients of her outpourings of both affection and ink were her three younger cousins, daughters of William Ritchie.[1] Emily, nicknamed Pinkie, was particularly close, but also included were the two older girls, Blanch[2] and Augusta.

Thackeray's mother had remarried Major Carmichael-Smythe, and they too had made their home in Paris; and during the times that their father was away, the two Thackeray girls, Annie and Minny were sent to stay with them. Augusta and Emily had been sent to stay with their two aunts, Charlotte and Jane Ritchie also in Paris, when Augusta was six, and they were to remain there for ten years. The girls quickly became bilingual, and developed a taste for reading in both French and English. Their father, William, was Judge Advocate General in Bengal, and in spite of the somewhat straightened circumstances in which his family lived, managed to amass a reasonable fortune. At least after he died, when Augusta was seventeen, his widow seems to have lived in some comfort, and his sons were fully educated. Very many years later one of his descendants remarked that he had never discovered the truth as to how a Judge, however distinguished, had managed to acquire such comparative riches.

On the death of her husband, their mother returned to England where the two girls joined with her and their sister and brothers at a country house called Henbury, near Wimborne in Dorset. The two girls from Paris found the change very depressing. The fox-hunting squires of Dorset were not at all to their taste, and Augusta complained that she only had to leave a book of poetry by her bed to be thought strange. In Paris the two girls had lived at the centre of a world of lively culture; musicians, writers and artists were fêted and were constant topics of conversation. New works of art and literature were discussed and criticized, and the girls had learned to accept this world as normal, and to regard serious conversation and discussion on topics seldom mentioned in stolid upper-middle class homes

---

[1] There were eight brothers and sisters, all of whom were born in Calcutta where their father was Legal Member of the Council of the Governor General, Lord Canning. At between the ages of four and six Augusta (Gussie) Emily (Pinkie), Charlotte and the boy Gerald,were despatched to their aunts Jane and.Charlotte in Paris where they remained until their widowed mother returned to England with the younger children, including a further girl, Eleanor (Nelly).

[2] For a description of Blanch (later Ware Cornish) see Hugh and Mirable Cecil's *Clever Hearts* ; Victor Gollancz, 1990.

in England as the very food of life. What the squirearchy of Dorset made of these young women is not known. They were asked once or twice to country house parties, the son of one such establishment being thought of as a suitable escort for Augusta.

'Blanche says we are like prisoners in the Bastille who have been shut up so long their spirits are broken, they beg to be allowed to remain in their cells' she wrote despairingly to Magdelen Brookfield[1] But it was evidently not entirely a desert. 'I was a good deal disillusioned with Mr Tuffnell though I do still think he is very nice to talk to – but the fact is he doesn't stand daylight.' Mr Tuffnell actually proposed, but though he was a very good dancer nothing else about him seems to have impressed. It is possible to sympathize with their mother; these two, almost strangers, mettlesome young women pressing all the time to disrupt her peaceful retirement and widowhood to plunge into the whirlpool of London. But she gave way, and in due course the two girls found themselves in the Capital, even if it was only for four months initially, taking up the threads of the life and culture they had learned from Paris. In very little time, through Annie Thackeray, they were drawn into the orbit around Little Holland House.

The singing of Mrs Sartoris, the playing of Joachim, the household and friends of Lady Somers, salons of Mrs Cameron, the Princeps, Millais, Watts, The Brownings, Leslie Stephen, Arthur Sullivan, Leighton, Doyle, the Darwins; her letters and diaries are peppered with the names of the antecedents of Bloomsbury that they in their turn would make such a cult of deposing. She felt herself to be very much on trial at Little Holland House – though Leighton gave his sign of approval. There was a game the sisters played: '... yesterday at the Monday Pop Pinkie discovered Mr Leighton was "Gifted Stupidity", Mrs Brookfield responded that she was "Brilliant Brevity".' Poor Mr James, an Eton master who had developed a crush on her was "Sentimental Stolidity" and Oscar Browning "Cultivated Stupidity"[2]

---

[1] Magdelen Brookfield – daughter of Jane and the Revd Brookfield. Jane had been the object of William Makepeace Thackeray's devoted love until it was brought to an end by her husband. Jane's family were distantly related to the Ritchies.

[2] Oscar Browning – for a good description of this extraordinary character who later became a famous (or infamous) tutor at Cambridge see E. F. Bensons *As We Were* published by Hogarth Press 1985.

'How else,' she remarks, 'to express denseness of perception.' By any standards, for a young woman of her age and in that period of English society, Gussie was no nonentity. She was proud, quick and passionate. She early developed a strong critical faculty, later witheringly sharp when roused; there was no reprieve once judged lacking. But she would remain staunchly loyal, and valued highly the friendship she judged worthy. She became a lifelong friend of George du Maurier, and a devoted friend and admirer of Joseph Joachim.

At this age she was beautiful too. She was proud of her long smooth neck and creamy shoulders. She was tall and slim with large brilliant eyes that conveyed great intensity of meaning; Mrs Cameron, the portrait photographer, used her several times as a model; here was no wilting flower of the common Victorian stereotype. She must have had a passable singing voice, for she sang in the presence of Mrs Sartoris[1] on a number of occasions, and stayed with her for some time before her mother finally moved to London. Though still young and mixing as she did with those with already established reputations, she was not awed by them – her sharp and critical eye missed very little.

She loved writing letters, constantly bombarding brothers and sisters, aunts and friends with news of her doings, and enquiries after the health and welfare of children. In the summer of 1868 she writes to her sister Blanche from Freshwater: 'We have just been buying some tobacco for Tennyson (with express warning not to say so). He gave us some roses in return to wear to the ball Mrs Cameron is going to give.'

And again a few days later: 'We breakfast at eleven, spend the rest of the morning in being photographed, or down to the sweet beach. In the afternoon we go for a walk with Tennyson ... I don't think you will like any of the photographs Mrs Cameron has done of me yet. The head is larger than life – more awfully like but hideous. The pretty one in the hat was spoiled by movement. The best are two commonplace little pictures which she did just as I came in from a walk.'[2]

And yet again: '... little Mr Walker arrived in the middle of the night on a visit to Annie – half frozen and scared by a twelve mile

[1] Born Adelaide Kemble (1814–79), daughter of actor Charles Kemble. She sang in opera in Venice and Covent Garden and also wrote novels.
[2] No trace of these photographs has been found.

drive in the dark, having been rejected by Mrs Cameron who had gone to bed. He was set down to a meal of curry and sherry in the kitchen with what he called fifteen or sixteen ladies looking at him – it was only Pamela and me and the two Miss Princeps, but he nearly burst into tears with emotion. Yesterday we took THE WALK with Mr Tennyson. He is exactly like himself and quite what he ought to be – there is something very grand and simple about him – his wife is like a Fra Angelico and ought always to stand against the blue sky – they are like Adam and Eve, somehow not the least like people of the nineteenth century. He was so kind to us all and made us sit in the summer-house and took us round his garden, showed us his cocks and hens and gave us tea.' At least Mr Walker escaped with curry and sherry, as the staple diet at Mrs Cameron's, for all meals at all times of the day, was bacon and eggs.

In the two years 1868 and 1869 she escaped almost continuously from the confinement of Henbury, and spent her time under the wing of Annie, or of Annie's sister Minnie Stephen, being whirled around the studios and drawing-rooms of London. While Douglas was in the Caucasus she was stretching her wings with Pinkie in Dresden, learning the language and warding off the attentions of a 'beast of a German student who used to sit near us at the symphonies in the Grosser Garten. He drank beer and smoked in our faces and wore a green cap and pink trousers.' It is not surprising that the next year she and Pinkie should find themselves roaming the Alps in the train of Leslie Stephen, in the company of her cousins and several young friends including Mr James, the stricken Eton master.

By this time Douglas was a figure that attracted a certain amount of attention, especially in mountain circles. Not many young men could boast – not that he did – such a formidable record of ascents, but, more important, and perhaps unique amongst alpinists, a well known exploratory expedition which included a claim to have conquered the highest mountain in Europe. In spite of his general lack of light conversation, and a restless inclination to always be on the move, others were drawn to him. Gussie would have heard a good deal about him, spending as much time as she did in the Stephen household, so that when Douglas, with his guides and two friends, serious and devoted climbers all, met the gay enthusiastic party which included the two Ritchie sisters and their Aunt Charlotte, his grave, attentive manners and quiet, gentlemanly concern singled him out.

Perhaps Jane Q was right in suspecting his susceptibility, for he seems to have fallen in love with the beautiful and seemingly unattainable Augusta almost immediately, and she too was not unaware of him, for, as he helped her into their carriage at Aosta, she flashed him a look that made his heart give a bound of hope.

A day or two later she wrote to her sister Blanche a long letter about the adventures of their party, and in the midst of her description of how their little brother Richmond fared, and the doings of their elder brother Gerald, there appears a new name. 'In the evening Mr Freshfield came back from the Shreckhorn and told us his adventures. He is very nice, adhesive, suave, conversational, and I have conceived a passion for the Alpine Club (Mr James is horribly jealous). It certainly has the power of transfiguring people for even Pollock[1] becomes interesting.'

When Douglas had told his mother that he was determined to fix his attention on things higher than 11,000 feet and not insignificant maidens of five feet ten inches he probably meant it – mountains do have the power to inspire some men to a kind of remote passion. But he detected a lofty quality about the intimidating Augusta that appealed to him as if she were some remote and guarded peak. The very words of his blurted proposal betray the nature and basis of his early feelings about her.

By accident or design we cannot tell, but the two parties met again on several occasions, until one day, as the Ritchies and their friends were preparing to make an early start to leave Zermatt and cross the St Theodule, Freshfield, Pollock and Carson, the three Alpine Club members, decided to join them for the walk, which was due to start at four the next morning. Augusta herself tells us what happened in her next letter to Blanche. 'It was great fun starting after a beef-steak candlelight breakfast, the whole cavalcade with Rudi Devouassoud [François father], a patriarch amongst guides. We had a gorgeous walk over the snow, and there as I trudged along between Rudi and Mr Freshfield he suddenly said he was more afraid of me than of the Matterhorn – which meant that he was making a love declaration. I

---

[1] F. Pollock (later Sir Fredrick Bart.) Member of a large family of distinguished lawyers. Contemporary of D.W.F. at Eton and a longstanding family friend.

The engaged couple.

promptly answered that he mustn't, over and over again – but he went on. We had a long conversation in which I begged him to let us be great friends always; in fact, as Pinkie says, it was my ideal refusal. That evening was rather wretched. My poor Mr Freshfield looked so miserable and white, ever so much more battered than after the Shreckhorn.'

This was hardly the conventional scene for a Victorian proposal; a young couple scrambling over a mountain pass before dawn. No prior declarations of intent to the girl's family, no stamp of approval from his. After that they parted again for three days, but they were to meet again at Chamonix. 'We took several long walks and had several conversations and at last, on Sunday, you know what I am going to say – I let myself be persuaded into saying yes. I have been perfectly happy ever since.'

Perhaps she had fallen in love with the young man as he was por- trayed in a contemporary cartoon, balanced coolly on the brink of some fearful mountain abyss, calmly ignoring poisonous snakes and other terrors, so that soon she was delighted to discover that he shared her love of poetry and appreciation of views and scenery; while he, in turn, remained awed by the young woman who roundly declared that the way to hold the love of a husband was through intellect.

With her father dead, her mother in England and evidently having given up trying to assert any real control over her very young and headstrong daughter, responsibility for Gussie would have fallen on her elder brother Gerald, who was with the party. It is true that aunt Charlotte's caring presence was in the background, but nowhere in the letters that have survived is there any indication as to their reac- tion to what was going on under their noses. There is no doubt that Gussie was more than capable of looking after herself, and Douglas could be relied upon to be the perfect gentleman, but he at least may have been wondering how his parents were going to react to the unconventional manner of his betrothal, and, by their standards, the bohemian and liberated attitudes of his betrothed.

It is difficult to trace the movements of the newly engaged couple during the period of their betrothal because of their habit of sending each other undated letters. But it seems that he soon had to return home to resume his studies, while she went back to Paris with her Aunt. But it was quickly arranged that she was to come over, meet, and stay with her future parents-in-law, with entirely predictable results. Mrs Freshfield may have made some slight break with convention herself, in that she had gone climbing in the Alps, but this intensely unpractical young woman, with everything to learn about household management, who actually spoke of the rights of women, with her head full of poetry and music, who talked of Paris and friendship with notorious artists and writers, was quite a different matter. The worthy wife of the solicitor to the Bank of England tried to talk of domestic affairs, the problems of setting up and running a home, the right way to handle servants and tradesmen, and all those subjects which she considered the true province of women; only to be met with evasion and disinterest. 'I am in the house of the Philistines!' was Gussie's anguished cry. To Blanche she wrote: 'I am dreadfully sorry not to be going to dine with you at the dear Cafe Anglais ... I expect that Mrs Freshfield is the opposition (it isn't a wig, only dye because I saw the grey roots). I rather enjoy the 'City Legal' in the form of big Robert Crawford the M.P.; he is very funny and jolly. I can't tell you how I hated them all the evening you were here, but it has never been so bad since. Douglas has gone to town today (Mrs F. would not let me go with him).'

But in spite of all she remained firmly attached to her Douglas, full of hope that her own love should grow to match his, and that he in turn would learn from her the passionate enthusiasm for the things which she, and those she admired, thought most important. She was making the familiar mistake of believing that it would be possible to mould his likes and dislikes to correspond with her own, and gave him little credit for the talents that were his already. During the engagement his book on his Caucasian travels was published,[1] and there is an air of patronage in her comments: 'I have just finished it and I can't tell you how delightfully interesting I found it. You must write another book for you have a real gift of graphic description. I understand what the critic means who reproaches you with a certain hardness where an older author would have given expression to feeling, especially in the first part about Bashan and Constantinople. You seem now and then, like Leslie Stephen, to be afraid of becoming sentimental – this is the only thing I feel wanting, and most

---

[1] *Travels in the Central Caucasus and Bashan*, Longmans, Green & Co., 1869.

people of course wouldn't miss it. Your description of forest and glacier scenery are beautifully vivid.'

Once again the steady determination of Douglas to have his own way was manifest, the wedding was arranged for 30 November in that same year, 1869. Although he was still studying for the Bar, there was apparently no pressing reason why they should not marry or, for that matter, take a long honeymoon abroad. To her aunt Charlotte in Paris Gussie wrote on the eve of her wedding: 'I am quite happy, and love Douglas so much that it scarcely makes me unhappy at the thought that I shall leave off for ever being Gussie Ritchie.'

Right from the start there is always the feeling that Augusta never accepted the social position that the Freshfields occupied. His riches were those of a new 'class' which, in spite of Eton and Oxford, would not, in her deeply ingrained opinion, match the standing of her own family. But the main cause of friction between the two was not yet apparent, nor was it to be the same as had already occurred between Douglas and his parents. The young couple were delight-fully happy, and had every reason to be so. Douglas had grown in wisdom and tolerance, as she was fiery and emotional, but this only served to increase his appreciation of her enthusiasms and freely expressed opinions. In days when women were not particularly well-educated, she was very much so, and in ways that he was not. Questions of taste other than in the classics were new to him, and he was quick to learn and appreciate.

They were married at the Church of the Holy Trinity, Brompton, on 27 November, in pouring rain amidst tears of joy from most of their relatives, and the lamentations of Pinkie who was grieving for the loss of her constant companion and confidante. Millais[1] was fulsome in his praise of the bride's looks and character, Mrs Fresh-field apparently looked magnificent in diamonds, and Mr Freshfield was 'arch' with one of the bridesmaids. All thought Douglas was most sensitive, kind and attentive, Jane Q considered surprisingly so, never having expected to see him so passionately attached.

They spent their honeymoon in Paris, Rome and Florence, with a short interlude in Capri, and they were joined at various stages by members of her family. On her arrival in Paris, where they had

[1] John Everett Millais, 1829–96; painter, later President of the Royal Academy.

gone in order to visit her beloved aunt Charlotte, she wrote to her sister Blanche, with all her usual feeling, of the wedding and its aftermath. Three years before, Blanche herself had married Francis Warr-Cornish, Vice Provost of Eton, and she too had spent the first few weeks of married life under Charlotte's care.[1]

'I have been thinking a great deal about you in this dear little apartment three years ago. There is a sort of French sentiment about it, the wood fire and the rooms opening into each other, which reminds one of that pretty poem in the "Revue des Deux Mondes" which you wrote out in your diary. When we got here on Monday at 7 dear Cha was waiting for us looking so radiant and overflowing with tears of joy in her eyes – don't you know how Aunty Charlotte cries for joy. She dined with us in our little salon, and yesterday we dined with her. I do think Auntie Charlotte's reception of Bridal Pairs in Paris is the most delightful institution. It gives a sort of respectability to ones situation & makes one realize that one is married. Little Hayes [the maid] also makes one realize it by her perpetual "madams". Charlotte and Little Hayes are the only two people we have seen.' She goes on to comment on various small items of gossip in letters from home, and finishes: 'I must say I enjoyed my wedding very much & should like it to have gone on much longer – Douglas's face shone so on me at the altar & with all the joy & love beaming out of his blue eyes I no longer felt the least inclined to cry but only a sort of triumphant happiness. You were a great comfort to me before, and in the carriage going & dear Frank[2] touched me so by the tears in his eyes. I felt that I had never loved him so much. Douglas is more sweet, romantic and beautifully loving than I can say.'

The honeymoon seems to have been an unqualified success. They visited ruins, picture galleries and attended concerts. She loved Florence and was disappointed in Rome. William Richmond, the fashionable portrait painter, started a sketch of her to be finished in London later. Douglas was not one who made intimate friendships easily; he liked to take his relationships for granted, without remark or demonstration, but for the present at least his manner as a lover and husband were all that Gussie could have dreamed of.

[1] For description and character of Blanch see *Clever Hearts* by Hugh and Mirabel Cecil, published by Victor Gollancz Ltd, 1990.
[2] Blanche's husband gave the bride away.

However he seems to have made little impression on his wife's friends or relations, although he never resented either, and made no attempt to prevent or curtail her going to the parties or functions she enjoyed. Nevertheless a certain air of Freshfield formality crept into their social doings, and their manner of carrying them out. Douglas disliked 'clever' talk, or the open discussion of those personal thoughts and feelings he considered better kept private; furthermore he was quickly bored in certain types of company, and showed it. He thus acquired a reputation for aloofness and even coldness that became a protective armour to his natural shyness. Many who had reason to be grateful for his understanding and kindness often did not appreciate it until years later. Another barrier was that, whatever his personal merit, his wealth was not earned; he gave no service in the way that the Ritchies and others like them understood it.

But some took the trouble to penetrate and understand the real man, and found themselves rewarded. One such was the laureate, Tennyson, for the Freshfields, later with their children, visited Fresh-water at least once a year, and when they were in London the Tennysons would almost invariably dine at the young Freshfields. A genuine affection seems to have grown between the two men that was based on mutual respect; their caped figures could be seen together striding out over the downs. Tennyson said he liked to walk with the explorer because he knew how to remain silent, and did not return home to repeat every word of the Bard as if it were some pearl – a habit that caused the women in the family a great deal of annoyance. There was one day when he returned after several hours of deep conversation with Tennyson, but infuriatingly maintained that he could not remember a word of it!

There was another day though when Douglas did repeat what had happened on a walk with Tennyson, as it had much amused the pair of them. It seemed that they had come upon an old local antiquary digging away with energy at a bank. 'I've got permission your Lord-ship, I'm excavating a Phoenician wall.'

'Why not a Roman wall?' enquired Tennyson with good humoured scepticism.

'Oh!' exclaimed the antiquary, who was stone deaf. 'Oh dear, oh dear! I've left my ear-trumpet at home, just the day when I might have had a conversation with his Lordship.' And he wrung his hands!

In fact Douglas derived a good deal of quiet amusement from the circle of admiring courtiers that congregated at Freshwater, and he produced a comic piece of doggerel. In this he was many years ahead of Virginia Stephen, who much later was to write a satirical play on the same subject.

The supposed speaker was A. D. Coleridge, a frequent companion on the poet's daily walks, of whom some of his rivals at times grew jealous.

TIME: Sunday morning 10.45
SCENE: Outside Freshwater lodgings opposite Farringford Lane.

> I'm a jolly barrister run down from town
> To air self and belongings on Freshwater Down,
> And Freshwater Down – I suppose you all know it –
> Lies conveniently close to the home of the Poet.
>
> The Laureate looks to my coming with zest,
> For in all the wide circuits my stories are best,
> My memories of judges, my tales at the bar,
> I'll rattle them off with unfailing éclat.
>
> Our dear Island at Easter it must be allowed
> Would be thoroughly nice were it not for the crowd
> Of idlers who troop up to tea, and to tease
> With their 'Read us a poem, your new one do please!'
>
> There's Stanford, my chum, I can't leave at the door
> But the Bard, I'll remind him, finds music a bore;
> Here's Freshfield with tales of Caucasian travel,
> He'll have had quite enough with one turn on the gravel.
>
> The Robertsons too: that spruce F.O. young man
> With his wife who's so charming; they'll come if they can;
> They must stop in the study, with Hallam take tea,
> While his father is pacing the garden with me.
>
> Mrs Allingham? No: let her stick to her paint,
> Her sketches are pretty, I don't say they ain't,
> But my stories are better, and no Easter card
> Must come between me and the ear of the Bard.

My word! Why here's Bradley! I'm fond of the Dean,
But so far from his cloisters he shouldn't be seen,
I'll fetch him a hymn-book; he must go to church -
Turned up Farringdon Lane, and left me in the lurch.

There is no doubt that by any standard the young couple were very spoiled. Through the years that followed, as one peruses their correspondence, there is scarcely a hint of the clouds that gathered from time to time on the national horizon, or of disaster and death unless it concerned their family or friends. Good husband and father though he was, there were many who would agree with Henry Freshfield that the years that followed Douglas's marriage, were wasted years for one with such advantages and gifts.

Their first house, acquired after a good deal of trouble as the most suitable they could find, turned out to be within a few doors of his parents, which would never have done. They eventually settled on 6, Stanhope Gardens; Augusta described it as: 'a wretchedly young place, unknown, with pools of water, but that is its worst fault and will cure. I am very glad indeed but appalled by the responsibilities of furnishing. Douglas has rushed blindly into the medieval and accuses me of coldness.'

But even this was hardly far enough from Sussex Square where her parents-in-law had their town house. Old Mrs Freshfield was determined to see that her son's home was being properly administered. 'In the afternoon we drive out and order crockery and glass. We talk about furniture and servants at all the meals ... Still frightfully oppressed by affectionate supervision. When I think we nearly took the house next door ...'

Just before they moved to Stanhope Gardens, there is another note in Gussie's journal: 'Douglas was called to the Bar on Thursday, which depressed him deeply. I rather sympathize. He says it is undertaking a responsibility in which he has not the slightest interest or ambition. He has even stronger longings for wander at this time of the year than I have, but I am quite sure that when he has real work to do, and when we are in our own house we shall be so much happier.'

So there it is, this reference to real work. It is not clear from her diary whether she considers the practice of law as better than nothing, but nor is it apparent that she had any particular desire for him to follow the path mapped out for him by his father. She was unhappy that he showed little inclination to use his gifts in some way that she considered meaningful. It was soon to become clear that she did not think that going off on distant and possibly dangerous exploring expeditions was a proper occupation for a husband and father, and that it was unworthy to spend his whole life in pursuit of a hobby. Much later in life, when writing his biography of de Saussure, Douglas gives us a hint of how he must have been thinking when he quotes from Candoll's reminiscences: 'As a matter of form and following a prevalent custom, I entered that of law, firmly resolved never to be a jurisconsult, or lawyer, but hoping to gain some knowledge of affairs.' Freshfield adds significantly 'The custom is not confined to Geneva: many Englishmen read law and are called to the Bar with a similar motive.'

There is little doubt that he loved Gussie more, as she herself pointed out, than she loved him. And for some years any departure abroad upset him as much as it did her, and this certainly had its effect in curtailing his exploring activities. But it can be argued that this was much to the benefit of the Royal Geographical Society.

So those years when the children were born and grew passed peacefully at least. We know so much of the doings of all their relations and Gussie's circle, they seem to whirl and explode about him; Douglas's brother-in-law, Richmond, for instance, after a brilliant scholastic career, scandalized London and infuriated Leslie Stephen by marrying his cousin 'Aunt' Annie Thackeray, rose swiftly and with distinction to a position of power in the India Office; the writings, the poems, the letters; the marriages, births and deaths; all so faithfully and dramatically recorded. Yet through it all he appears only as a shadow, lit for the moment by the light of some shooting star in a firmament that, as the precursors of Bloomsbury, are one of the most faithfully recorded in English literary history. It was little wonder that Augusta began to despair of a man who devoted his talents to producing what were little more than guide books, at least in the eyes of her circle.[1] Still Douglas Freshfield's day would come, even if not in the field or manner that others saw for him.

---

[1] He was commissioned on a number of occasions to write for sections of Murray's *Guides*.

During the years between his marriage and his second visit to the Caucasus in 1887, perhaps the one thing that would give his growing family more pleasure than anything was the purchase of Kidbrook by his father in 1874. The house stood just outside the village of Forest Row in Sussex, in the midst of a delightful park, whose giant trees, meadows, lake and woodland ridges made a wonderful setting for the children. Henry Freshfield and his wife loved the position and the responsibilities that their new acquisition brought them; they purchased adjoining land whenever the opportunity offered and became very interested in the preservation of Ashdown Forest, which even then was coming under pressure from all kinds of development. On their many and frequent trips abroad Douglas and Augusta would leave the children with their grandparents at Kidbrook, in the charge of their indulgent and doting grandfather. There was a little donkey cart for rides around the park; there were picnics and walks in the forest. The only drawback was that their mother never seemed happy there, but seemed always anxious to escape from an atmosphere she considered too oppressive to be borne.

The Freshfields continued to travel frequently; it might be to Greece, Constantinople or Italy, but most often to the Alps, where he continued to climb, search out new paths, and write his particular type of travel guides. So much so that even Augusta, with her professed love of mountain scenery, confesses that on occasions she was bored with mountains and bored with Mr Tucker, too often their companion. But always the faithful François was waiting at the station when they arrived, and when they brought the children with them he was ready to play nursemaid and carry them on his broad shoulders, so that sometimes the whole family would achieve a peak.

> Two sisters and one small brother, raised my frame
> As part and parcel of their daily game;
> Spare me, rude cowherds, idle tourists, spare,
> To show how far British babes may fare.

Thus wrote the father for the stone man that his children erected on achieving the Prarion.

He did not however always stay on the easy slopes with his family. There were days when he and François would vanish together to explore and climb with serious intent. There were other occasions when he came alone to the mountains, leaving the family at home, or, as on one occasion, leaving them on holiday in England. Once as he departed over the hill leaving his family below, he was filled with guilt and gloom at leaving them. 'When I got to the top of the hill and saw Woodey Bay with all that is dear to me below,' he wrote, 'I felt rather like a suicide might, five minutes after the deed.' He was devoted to his family and it was always a struggle to leave them. Augusta knew this, and realized that at the slightest hint of trouble he was ready to hurry home.

'You may imagine what a sensation Douglas's appearance caused last night at ten o'clock when the door bell sounded and he strode in looking very brown, gaunt, and slightly offended with us all; but very pleased and triumphant. I felt dreadfully ashamed at having brought him flying back, almost too guilty to be very glad; Mrs Freshfield was quite horrified.' By what means she had managed to scare him into an instant abandonment of his travels is not known, but, from her own words, it would seem not to have been a real crisis.

However they were developing a new interest that they could and did share. They started their own collection of pictures. Their favourite artist was Corot, and they had already acquired one such, when at Christmas 1875 Gussie wrote to her sister Emily: 'My Christmas present from Douglas was – The Sunset Corot! Which he firmly planted on my bed before I was up. Anything more exquisitely beautiful than they look in different lights in our room, impossible to imagine. They still so equally divide my imagination that I turn from one to the other in rapture. It is quite a new sensation having such great pictures near one all day long – like when one has learned a great poem by heart and discovers in oneself a new sense for poetry. Douglas and I are so furiously bitten that I can imagine perfectly well going in rags and feeding on bread and water to have a lovely collection of pictures.'

But there was no need to contemplate such extremes. They patronized fashionable portrait painters too. Augusta's journal for 10 January 1874 reads: 'Mrs Freshfield and her carriage were at the door at 10.30. Nauseating expedition to Hammersmith. Sat for my portrait to William Richmond, who was far from pleased by his subject. Complained of coldness of my complexion.'

In this portrait she sits composed, perhaps resigned, against an Italianate background. Heavy lids half obscure the great eyes, and one gets the feeling of a somewhat impatient Madonna. But she was delighted with the finished product: 'My picture on the eve of being finished, exquisite symphony of greens, blues, and purples, with lovely Capri at my back ...' Much later generations of the family did not share her pleasure, it was shuffled from house to house for a long time before it found a home.

Throughout the years they added to their collection. Watts, Corot – there were five of them in the end – Constable, Gainsborough; Italians, English, Flemish; modern and medieval, in a glorious jumble and confusion on every wall of their London home. A collection for which at last they were to build their ideal setting, their 'fairy palace' on the fringe of the forest.

Although Augusta may have felt that Douglas was at a disadvantage in not having a real occupation, this did not mean that he was idle, and doing nothing whatever to forward his real passion in any way he could. In 1872 he took on the job of editing the *Alpine Journal* from Leslie Stephen, a task which he continued to fulfil for nine years, until he took the more important office of Honorary Secretary to the Royal Geographical Society. At the same time he continued to contribute to the journals of both these bodies, published his book on the Italian Alps, edited *Hints for Travellers* in which he himself wrote the section on mountaineering, and was commissioned to bring up to date the mountain sections of a famous European guide book. He still wrote in his serious objective manner, even the descriptions in his letters to his wife are accurate rather than imaginative, but that is what he did best. The thrill of meeting danger, however, had begun to pall with the development of family responsibilities. He said himself in a letter home: 'I am beginning to doubt whether I enjoy as much as formerly the sensation of danger, even without the reality.' Although he remained faithful throughout his life to the welfare and activities of the Alpine Club, more and more it was the Royal Geographical Society that claimed his attention; studying reports and writing notes and recommendations on the exact position and nomenclature of the 29,000 foot peak in the Himalayas; making a detailed study of the passes Hannibal may have used in making his famous crossing of the Alps; or studying the

Alpine Notes of Leonardo da Vinci. The period from 1870 to 1880 can be described as a long period of transition for Douglas Freshfield, from the typical Alpine Club enthusiast to the behind the scenes advocate of the increasingly important science of geography.[1]

Much as Douglas admired and was influenced by the mountain writings of Leslie Stephen, and as much as their approach to the art of mountaineering were similar, there was nevertheless a profound difference in their attitudes. Stephen had two pet hates: the celebrity, whom he would ignore rudely for no specific reason other than that he was a celebrity, and the scientist, who climbed mountains and studied glaciers in order to try to add to the sum of topographical knowledge. Perhaps there was a certain amount of excuse for the latter aversion, for undoubtedly some of the amateur scientific climbers must have made very boring company. Freshfield had a foot in both camps, for not only was he moved by mountain scenery, but he was intensely curious about its formation and origins. Stephen came to the mountains to prove himself to himself, but this was not, for long, enough for Freshfield, so we find him lending weight to current arguments – Do glaciers gouge or bore? How much is the rarity of air a hindrance at great heights? – and so on. Thus there came about a paradox. When Freshfield took over the editing of the *Alpine Journal* his influence was to make that paper somewhat more scientific in approach, but as a contrast over the years he used his influence to make the journal of a scientific body, the Royal Geographical Society, more interesting to the general reader. Both Ruskin and Stephen had influenced Freshfield's literary style – but as to content and matter – that was his own choice.

As an Alpine Club member he differed little from many others. Not as cantankerous as some, and true, he might have been able to claim more than most in the way of maiden peaks and passes, but there were few that were able to devote so much time to their chosen sport as he, and it is perhaps surprising that he took so long to arrive in the Alps with some other motive than to search for some untrodden yard of ground or some new scenic sensation.

[1] A much later Secretary complained to the author that D.W.F. left no money to the A.C. nor any pictures or papers, though he knew that they were having financial difficulties.

His family had much to do with this, for his wife made no secret of the fact that she could hardly bear the thought of the long separation that any serious expedition of exploration would entail, and furthermore he loved to display the delights of alpine travel to both his children and younger in-laws. In the early years of his marriage they sometimes took his younger brothers-in-law. Augusta wrote to 'Pinkie' (Emily) 'Richmond's Pyrenean tour would have been very incomplete without coming to this delightful place, where the last three days have been best of all … Douglas and Richmond went up the Porte di Vinasque which looks down upon Spain. Eleanor and I dashed down the dewey valley in the morning and met them at the station where they were standing burnt a bright brick colour, surrounded by their enthusiastic Pyrenean guides, there was great clasping of hands and congratulations.'

Douglas's son was yet too young to be a climbing companion to his father. Henry, called Hal, was born at Kidbrook in 1877, the Freshfield's third child.

Altogether they led the full lives of cultivated, independent people that are sure of their place in the world and the love and esteem of their friends and relatives. They had their griefs, as when Minnie Stephen died; but grief in its way served to make life more meaningful. Gussie's letters to Paris and India burst with lively gossip, news, sympathy and adoring tales of the children. Aunt Charlotte was immersed in charity work in Paris, and there was much worry over her safety at the time of the riots and the German siege. But generally it was news of how she could never do right to please Mrs Freshfield; news of the latest play, book, or party. News of the picture galleries: 'At the private view of the Grosvenor House there was a fearful young man, stout, fair, with curling fair hair on his shoulders and a splendid, thick frock coat who Magdalene and I severally put down for a Jew-boy and a Lord. He turned out to be Oscar Wilde – poet – who made the celebrated speech of trying to live up to his blue china – such a beast.'

Sometimes she sees in the stolid respectable life at Kidbrook, pure farce: 'Languishing in the incredibly dull, narrow, egotistical moral atmosphere of this lovely place, where no ray of intellect or reviving wit, or blessed humour ever penetrate. Yet they are very kind and devoted to us; deeply hurt when Douglas mildly said that the Bishop and neighbouring clergymen who are invited here next week are "Not in his line". Mr Grove, Augusta Irvine's little husband, and Augusta herself were down here, he, as clergyman to do the services of Holy Week in the absence of the proper clergyman of the Parish. When we arrived they were in high favour. She is a terrible vulgar little chatterbox, but he is a nice little human being, well read, interested in things.

'On Easter Eve Mr Grove retired to bed early with a bilious headache. Mr Freshfield, as kind host as well as churchwarden, supplied him with blue pills and went to bed rather nervous. On Sunday morning the poor little parson could not lift his head from the pillow, was far too sick to be able to think of performing the Paschal ceremonies. Mr and Mrs Freshfield were pale with dismay and displeasure. Then Mrs F. remembered that the poor wretch had eaten cream tart the day before at dinner; that he had mixed his sherry and claret; and that in his folly had gone so far as to stand sketching Douglas's Constable in the cold hall! Mr F. kept trotting off with tea and toast to his bed-side, and insisting on pouring it down his throat in order to make him sick and so relieve him in time to do the service. Fortunately at the eleventh hour a clergyman from East Grinstead arrived and the souls of the Parish were edified and the honour of the Kidbrook churchwarden and patron saved. In the evening Mr Grove appeared not at all crushed, in excellent spirits, prepared to discuss the French plays, and actually mixed his sherry and claret again at dinner.'

They were unable to attend the wedding that was the cause of great family strife, between Gussie's brother Richmond and his God-Mother cousin Annie Thackeray. She had been looking after her widower brother-in-law Leslie Stephen, and his subsequent rage, which was was at least in part jealousy, was only kept in control by the practical understanding of Julia Duckworth, the widowed niece of Mrs Cameron, whom he later married. Had she been able to attend no doubt Gussie would have left a very vivid description of the event. As it was she wrote to her brother in India: 'I feel just as if I had been at the wedding thanks to the graphic accounts from Blanche, Pinkie, and Magdalene, of Leslie crouching like Mephistopheles during the religious service; Julia the queen of the night presiding in her sables.'

Augusta Freshfield by Sir William Blake Richmond.

Gussie had a gift for graphic characterization, especially if the subject was someone for whom she held no fondness. 'Lady Ida Macnaghten, Malcolm's wife, who is an extraordinary compound of low church principles, blue veins of the Hapsburg House; a lovely aristocrat with a passion for economy in every department and a sort of holy enthusiasm for the subject of pounds shillings and pence; she makes it her mission to tell all her friends how much cheaper they can get their butchers meat.'

As time passed and the children arrived and grew, the relationship matured, as relationships do, Douglas giving time and seriousness to geography and geographical research, Gussie to the family and her social friends. They were becoming well-known as hosts, and Gussie too was sought after for her support during times of crisis. Her sister-in-law, William's wife Magdalene, often her companion and frequent correspondent, died after a long illness, and she spent much time as in the Victorian way of death, comforting the distraught husband, and writing to their brother in India with words of consolation and intimate description of the rites of death. She herself was becoming sceptical, as was Douglas, of Church of England received wisdom and contemptuous of clerical performance, but unable to face the prospect of entire loss of faith. Such matters were now openly discussed and written of in a way that had not been generally so amongst women as well as men, and the company at her table was such that anything could be called into question.

'A person who is the best company possible is William Sidgwick.[1] ... Talking to him is like riding a buck-jumping horse, one never knows where his paradoxes will fling one and must hold on tight and be ready to follow him up and down his vivacious and surprising arguments. He is best talking to a whole table, only he offends people sometimes. Mrs Green flounced away one day upon his saying that it appeared the rottenness of Ireland extended even to the potatoes ... But for tête à tête conversation, the only person I ever have that treat with is my dear Mr Du Maurier – how I should like to talk with him for an hour once a week – we do not meet once a month.'

[1] William Sidgwick, tutor at Merton College, Oxford, brother-in-law to E. W. Benson, Archbishop of Canterbury.

In 1881 there occurred a domestic incident which throws a light upon the family relationship: Douglas's sense of guilt on his travels, and Gussie's impatience with his absences. Gussie's younger sister, Nelly (Eleanor) had been travelling with her mother in Italy, and whilst in Rome had been struck down with typhoid. It is not clear whether Douglas had hurried from the Maritime Alps to be of assistance, or whether he had already joined with the two women on their travels. However he found himself having to take charge of the situation, arranging for nursing, doctors and accommodation at the Hotel Bristol (he writes home that the sanitary arrangements were excellent), and daily sending bulletins home to the sisters. While he shows every sign of sympathy for the poor fevered patient he obviously finds the job of sickroom attendant for a long period, difficult, and writes to Gussie pleading with her to come out and assist. The answer he received from her obviously upset him, as for the first time there is a note of hurt when he again writes saying that no, he is not having a nice easy time enjoying himself. [1]

By 1885 Douglas and Augusta had completed their family of five children. They were lucky, all four girls and their son had been born and reared without major problems of health. Although, besides the death of her sister-in-law and the earlier death of the much loved Auntie Charlotte in Paris, there was no sign of the cruel revenge that the fates had in store, so now at last Douglas allowed himself to contemplate going slightly further afield.

[1] In 1883 Nellie was to marry Herbert Paul M.P., historian and author.

CHAPTER 6

In 1882 Freshfield had toured the Alps yet again, collecting material
for articles published by him in both the journals of the Royal
Geographical Society and the Alpine Club on the subject of Hannibal's passage of the Alps. This subject interested him for many years,
and he was eventually to publish a full length book on it. His arguments are now generally discarded in favour of another route and
his writings on this subject forgotten. Apart from this however he
was still going further afield as far as the Dolomites, Corsica, and in
1886, the Atlas mountains. Later he was to publish a popular travel
book called *Below the Snow Line*,[1] which remained in print for
many years, and still has its devotees.

The decision to take François and visit the Atlas was taken whilst
he was having a holiday with the children in Normandy in the
summer of 1885, where he had discovered two books by a Frenchman called Fromentin, a painter, which had interested him greatly,
Une Année Dans Le Sahel and *Un Eté dans le Sahara*.

The arrival of the two men in Algiers passed unnoticed until they
had departed for the hills, when a newspaper published that an
English Milord with his Swiss guide had started to walk across the
Sahara to Khartoum – a story which almost matched that of an
English paper published when he was about to depart on his later
expedition to South Africa, and telling of how he had, in his youth,
walked up Mont Blanc dressed as for town, wearing top hat, tail

---

[1] Published by Constable & Co. in its final Edition in 1923.

coat, and carrying a cane. Often in his more distant wanderings he was dogged by terrible rains; in Sikkim he was to be nearly prevented from making his tour of Kanchenjunga by tropical deluge; the summit of Ruwenzori was to be denied him because of rain and attendant mud, and for the first ten days in the Kabyle Highlands he was attended by similar weather, so the two men made a tour by train and coach over the central highlands, arriving at Bougie just as the weather broke for the first time. Whatever he may have thought of the French as artists and writers, Douglas had a very poor opinion of their powers on the mountains, even their own. On one occasion, when describing the Dauphine he says; 'The Meige is superb and beautiful on one side, majestically ugly on the other. I cannot conceive how any human being ever got up it, much less a Frenchman!' On this occasion he and François had a good deal of superior fun at the expense of the Club Alpin Francais who were paying a simultaneous visit to the region. Several times their flamboyant cart-born procession passed the two solitary foot-born but more businesslike climbers. 'We encountered three diligences – the vanguard of the Alpinists. Lower down we met the main army. Flags waved and horns blew. We quickly passed, unobserved by at least a third of the company who, happily unconscious that a note-taking 'chiel' was on the road, had their heads buried in polychromatic handkerchiefs, which doubtless assisted them to highly coloured dreams of the Algerian Landscape.'

Hardly the manner in which members of the English Alpine Club thought it appropriate to conduct their expeditions! Three days later at Taourirt Iril they asked a woman if a number of tourists had passed that way three days before. 'Ah, yes, Monsieur,' she replied, 'such a pity: the fog was so thick we did not even see them go through. What a spectacle we lost!'

Douglas was intrigued with the Algerian landscape, but did not think it compared well enough with better known ranges to bring his Alpine Club members streaming out in his footsteps, although he was very much interested in the native Kabyles and their origins.

They had secured for themselves a little Kabyl and his mule as guide and baggage carrier respectively, and they had attained Fort National, in sight of Eas Timedouin the 7,546 ft. peak that was their objective. As a guide the Kabyl was less than helpful; in the first place leading them in directly the opposite direction to their proper path. When this was pointed out to him, he shrugged happily and said '*La même chose*.' They led him to the top of a convenient knoll and pointed out the conspicuous peak that they wished to reach. 'Lella Khedidja' murmured the guide. 'Not at all,' said Freshfield, 'that one,' pointing many degrees further west. '*La même chose*,' said the guide. The best way to proceed they found was to take a careful eye survey of the ground from their vantage point and then guide the guide.

They spent the day clambering up and down a series of ravines, through varying degrees of cultivation, forest and stony ground. Perhaps the guide knew more than they gave him credit for. They ate their lunch under a sycamore tree near a small hamlet, where an orphan boy offered himself for adoption, and then entered the oak and olive covered slopes of the Jurjura. In a village that lay conveniently near the foot of their peak they took a small flat-roofed mud house for the night; sharing with a number of cows, whose heads loomed dimly in the two openings which led to their subterranean den below, and a donkey which was allowed to stand in the passage with its front legs in the room and proceeded to exercise its apparent right to join in the conversation. In the circumstances they did not sleep very well and were glad to make an early start into the twilight. It must have been a great relief to the two friends, after all the years of tame domesticity and tourism, to find themselves roughing it in a land that was totally unfamiliar, however well explored and mapped. They had a very steep but by no means difficult ascent, mainly by snow gully, and in three hours from their sleeping quarters they were examining the snow-filled, cauldron-like hollows on the top. On the farthest summit, for there were several of them, they found rings of stone that were of native origin, and concluded that Kabyl goatherds had preceded them; but of European climbers they had no knowledge.

They were treated to a most interesting view, even to a connoisseur; Algiers, sixty-five miles distant, was clear in the morning light, while to the north the blue Mediterranean and to the south the golden haze of the Sahara made a magnificent contrast.

Their return was soon accomplished, as they were able to glissade most of the way, and by 10 a.m. they were back with their baggage having enjoyed a bathe in an oleander shaded pool on the way. Their

Kabyl enquired if they had been to the foot of the cliffs. 'To the top of the snows', replied the climbers, in tones of quiet rebuke. 'La même chose,' was the imperturbable reply.

During all those years of marriage and family life, that first visit to the Caucasus receded in his mind to become like a far-off dream, a wonderful unique memory, to be recalled and mulled over in climbing reminiscences. Every now and again discussion would break out in the Alpine Club or the Royal Geographical Society on some matter of interest or argument concerning that distant range, and when that happened he was happy to lend the weight of his personal knowledge. There were times too when his own tales and descriptions were called in question, but this failed to arouse him to any great desire to argue, for, after all, others would soon confirm what he had said. It was in fact the reports of a number of new expeditions to the Caucasus that once more brought his attention back to those frosty peaks, and woke in him the desire to see again the summits that in his day had been unsuspected and unnamed. Surely now, with improved transport facilities and the gradual percolation of civilization to those isolated valleys, the time had come for positive identification of the major peaks that remained in doubt, and the careful correction and correlation of the growing mass of material.

In 1884 a Hungarian, M. de Dechy, led a small expedition into the area, climbed Elbruz and a number of other peaks and made useful scientific observations with regard to the extent of glaciers, snow-fields and so on. He made further expeditions during the next two succeeding years, and eventually the results of his work and travels arrived with the Alpine Club. The greatest excitement was caused by the fact that the most significant feature of the reports was that they were accompanied by numerous photographs, the first ever from the region. They had an immediate effect on climbers and explorers in this country, for they confirmed Freshfield's and Grove's descriptions and fully opened the eyes of many to undreamed of possibilities. On Freshfield too they had an immediate effect, awakening in him the desire to find some of the answers to the questions now being posed, and to see again the luxuriant valleys and unrivalled views to which he had sought to draw others by his book of nearly eighteen years ago.

It would have to be a short trip this time, for Augusta was not

compound to the well remembered guest hut they had occupied all those years before, and where they had celebrated their victory.

But if Freshfield remembered the village of Urusbeih, neither had its inhabitants forgotten him. Two of the Princes were still alive; there was a dark tale concerning the fate of the third, but they attributed most of it to the native love of romancing. But the other two, shorn of the last shreds of their feudal power, of which they had retained at least some effective measure at the time of Freshfield's first visit, were still able to make travellers welcome. They were treated to a glimpse of a carefully guarded treasure in the village archives, their own visiting cards. That first expedition had become a legend to the rising generation of villagers, and their porters were venerable local heroes, happy now in the opportunity to recall past exploits. One of them went so far as to ask after Moor and 'the little Gospodin who walked so well', meaning Tucker.

They hired eight Urusbieh men as porters, and this time set off in a south-easterly direction, up a tributary valley to the Baksan, which would lead them to the Mestia Pass over the main ridge and down into Suanetia once more. They found that the wild, surly, knavish people that they so well remembered had, to some extent at least, been tamed. They still retained their ability to go back on a bargain without the slightest compunction, or to steal or lie as the occasion offered, but on the other hand their fierce truculent manner had become a sort of pantomime to be put on for form's sake, with very little real evil intention behind it; a man would make a great show of going for his dagger or his gun during an argument, but they soon realized that it was quite safe to ignore the gesture. However, they were just as much objects of interest as formerly, having to submit to an attentive audience for every act, from shaving to eating. But at least the attention was not hostile, and in fact there was now a representative of the law in each village, in the form of a locally appointed mayor, directly responsible to the government. Robbed of the tension that had been caused by the inhabitants, Suanetia was indeed the most delightful region, with its beech, alder, and poplar groves; its hayfields bounded by wattle fences and fringed with flowering azaleas and rhododendrons, and everywhere the collections of villages with their clustering white towers. They continued westwards down the valley for two hours to a large collection of villages known as Latal, where they sat for lunch under the shade of a giant sycamore, once again the objects of amused attention. This time there seemed to be more women than usual amongst the crowd, and in fact one of them went so far as to take a bath in the wooden trough of the village fountain, quite unconcerned by the proximity of the party of strangers. This idyllic scene was described by Douglas in a letter home, and revived all the old fears as to his vulnerability to the wiles of women when away from home. But they escaped unensnared, and pushed on to Betsho, the new capital of Suanetia, and the official residence of the Commissioner who now ruled the country.

In fact the place was not a bit as pretentious as its description might sound, consisting of nothing more than the bungalow that was the official residence, a ruined barrack, a low shed which was the quarters of the police staff, and a courthouse that was sometimes placed at the disposal of travellers. The only remarkable feature of the place was the view it afforded of Ushba, the immediate objective of the explorers, which rocketed skywards 10,700 feet above them, a bare ten miles distant. But unfortunately, apart from its position, Betsho proved a poor place from which to try and mount a sortie of mountain exploration; provisions proved scarce, porters hard to obtain, and it was obvious that little more than a reconnaissance could be effected.

Accordingly de Dechy decided on a photographic expedition, while Douglas and François were bent on trying to climb a neighbouring and lesser peak in the hopes of being able to obtain a close and useful look at Ushba to determine if possible a practicable route to the summit of the twin-toothed giant. They started at 5 a.m., and in trying to take a short cut were soon lost in a seemingly impenetrable thicket of hazel and azaleas. But eventually they found a horse track that led to the snout of the Gul glacier, where Russian officers sometimes sent in summer for a load of ice, and the way became obvious and easy – a steadily mounting path through fir forest and flowery pastures. Later, as they climbed to the side of the glacier, they could see that it was encircled by a rocky ridge that terminated to their left in the lofty spires of Ushba itself, and to the right in a lesser peak. By comparison with its giant neighbour, the latter peak, which Freshfield called Gulba, was not very imposing; but none the less it rose to a height of over 12,000 feet: as Freshfield points out, the height of the Wetterhorn and fully entitled to be regarded as a mountain in its own right. A careful survey of Ushba from its very base, however, decided Freshfield that conditions that season would render an assault impossible. As they ploughed up the first slope of névé above the icefall this opinion was confirmed. The snow was exceedingly treacherous, giving way at every step under their feet, and in the still air they could hear the soft 'ominous hissing sound, like that made by a disturbed snake', as the upper layer became detached and slid smoothly downwards. On the higher slopes of the mountain, too, they could observe the continuous discharge of miniature avalanches, which forced them to the conclusion that coupled with the difficulty of obtaining porters, for this season at least, Ushba must remain unattempted. Perhaps the intervening years had made him soft and dulled his attacking edge. Certainly in later life the failure to make the attempt was the cause of considerable regret. He was often assailed with the thought that with a little more determination they might have overcome the difficulties that had seemed insurmountable at the time.

From Betsho, Gulba had looked uninteresting; 'blunt and stumpy' were Freshfield's adjectives. But as they pulled themselves, mostly by arm-work, to the top of the buttress leading to their peak, they found that it was in fact a very thin wedge, whose far side was a grim precipice dropping directly down to the Chalaat glacier which lay beyond. They amused themselves for a moment tossing stones down the sheer rock face, before proceeding to the nearest summit, and then over an ice gully to the second, slightly higher crest. The first part of the descent required caution because of the loose boulders, but they soon came to a snow slope which did not seem to be crevassed, at an angle not too steep to allow a slide. They reached the foot in fifteen minutes at a point at which it had taken them two hours to climb by the rocks. Freshfield was an indefatigable and very fast walker, and on reaching safe ground hurried ahead in order to avoid the storm that seemed to be brewing, leaving the exhausted guides to follow at their leisure. There are many descriptions of Douglas's walk, especially in his middle and old age, but it seems that already he had developed the rapid, almost jog-trot shuffle which became the hall-mark of his progression. 'Four hours after leaving the top of Gulba I pushed open the door of the courthouse at Betsho and discovered my companion sedulously immersed in those tiresome occupations which are the price the mountain photographer pays for his success.'

Although Ushba was to retain its icy maidenhood for some time longer, Douglas and François had one objective on this journey that they were most anxious to attain. In the year after de Dechy's reports had first arrived at the headquarters of the Alpine Club, Freshfield had prevailed upon his friends, W. F. Donkin and Clifton Dent, to try their luck in the Caucasus. The mountainous country of Suanetia is dominated by yet another major peak besides Ushba, which had been identified as the Tetnuld, and it was this peak that Donkin and his party decided was to be the main object of their expedition. Having arrived at the foot of the mountain, they selected their peak, and were successful, except that on attaining their summit they discovered that they were in fact on the wrong one, and that the true Tetnuld rose serene and unconquered, some distance off. It was to clear up this confusion, and to conquer the real Tetnuld, that Douglas and François were embarked.

They set out for the village of Adish, lying on the lower slopes of the range, some two miles from the skirts of the mountain, via Impari; a journey on which they encountered all the usual inconveniences and attendant scenic wonders. 'Fancy the valley of the Lyn,' reported Douglas, 'with two mountains over 15,000 feet closing every vista, the white pyramid of Tetnuld in front, the rock towers of Ushba behind. One of the views of Ushba was the most perfect imaginable. But there are so many perfect views of Ushba! The particular charm of this one was in the water, and the foliage of the foreground, and the way in which the lower hills formed a framework for the two great peaks. The path continued by – and often in – the stream, until the barley fields and towers of Adish came suddenly in sight.'

Adish was perhaps the most isolated village in Suanetia, and for this reason was one of the least law-abiding; but on this occasion they offered no trouble other than the usual pantomime resorted to whenever their exorbitant charges were resisted. One man seized Freshfield's ice axe and demanded ransom for it; another tried to make them pay for the privilege of having eaten their lunch on his land, but, secure in the knowledge that this time they had the protection of their two Cossacks, the party were able to settle all questions by the distribution of a few copecks. It was often said that wherever Englishmen travelled they paid such high prices that others were quite unable to follow. This charge could never be levelled with substance at Freshfield; rather the reverse. He seems to have taken a pride in paying as little as possible, and enjoyed the opportunities for Byzantine bartering, perhaps something he had learned from Jane Q's good housekeeping.

They camped for the night an hour above the village in a grove of birches close to the foot of the great Adish glacier. It was to prove an unfortunate choice of site. At dawn François pushed his head out through the tent flaps only to exclaim, 'Our mutton has been stolen!' Investigation proved that it was not only their supplies of meat that had been taken, but more seriously, a corner of the waterproof that covered the pile of baggage between their tent and that of the two Cossacks had been lifted, de Dechy's case removed, and his clothes and revolver gone. To add to the difficulties it was pouring with rain, and it was decided that they could not possibly start climbing the Tetnuld, leaving the rest of their luggage to the tender mercies of the men of Adish, whom they had no doubt were responsible for the theft.

They sent off a Cossack to inform the representative of the Russian Government at Betsho of their loss and spent the morning moving their camp to a village called Mujal on the south-east of the mountain, a mile below the point where the southern glacial streams unite; a miserable journey, the rain making it exceedingly difficult to keep their photographic material dry. The following day a man was sent back to Adish with 15 roubles to offer as ransom for their stolen goods, and at about midday Freshfield and the Chamonix guides set out on an abortive attempt to reach the mountain. However they were forced to return, the misty weather making it impossible to identify the various slopes and glaciers.

They now had to fill in several days of idleness while they waited for better weather by allowing themselves to be entertained by the various comings and goings of the village. First there was the arrival of 'a splendid old Cossack sergeant – quite the popular ideal of a

Cossack – and his two men, to avenge' as Freshfield puts it, 'the Rape of the Shirts,' who set off and much to everyone's surprise succeeded in arresting ten of the villagers. The sequel to this determined action was the return of all their property with the exception of the revolver, and a telegram which somehow came into the hands of the German press, and from thence to England, where it was reported that Freshfield was being forced to abandon his explorations owing to the loss of all his goods.

The adventure they now proposed was a bold one. Freshfield and the three alpine guides were to set out twenty-four hours ahead of the stores and de Dechy, bivouac high, and attempt the mountain. In the meantime the other party would move up and make camp at the side of the Zanner glacier and wait for the climbers to join them. Should the parties fail to meet, they were to light fires to give an indication of their safety and their whereabouts, and the following morning the climbers would take steps to catch the main party as they pushed upwards to force the unknown pass that was thought to exist behind the Tetnuld, over the range into Europe once again. They had some difficulty in persuading porters to go with them on this trip, for the existence of such a pass was doubtful; it had not been crossed in living memory.

On the first night of the attempt on the Tetnuld Douglas and his little party camped at around 9,000 feet under an overhanging rock to the side of the Nageb glacier. 'The space under the rock was soon levelled, stones thrown out, and a flooring of elastic twigs and grass laid down. Then we piled up a blazing fire, toasted Suanetian loaves, and watched with satisfaction the last clouds melt into the sky and the peaks of Ushba stand out against a golden sunset.'

He was woken by a brilliant moon shining down upon them, and at once roused the others to take full advantage of the light in an early start. At first it was easy, but before long they were faced with a frozen cascade a mile wide and at least 500 feet high, and were forced to bring the rope into play. Freshfield had several times complained of the dullness of alpine writings, how dreary and alike the members of the Alpine Club made their adventures when they came to let their contemporaries know of them. He realized that they had become uninteresting to the general reader and it was for this reason that he attempted to make his books, rather than his Royal

Geographical Society papers, a moving story of travel and adventure, and not just a catalogue of glaciers, passes, ridges and peaks, all much the same to the uninitiated. But when he was forced to take the reader on a long climb with him he learned many lessons. He wrote of the next stage of the assault: 'The whole situation was stirring. The scenery was more fantastically lovely than a child's dream after the pantomime. The snows around us seemed to emit an unearthly light. Huge towers of milk-white substance shone against the dark background of sky, green icicle-hung vaults yawned between them. Presently the clefts and caverns grew more frequent and troublesome, the bridges over them more frail and ill-adjusted. At moments all progress appeared to be barred.

'In such cases the boldest course is sometimes the best – at any rate before dawn while the frost holds. We struck at the slope where it was steepest, and the crevasses were filled by pieces fallen from the impending cliffs. By the help of small and half choked crevasses, François dashed through and up the sides of a huge tumbledown snow quarry, and we found ourselves at last on the platform which stretches under the western base of Tetnuld. The final peak, previously hidden for a time, was again in full view; the stars still formed a coronet round the highest crest. Slowly they faded, and a glimmer of coming dawn played behind the southern shoulder of the peak, and rested on something vast and white, far and high in the west – Elbruz. As the sky grew paler, arrows of daylight flashed round the edge of the world across the upper vault; other arrows seemed to rise to meet them from the depths of the distant sea. It was very long before any light touched the Earth, but at last the great dome of Elbruz was of a sudden illuminated, and the twin towers of Ushba caught the flames, first red, then golden. In a few minutes the lesser crests of the "Frosty Caucasus" were kissed by the sun, the shadows fled away for shelter under the loftiest ridges. The upper world of the mountains was awake. The inhabited world – the grey hills and dales of Mingrelia and the sea-spaces beyond – still waited in sombre twilight.'

It was for such moments as this that Freshfield climbed mountains.

The next stage was unpleasant, for they were climbing in shadow, and it proved uncomfortably cold, but by 9 a.m. they had broken through a cornice and climbed into sunshine on a small terrace that lies at the base of the long southern ridge of the mountain, and here, nine hours from the bivouac, they sat down to eat lunch. For the next three hours they climbed upwards on the broad snow covered crest of the ridge that led them towards the summit, occasionally having to use their axes to surmount an obstacle, and once they had to step on to the broad back of a cornice that would have 'borne an elephant'.

'So three hours or more passed; my aneroid was marking 16,500 feet (equivalent to 15,700 to 15,800), but ever in front rose a fresh frozen bank. I looked across to the north-west ridge, and an eminence I had noted on it was below us. "Nous approchons", I said to François. "Nous allons arriver," he replied cheerily. The snow grew thin, some steps had to be cut into ice. There seemed less bulk in our peak; the converging ridges were below; there was little but air above us. Twenty minutes later a white bank cut the sky; it sank, our eyes overlooked it, our feet trampled it. I ran on for a few level yards; there was nothing more; two ridges fell steeply beneath me. Tetnuld was ours; another great peak of the Caucasus was climbed.'

Whatever the reason for their failure to attempt Ushba, at over forty, after a long period of relatively low-level climbing, Freshfield was right back on form. It had taken twelve and a half hours from their bivouac. Once again it is the view that claimed his attention, rather than the observations that might become the member of a scientific body. He made excuses for this himself, saying that on a first ascent it is enough to have got there, making the way easier for others to follow and make their observations. To stand for the first time at the summit of some vanquished giant is a thrill and for some a moment for silent worship, a moment of ecstasy still sought by every generation of climbers. It is not for pulse taking or boiling water tests.

The return journey was accomplished without difficulty, and with general lightheartedness, although at one stage Douglas suffered a harsh headache, possibly the result of altitude and lack of substantial food. They reached the bivouac, with its overhanging rock and bank of white rhododendrons, at 7 p.m., and at once strained their eyes to see if there was any sign of the others on the sides of the Zanner icefall opposite, but saw nothing. Douglas decided that they should remain in their old bivouac for the night, as the fires of the other party would give them a good idea of their exact position once darkness fell, and they should be able to catch up with them the following morning without difficulty. Presently their own beacon was signalling to the night sky, but there came no answering gleam from the darkness.

They spent a troubled night as a consequence, wondering what might have happened to the remainder of their party. But their doubts were soon set at rest when they reached the Zanner icefall and found tracks. They set off in pursuit, but not hurrying, so as to let the others have the task of leading and making a path. But none the less they came up with the baggage party by 11 a.m. After they had eaten a good meal they resumed the climb upwards towards the pass, but the going became difficult for the heavily laden porters, and Douglas went ahead to make a trail.

Suddenly he realized that he had gone too fast and the caravan was lost to view in a white fog that had risen behind him. Then strange sounds were born up to him, and he hurriedly retraced his steps until he came upon the party once again. It was a fantastic scene. As he describes it the whole motley crew were squatted on a snow bank praying at the tops of their voices. 'The Suanetians, in order to avoid sore eyes and sunburn, had blacked and greased their faces, which gave them an appearance which suggested anything but devotional associations. They were however, very much in earnest, and absolutely declined to shorten their service. Suddenly the fog lifted, and the pass was revealed to their front, and the hymn, eminently successful, changed to a howl of triumph.' One cannot help being sorry for the poor villagers being dragged into regions where they and their ancestors knew quite well there was nothing but pain and awful death to be contemplated.

The eight porters of Urusbieh who had accompanied them over the Mestia, had expressed doubts as to whether the grey haired veteran, the legendary conqueror of Elbruz, would be able to cross the mountains. It was now Freshfield's turn to wonder if this party of awe-struck Suanetians would be able to repress their terror and make their way down the pass. They found themselves standing on the top of a corniced wall with an icy moat at its foot. It was obvious that the porters would be unable to climb down, in fact they were all making a great hubbub 'praying or swearing – we were not sure which – on the cornice. One after the other peeped over the edge, and, drawing back with horror, expressed his feelings in a brief solo, which was followed by a chorus from the whole strength of the company'.

At last the Europeans left their Asian companions and climbed down a rock spur to one side and in a few moments were safely back in their mother continent. At first this had an even worse effect on the unfortunate porters, who merely set up a fresh wailing, and seemed to be on the point of attacking each other. But at last the watchers below became aware that they were resolved to follow, for the baggage was pitched down the wall in an agonizingly reckless manner. Then, surprisingly, for they had steadfastly refused such a modern innovation, they roped together, and started gingerly down. They had reached the last snow slope, when one of them missed his footing and the whole party catapulted through the air to land in a panting terrified heap, quite unhurt, at the feet of their masters. 'This screaming farce', as Freshfield called it, took no less than an hour to play, and it was quite dark before they were able to find a good place to camp.

The next day in pouring rain, they descended towards civilization and the letters that they hoped awaited them at Bezingi, but it was not a happy party that made camp that night; Michel Devouassoud proved to have a painful frostbitten foot acquired on the face of the Tetnuld; one of the Cossacks was almost snow-blind and in great pain, and as a final additional misery, it was too wet to light a fire.

They made an evil-smelling guest house in Bezingi their headquarters, and received their letters from the depths of the robes that draped the six foot three inch chief, and set about making their plans for the last exploration before de Dechy was due to return home. Freshfield was energetically anxious to climb Koshantau, and accordingly they set off, but de Dechy declined to accompany them further than the foot of the mountain. François had also been forced to give up as the efforts of the past few days had been more than enough for him, so Douglas took one of the younger guides and reached the summit of Ukiu, hoping that from there they would see their way clear to the crest of their target. They found in fact that they were mistaken, and were forced to return somewhat despondent.

François Devouassoud in old age.

De Dechy accompanied them as far as Vladikavkaz, from where Freshfield intended to make a rapid trip south to Tiflis where Devouassoud could receive proper attention and be despatched home. But he certainly did not regard the trip as over and could not foresee any difficulty about this, and fully intended to take the rest of the expedition north again into the mountains. De Dechy however, seized the opportunity of their arrival at Vladikavkaz to abandon them and return home. Relations had not been good; de Dechy had declined to accompany them on many of the more difficult climbs, and had made a great fuss, in Freshfield's mind, over the theft of their belongings. He regarded him as a deserter, and immediately on his return to England fired off a letter to the Secretary of the Royal Geographical Society: 'Freshwater. Isle of Wight. Dear Bates, I am back today all right after a successful journey. Dechy turned out a Muff – and is turning out something worse. But I got up a mountain higher than Mont Blanc, and learned no end of geography and saw no end of scenery, on the whole favourable weather. I had perfect health the whole time. Our chief contretemps were a guide being badly frostbitten, and the amount of snow, altogether abnormal according to Radde. The theft from our camp was a trivial affair (I suppose you saw the *Standard*) and has been, I find, made the most of by Dechy to cover his desertion of me in the middle of the journey. In these circumstances I must have space (a page or two for a note only) in the next Number to tell the true state of the case, not of course in terms of controversy, and briefly summarize results ...'

The Secretary, wise in the ways of explorers wishing to get their word in first, must have written back asking for more details of what it was Freshfield wanted to write, because a few days later another letter arrived at the Society.

'I want to get something out that will stop Dechy making a fool of both of us by committing himself to something I should have to take up – however I don't mean to take up anything I can help, then I can rest quietly until I have got all my material for a serious article. I hope Dechy will behave properly, but he is volatile and vain to a point, and old Devouassoud says, "*Tout au fait enfant et egoist.*" And after his saying that our time was broken up by the robbery, I cannot tell what he may not say ...'

Douglas Freshfield had all the traits of many more famous explorers in jealously guarding the right to be the first to tell the 'truth' of an expedition, and his own stoical indifference to hardship made him contemptuous of those who did not have those same qualities.

There was perhaps one more incident on this journey, that is worth repeating. Douglas and François set out on a private pilgrimage, a visit to the village of Jibaini in the Ushkul collection where, nineteen years earlier, they had their tensest encounter with the local inhabitants. This time as they crossed the yellowing barley fields and the well remembered towers came in sight, neither of them could help feeling apprehensive, especially, they reminded themselves, in the light of their experiences at Adish two weeks previously. The two men concealed their nervousness and strode boldly within the grim walls. But they soon discovered that of all the villages in the country this one had changed the most, at least so far as the disposition of the inhabitants was concerned. There was now a village schoolmaster who exercised considerable influence, and little sign of the previous atmosphere of stalking red-handed terror, or the vengeful violence that had seemed to lurk in the eyes of all, and moreover the visitors were allowed to move about freely without being molested. Freshfield was interested in the native people of this beautiful country, and now spent the remaining days of the expedition exploring the villages, examining their churches, their archives, their customs and administration, the results of which were incorporated in his final *Exploration of the Caucasus*. The fascination of this work today lies largely in the fact that the great purges under Joseph Stalin in the 1930s, and the stamping of a uniform mould on all the peoples of the vast Socialist Republic, and above all the tremendous industrialization of parts of Caucasia have so changed the peoples of the area as to make it a lost world, of which without Freshfield there would be little record.

At last the move that he hoped to encourage by his first visit came about. The expeditions of 1886 and 1887 focused the attention of many climbers on the possibilities open to them in the Caucasus, and the following year saw several strong expeditions in the field. One by one the most important and dramatic summits were conquered. This time Freshfield was not directly involved but, as the man with more personal experience of the central range than any other, his

advice was very much sought. The most successful party was that of
H. Woolley, accompanied by Holder and Cockin, who successfully
climbed Ushba, a success which brought Freshfield a moment of
regret, for this was his favourite peak both for its drama as a spectacle and the difficulties that it presented. They also climbed Dykhtau,
Katuintau and Salynan. Cockin continued on his own to climb
Shkara and the eastern peak of Janga.

There was one party that particularly interested Douglas, as one
of its leading members was a lively young climber, W. F. Donkin.
Douglas complained of the dullness of the fast growing mass of
alpine writings, and was pleased to find in this young man someone
that he considered had all the qualities of a good mountaineer
coupled with a lively literary style. Donkin had discussed his forth-
coming expedition with Freshfield at some length, and had firmly
fixed his sights on Koshantau as one of the major objectives. The rest
of the party consisted of Clinton Dent, H. Fox, and two alpine
guides, Streich and Fischer.

During the month of September 1888 Douglas was caught up in
the general *mêlée* of family affairs. His son was taken to boarding
school at Broadstairs for the first time, and, having accomplished
this mission, he parted temporarily from his wife and the rest of the
children in order to return to London; one reason being that he was
anxious to hear if there had been any news of the explorers. But the
news was bad. He found Dent returned to London because of ill
health, who informed Freshfield that he knew that the other two
were still, at the time of his departure, bent on trying to make the
summit of Koshantau. He had been expecting to hear at almost any
time how they had fared. But instead a telegram came from the
German dragoman that had been serving the climbers, saying that
he had parted from them at the start of their assault with instructions to meet them again in three days at a certain spot. He had gone
to the place as directed, but the climbers had never shown up, and
they were now twenty-seven days overdue.

After hurrying down for a consultation with his family, and
returning to London for further talks with Dent, Douglas came to
the conclusion that it was no good leading a search party so late in
the season. He was certain that there must have been a climbing accident, and that being so it was bound to have happened at some point

which would be inaccessible in winter. At the express orders of the Tzar, search parties had been organized; but they were hampered by the already prevailing winter conditions and their total lack of climbing experience. There the matter might have been allowed to rest. To Freshfield and his friends there had certainly never been any hope of a rescue, because any survivors of an accident must have perished before any competent climbers could have received the news. So sure were the friends and families of those lost of what had happened, that they had a memorial brass, recording the facts, set up in the chapel in Eton College. But there were others who were not so sure. Suddenly rumour and speculation became rife. Russian officials in the area were reported to be openly suspecting foul play. Several mountain communities were being regarded with grave suspicion and were thought by some to be ripe for retribution. The basic cause for all this seemed to be the fact that the Russians, who had no knowledge of the uses of the rope in climbing, could not imagine an accident in which both men and their two guides could lose their lives. In view of all this Freshfield decided that a careful enquiry must be made on the spot by competent mountaineers who knew that particular section of the range well – and there was obviously no man better fitted to discover the fate of the lost climbers than he.

For the rest of the party he invited Dent, who was an obvious choice, Captain C. H. Powell, an army officer and friend of Fox and more importantly a Russian scholar. Also with them was Woolley, who had been within a few miles from the spot where the accident must have occurred at the very time, but because of intervening high ridges had known nothing until his return to England.

By this time there was of course no question of urgency so far as the search was concerned, unless it was to put the unfortunate suspects out of their misery, and so Freshfield proposed to combine detective work with a further extensive exploration of the area. As he had done in 1868 he planned to start from Kasbek or the eastern end of the central range and make a high level route westwards, but this time on the north side of the watershed.

They started on 6 July taking the overland route south from St Petersburg. Once again he sat with his companions in those comfortable chairs watching the plains of Russia slide smoothly by, but this time the faithful François was unable to share his master's fortunes nor share that first sight of Elbruz gleaming in the morning sun. Neither did they disembark at Patigorsk but remained on the train as it bore away eastwards on a course more parallel with the mountains, leaving Elbruz to fall away behind them, while another noble peak took its place in the centre of their vision. A Russian officer named it to his fellow travellers, 'Koshantau', and they all peered with interest at the slopes where the Englishmen had perished the previous year.

In the course of time, which included having to spend an hour or two sitting on a bank beside the track admiring the mountains while awaiting the arrival of a fresh engine, their own having broken down, they arrived at Vladikavakaz. The town is situated on the main road that leads under Kasbek and through the Darial Gorge to Tiflis, and is within half a day's drive of the mountain. In 1869, when Freshfield and his two companions returned to the village after their successful climb over the summit of Kasbek, their two porters, Toto and Zogel, in the course of the general congratulations and story telling, had said that they had followed the climbers to the summit. That they should say so was entirely to be expected from the peasants; that they should actually have done so, no one was able to believe. In the first place the climbing party would have been bound to see them following up the steep ice slope, and in the second, to have mounted that same slope shod only in sandals and without a rope, was impossible. But in later years, given credence by the writings of a man called Muromzoff, the story came to find general acceptance in the region. On discovering this Freshfield wrote, 'May Toto and Zogel live long to enjoy the honour thrust on them by the provincial or national feelings of the good people of Tiflis.' A statement which in modern ears might ring of some condescension.

They engaged a local Jew to accompany them as interpreter, and started the journey by going to Alagirski, and from there south up the valley of the Ardon to the Mamisson pass, traversing the gorge that divides the main central range from the Kasbek block. From Mamisson, where they looked down upon Gebi and their road taken out of the region two years before, they turned north again towards that range and Adai Khokh, beneath which they crossed into the Zea valley. The story of the next stage of their travels can be found in detail in *The Exploration of the Caucasus*. Briefly, they marched westwards, crossing the ridges that divide the sources of the Urukh until they reached the valley of the Cherek. As they progressed they were warned several times that they were courting disaster in entering, unguarded, an area where four travellers had so recently been murdered, a warning which Freshfield ignored, but which caused their guides to proceed wearing an air of 'woeful anticipation of the worst'.

Their tour that summer was a long one, but the three highlights, the discovery of the fate of Donkin and Fox; the ascent of Laila, the principle mountain to the south of Suanetia; and the exploration of the 'lost' land of Abkhasia are more interesting than usual mountain literature to the general reader or traveller.

Douglas had a very good idea as to what the plans of the ill-fated climbers had been, for he had discussed the best method of attacking the mountain with them before their departure, and Donkin's diary, which had been brought back with their baggage, and the orders which he had given to their dragoman confirmed that he was more or less following the route forecast. Their last base was situated at the foot of the Ulluauz Glacier, on the north face of the mountain, and to Douglas it was obvious from the diary that they intended to climb to the high snow pass that was at the head of the glacier, and just east of the summit of Koshtantau, He was convinced that if he was to climb to this pass he would surely find some traces of the party's last high bivouac before they tested their skill against the peak itself. The evidence given by the searchers the previous year confirmed this opinion, as they claimed to have found tracks leading upwards on the left bank of the glacier.

There was one piece of evidence which did not fit into the general picture that had formed in Douglas's mind. The headman of Bezingi reported that his hunters had found the tracks of the party leading eastwards over the ridge to Balkar in the Cherek valley. For the moment at least he decided to ignore this statement, as it crossed his mind that if there was suspicion of foul play, then the men of Bezingi would be most anxious to furnish proof that the climbers had left their territory.

The best plan therefore seemed to be to establish a base at the head of the Cherek valley, at the pasturage called Karaul, where

Donkin and Fox had arranged to rendezvous with their baggage, and climb over their intended route in reverse. Karoul was a convenient spot for what might turn out to be a prolonged stay; within easy striking distance of Tiutiun glacier, which led to the pass in question from this side. It was further provided with the amenities of civilization in the form of two Tartar guards who lived in a stone hut, the only habitation for many miles, who were ready to supply them with milk. The position chosen was at the junction of the routes to three major passes over the main range, so that it was hardly surprising that they should find an officer of the Russian Survey camping there. 'Our camp was pitched on a grassy terrace, at the mouth of a wild gorge. Grey granite screes, scantily clothed with azalea bushes and green flowery grass, sloped down on all sides with extreme steepness, enclosing in their midst a flat open meadow, a mile perhaps in length, by half a mile in breadth. Our tents were erected on a little triangle of land above the junction of two roaring torrents, the Cherek and the Dykhsu, side by side with those of Mr Bogdanoff of the Russian Survey – six in all.' As one of their party was sick, a day or two had to be wasted, during which they were entertained by the constant comings and goings of colourful bands using the great passes to the south, and occupied themselves in some serious reconnaissance. Woolley explored the approaches to their intended route up into the mountain, which the surveyor had reported as impossible; while Freshfield climbed a spur on the east side of the valley in order to get a complete view of the glacier by which they intended to mount to the pass that had been the first objective of Donkin's party from the other side. The view of Koshantau they had was terrific, and the brother of the missing guide Fischer, declared with tears in his eyes that he was glad his brother had found so noble a resting place.

The next day, 28 July, was to have been the start of their major search. They were just about to leave camp early in the morning when a message came asking Freshfield to speak to the surveyor leaving. On entering the tent he was handed a letter from a geologist, Baron Sternberg, who was known to be working in the area. In it the Baron maintained that he had just crossed a very difficult and high pass from Bezingi to the Cherek valley, approximately in the direction that the headman of Bezingi had maintained the missing party had vanished. At the summit of this pass, which was too high and difficult for native use as there were easier and safer routes further north, the Baron had found three stone-men which he declared must have been made by Donkin and Fox.

Immediately Freshfield called for a horse and, accompanied by Powell, set off to find the Baron, who was reported to be camping some distance further down the valley.

Some time after sunrise, following a stiff ride that was longer than they expected, they found the Baron's little encampment on a piece of flat ground near the highest bridge over the torrent. He received Freshfield and Powell hospitably, and told them that he had recently spent three days on the Ulluauz glacier; that he was convinced that the missing party could never have attempted such an impossible route; that he had discovered the path they must have used and the stone men they had built. Further, he went on to tell them a good deal to the discredit of the interpreter that had accompanied the lost party, and of how a native had been found with a wound that might have been inflicted by an ice axe.

But Freshfield was adamant. 'Nothing of all this carried weight in my mind ... I could only reply that the point was one for expert's opinion, and that my experience convinced me that I was not in any risk of being mistaken.'

In the Baron's party there was a native of Bezingi who had been a member of the search party of the previous year that had reported finding the tracks of Donkin's men leading into the Cherek valley. Freshfield took the opportunity of questioning him. He was a member of the party that had found both tracks and stone-men, and conversation with him through Powell convinced Freshfield that the leader of that search party, having been told to find traces of the Englishmen, had taken the first clue that could mean that they had left the district, thus relieving the people of Benzingi of all responsibility for the ultimate fate of the climbers.

It was a hot weary ride back in the midday sun to the head of the valley and their own camp; they dismounted stiff and tired after such an unaccustomed form of exercise. But there was no time to pause. After a sharp 800 foot climb they caught up with the rest of their party, heavily laden, zig-zagging their way upwards through groves of birch and mossy crags. 'Flowers covered everything. Our path was buried in them. Dense beds of cream rhododendrons in full bloom clothed the lower slopes, the river banks were painted blue and white and yellow with blossom – gentians and forget-me-nots, daisy-like pyrethrums, primulas, and many other less familiar blooms. The ground below the glacier was so densely carpeted that walking was made difficult by the complete concealment of the uneven surface.

They had to make their camp that night amidst the dripping leaves of a plant not unlike giant rhubarb, and emerging sleepers in the half light of the following morning reminded Freshfield irresistibly of Doyle's[1] elves. They started at 5 a.m. They had one hour of steep easy climbing and then plunged into the midst of the icefall, which proved more difficult; so much so that at one time it looked as though there might not be a way out. But at last they found themselves facing a broad, frozen corridor, that led, as Freshfield described it, into the secret heart of the mountains. The Swiss, not trusting Freshfield's confidence, asked dubiously how he proposed to get them out of such a seemingly impossible place, barred as it was by a steep ridge with two precipitous gullies and the summit of Koshantau.

But to Freshfield at least, the path they must take was perfectly clear. He knew that round the next buttress they must see the pass, and be able to climb to it up steep rocks. He instructed his companions to keep careful watch, for they were entering the area in which it was possible that they might find traces of a bivouac left by the lost party, or some sign of the disaster that had overtaken them.

Then the pass came into sight. As he had surmised it was approachable from this side to skilful climbers, an almost vertical rock face of near 1,400 feet. Before tackling its craggy face they made a careful examination of the glacier at its base for signs of previous climbers, but there was nothing.

They set their faces to the rocks, roped together, each man silently absorbed in the task of heaving himself upwards, conscious of the hot sun on their backs and the rush of melting snow that poured down the snow gulley at their side. They were about 300 feet from

[1] Richard (Dicky) Doyle. Best known for the old cover of *Punch* and for his children's Fairy Book.

the top when their leader suddenly gave a gasp. They all looked upward to see not many feet away a low wall of loose stones, obviously man-made, balanced round the outer edge of a narrow ledge that was partly sheltered by overhanging rock above. Quickly they scrambled up and peered over the wall. There was a revolver in its case hanging under the rocks, while on the floor, projecting through the thick layer of last winter's frozen snow and ice, were portions of rucksacks and sleeping bags. This then was the last bivouac.

The searchers set about the long task of extricating the various pathetic, personal belongings from the tough embrace of the often re-frozen snow. 'Surrounded by so many memorials of the missing, so many objects that spoke of individual traits of character and habit, it was difficult to believe in the catastrophe. It almost seemed natural to expect that our friends might at any moment be seen coming quickly over the crags to regain the bivouac where all still lay exactly as when they quitted it for their last climb.'

While the others continued with their sad task, Woolley and Freshfield climbed the last 300 feet to the pass, for there was hardly room for them all to work on the tiny shelf with nothing but space on three sides. It took them half an hour and entailed an icy chimney and a steep narrow rib of rock, then a traverse across a broad, frozen slope before the earth fell away and a wide view over the foothills and the northern plains was fully revealed. On the pass they found a small stone man, a true record this time of the vanished climbers, but there was no message concealed within it. A careful examination of the mountain through a powerful telescope failed to reveal any sign that they had reached the top, and this was confirmed a few weeks later when Woolley conducted a successful assault. So it had to be somewhere on the ascent that the tragedy occurred.

Freshfield sat down on the pass and pictured the fatal course of events to himself. 'The mountaineers, all heavily laden, travellers as well as guides, had reached about noon the crest of the range at the point where we stood. They had given up all thoughts of an attack on the great peak from the side of the Ulluauz, and, following the suggestion made in my notes, and the intention so clearly expressed in Fox's diary, meant to go down to the Tiutiun snowfield, and "climb Koshtantau from the south side". As they descended, the southern cliffs of the ridge they were on came partially into view. For a short distance these were practicable; beyond, they became more formidable, but, owing to foreshortening, how formidable must still have remained for them a matter of speculation. Afternoon clouds probably played about the crests and obscured their features. They saw frozen gullies which might be cut across, ledges that might lead far. A month later in the year, the broad sheets of ice, which now would have rendered the attempt too obviously hazardous, had probably in great part disappeared under the sun of August. They had in their minds the smooth upper snows, that pleasant ridge which, once the great towers passed, leads in continuous curves to the crowning peak. They had never examined from any distant vantage point the full breadth and height and formidable nature of the crest that separated them from the last tower. Its passage, they persuaded themselves, was worth the attempt, a *mauvais pas* to be faced and surmounted. The alternative was to descend many hundred feet to the Tiutiun névé, to lose all this height for the morrow, to carry down the wraps and provisions they had laboriously raised.

'The ledge was found, and the fatal decision made. The loads were laid down and all went cheerfully to work. Fox doubtless set the guides to wall-building and hard at it himself; Donkin laboured, looked to the fire, adjusted his camera, made his boiling point observations, unpacked and repacked some of his instruments, meeting the occasion, after his manner, by nice adaption of homely articles to purposes for which they were never intended. Thus we discovered some delicate instruments done up in the neatest possible parcel in a sock and glove, all tied together with a bootlace. The red flames of the little fire (we found remnants of firewood) shone for a short time on the icicle-hung rocks, and then the mountaineers rolled themselves close together in their wraps.'

And that was all they could ever know for certain. The party had set out in the morning, clad in light climbing gear, leaving their belongings to be collected on their return. And somewhere, out on that terrible slope, so deceptive from the only angle from which they had viewed it, the end had come. One slip and there was no salvation, nothing to break their fall to the glacier and the blue vaulted ice below.

It took Freshfield and Woolley forty minutes to return down that precipitous face to the bivouac ledge. It was an area that could only be visited by experienced mountaineers, so much was abundantly obvious; no native robbers could have arrived at such a place intent on violent crime. The burden of suspicion was removed from the shoulders of the mountain people who lived between Elbruz and Ossetia. When the searchers returned to the villages below, and unfolded the tale of their discoveries, and produced a few objects from the bivouac as proof, the people were profoundly grateful. On several occasions what might be described as a formal speech was delivered by the headman, praising the English that had come so far, and ventured with such bravery into inaccessible places in order to prove their innocence – they could never have expected so much from the Russian authorities.

Again that night they slept in their 'rhubarb' patch, and the following day returned down the valley of flowers to Karaul. Here the party was to split. Woolley had decided to remain in the area to explore thoroughly the surrounding heights, and make a second attempt on the fatal mountain with two of the guides. An attempt that was finally successful. Before leaving the area Freshfield made a three day expedition to have one last look at the mountain, and then returned to the villages in the Balkar and Bezingi neighbourhood to make the result of their searches known. Then leaving their heavy baggage at the latter, with Dent and the alpine guides, he went south up the Bezingi glacier in order to force a high pass over the main intervening ridge into the Chegem valley. This they succeeded in doing, although they had an uncomfortable moment during the descent on the far side. They had been using a steep furrow which had become glazed with ice and unsafe, so they decided to leave it. The only way they could find to do so was by climbing round the bulging face of a rock that hung over an ice bank. Fischer, the first guide, worked himself over and round the protuberance with skill, but the second guide became stuck half way. Freshfield and Dent were waiting patiently, calling instructions and encouragement to the poor man, when with a harsh whistling the mountain hurled a volley of pebbles past their ears. The volley proved to be only the opening shots in a very one sided engagement, and soon their shouts to the guide, still in the attitude of Prometheus, came couched in less patient terms. Eventually their eloquence persuaded the guide to continue over the rock. But stones and small boulders that have an almost uninterrupted fall of a thousand feet or more, can be lethal. As it looked as though there was to be no let up in what was rapidly becoming a barrage, there was nothing for it but to try to find some way down that was out of the path of the missiles. This entailed a dangerous five minutes while they passed over black rock that was already covered in grey gashes caused by falling stones, but it was difficult to hurry when every third step had to be cut in ice. The rest of the descent was difficult, slow work, with the stones constantly rattling down to one side of them, but no longer an immediate danger. As they worked Freshfield admits enjoying with 'strange intensity' one of the most glorious sunsets he had ever seen. They were nearly out of range when there was a yell, one of the guides had been struck by a particularly malevolent ricochet, but it was the last of the action, causing nothing worse than a severe headache. Under these exceedingly difficult conditions they descended a rock wall of 1,400 feet. They then continued down the glacier by the light of a lantern, feeling a little lightheaded. 'The long strain of seven hours incessant occupation in finding foothold for oneself and watching one's companions, of constant apprehension of some sudden divergence of the missiles, which though they, for the most part, flew past too swiftly to be seen, had kept up a constant scream in our ears, was now over. The relief was immense.'

They continued down the glacier as far as possible by the light of their lamps, and later the moon, but the region was quite unexplored and they decided, at about ten, that they had better halt for the night. They had the barest minimum of equipment and there was little chance of sleep; Freshfield lay down with a volume of Dickens for a pillow and a number of maps for covering, while the others tramped back and forth in an effort to keep warm. There was little comfort to be had in remembering the advice of his old friend A.W. Moor: 'In a strange country avoid new passes you do not know the other side of.'

The lower parts of the Chegem, by contrast, proved most delightful. Freshfield admits to committing the mountaineers cardinal sin, taking a solitary ramble. The woods were full of wild strawberries, and the temptation to lie down near a little waterfall with a handful was irresistible.

After exploring the head of the valley they took a high pass over the western dividing range, close to one that had been used the previous year and in the opposite direction by Donkin's ill-fated party, and once more entered the familiar Urusbeih, to rejoin their porters and heavy baggage which had arrived by a lower route. Here they took leave of Dent, who was due to start home now that the search for the missing climbers was over, and Freshfield, with Powell and the two guides for company, started south once again, up the Baksan to find yet another new pass to Suanetia. They were assisted in the finding of this pass by a young shepherd whom they met with an older companion on the lower slopes of the north side. They spent a disturbed night in the company of these two, whose monotonous devotions extended far into the night.

Freshfield had developed a deep love for this landscape, and to some extent even for the people of Suanetia, in spite of the grim reception they had had all those years ago. He felt happy to be returning as they passed to the west of the familiar walls of Ushba and descended steeply through the woods to Mazeri. They passed beneath the walls of the Dadish Kilian's castle, grandson of the Prince who had murdered a Russian official just prior to Freshfield's first visit, but now restored to his estates. A mile or two down the valley they came to Betsho, whose twinkling lights they had observed for some time with their promise of shelter and food. But they were to be disappointed. The Russian chief official for the area was absent with his secretary, and there was only a police officer in charge who greeted the travellers with the surliness and ill grace they had come to regard as habitual amongst the junior employees of the government. They were directed to a roofless, floorless shed and treated as objects worthy of the deepest suspicion, until the chance arrival of the two sons of the late Prince Murat, who had been educated in England, put all to rights. Realizing his mistake the police official at once became confidential, and regaled them with stories of how he lured murderers who were hiding in the forests, to return to their homes and into his clutches. Freshfield made a mental note not to ride around the country with this gentleman for company, as he says: 'Culprits who go to Siberia leave relatives at home; the natives of Suanetia have not yet been deprived of their firearms, and a shot is easily fired from the forest.'

It was not long before Freshfield and Powell received an invitation from Prince Atar Dadish Kilian to become his guests during their stay, in the castle at Mazeri, that had been restored to his family. The grandfather's lapse from grace may have been a blessing in disguise for his descendants, for during their banishment they had seen something of the world and the advance of civilization. Now their lands were restored and a document issued by Tzar Nicholas confirmed them in their rights as feudal lords of the country. The Prince was an educated man who spoke French, had travelled to Japan on Government business, and kept more or less open house to guests while at home, where he lived in truly feudal style, his people paying rent in service and kind. The actual castle was abandoned; the family now lived in a large Swiss style cottage close by. For Suanetia it was luxurious. The visitors' bedroom was filled with divans and Persian carpets, meals were served in a feudal hall with ranks of retainers looking like something from an historical play, and they sat out on a great balcony watching the Prince dispense justice. The food was excellent and the contrast to baking their own bread in an open fronted shed was extreme.

But there were more surprises in store. On Sunday morning when they awoke to the sound of a church bell it seemed hardly credible that they were in Suanetia, where previously the churches had been crumbling and barred, objects of pagan superstition. During the afternoon they were privileged spectators to sports held on the village green; games were played, the girls danced, and young boys wrestled with bears that had been caught in the forest. In the evening after a late meal they were entertained by a chorus of women who sang a long ballad, dancing in a circle to the refrain. The Prince translated for them the meaning of the verses, in which it was apparent that the lost history of Suanetia was buried. One particular tale told of how Turkish invaders had attacked a company of Suanetians on the Tuiber glacier, and in the midst of the battle an avalanche had fallen, wiping out in one blow both armies 'stilled in a moment of clamour and strife'. They were told that this story had recently been confirmed by the discovery of human bones and armour at the foot of the glacier, relics of the legendary catastrophe.

On the first occasion the weather prevented their intended assault on Laila, although the journey through flowering forests and meadows was a great consolation. When they were ready for the second attempt the Prince announced his intention of coming too, which had the effect of slowing Freshfield's normal impatient progress. They paused at one place to take tea with an uncle of the Prince, which delayed them still further, and then Freshfield forced them to travel at a brisk trot through the gathering gloom, in danger of being swept from their saddles by low branches. They found a suitable shepherd's hut in which to make camp for the night, but Douglas was forced to sleep outside, where he was sharply nipped by the frost, because he absolutely detested the smell of boiling mutton – and a whole sheep was being boiled inside the hut.

The Laila proved an easy ascent. It was a great pity that the Prince allowed himself to be misled by his hunters, who maintained that Freshfield's intended route was impossible; as a consequence they parted company, and the Prince never attained the summit. It was a wonderful vantage point. The whole central range of the Caucasus mountains was revealed in every detail through the soft clear air, so that they could trace all their previous wanderings. At their feet the valleys and rivers of Suanetia were laid out, 'a carpet of green and gold'. Signor Sella, the greatest of all mountaineer photographers, was that year spending his first season in the Caucasus, and ascended to this very point a few weeks later to rake the opposing range with one of his tremendous panoramas.

The next day Freshfield took a walk to a comparatively low vantage point, Mesik, from which there is a fine view of Ushba. He speculated that at some time during the twentieth century it would be a popular walk for ladies. It was Ushba that was to haunt him, the mountain that he most regretted not having attempted. He wrote 'The double-headed giant of Suanetian mountains is justly named Ushba – the Stormpeak'.

The final stage of this journey had a most romantic flavour. West of Suanetia, over the Ingur river between the mountains and the sea, lay an almost unknown land. Travellers' tales that had reached England in the past spoke of vast forests teeming with wild life; of an almost vanished race of men that ran naked through the glades; incapable of speech and living solely on fruits. In Suanetia, however, they were able to obtain a little more substantial information, and an offer of help from the Prince. It seemed that men did occasionally penetrate the region, mostly either hunters seeking the game that was said to abound in the forests; or outlaws, seeking sanctuary from the justice of their own people in the pathless and impenetrable valleys. The Prince warned them that if they were adamant in choosing to leave his domain for such a region, they were to proceed with great caution, never allowing their party to become split thus giving a cowardly robber a chance to strike. By way of help he offered to obtain for them two outlaw hunters as guides, for they were the only type of people who would stand any chance of being able to lead them through the forest. As promised the two guides were procured, bringing with them two mules that were to carry the camping gear, luggage, and one week's food supply for the whole party. It soon became hard to decide which were the wildest, most impulsive, and unschooled, the mules or their guides. The latter soon confirmed that they were all that might be expected as outlaws living wild, far from the paths of men; 'barbarians in speech and gesture, yielding to every impulse and little accustomed to control.'

They said goodbye to the Prince, under whose patronage they had enjoyed what Freshfield later remembered as one of the most pleasant interludes of his life – as well as one of the cheapest, for he writes home to say: 'We have had great hospitality, so that since leaving Vladikavkaz my share of expenses for food and travel is about £12 – for five weeks.'

They set out in the evening, chiefly to avoid the Prince's late evening meal of pomp and entertainment, for had they shared it they would have been in no fit state to make an early start the next morning, which might lead to the deduction that there were elements to the Prince's hospitality that were not mentioned in letters home. However they camped only an hour or two away from the home of the generous host, and the early light found them passing through Pari, which, during the banishment of the ruling family at the time of Douglas's 1868 visit, had been the quarters of a company of Cossacks. The place seemed unchanged; even the house where they had lodged looked only a trifle more dilapidated. Beyond the village they had their first foretaste of the capabilities of one of the mules; on the very first steep slope he swiftly kicked off his load.

In the first villages, as they moved west, they met with a friendly reception, the people happy to provide milk, eggs and bread. But as they travelled further from the influence of government and into wilder and more thinly populated areas, the change of attitude became marked; although they found that they were sometimes given for nothing that which they had been jeeringly refused, even for payment, only a few hundred yards away. Soon their path became no more than the merest suggestion of a track which twisted at times almost vertically up a 5,000 foot slope, laced with the twisted roots of giant beeches and firs, that closed in welcome shade over the heads of the hot and aggravated party – for the mules were displaying a fine repertoire of perversities. But the fairyland scenery continued, they made their first halt in 'a garden of gigantic ferns and golden blossom'.

At the top of this slope they found themselves wandering through grasses and flowers that were sometimes over their heads, so moist and fertile the ground under the summer sky, until, as they gained height, they were able to find a place to camp, an hour below the pass and on short grass among stunted birches. But they were in for a disturbed night. Before the sun had set they had been admiring the view of Suanetia below, and the dramatic effects of a thunderstorm that played about the heads of Laila, the more so because its position and course held no apparent threat for them. But a second storm had crept up the hill behind them, and broke overhead with terrifying intensity. Freshfield had never experienced anything like it before. The lightning crackled and spluttered all round them while rain and then hail battered against their little tent with such force that they thought it must drill its way through. All this was punctuated by tremendous rushes of wind that seemed about to sweep them from the mountain. The guides pushed their heads inside the tent doors, screaming in broken Russian that they were all lost; every fresh blaze of lightning and crash of thunder made them redouble their cries. But at last the storm gradually died down, until the steady patter of rain lulled them all to sleep. In the morning 'the peaks of Tetnuld and Shkara showed deadly white against the black skirts of the retreating storm cloud, still fitfully flashing, and its upper edge cut sharp against the pale amber of the sunrise'.

As is often the case, the stories of an unknown region are more dramatic than the facts allow. True it was a region of great silent forests, of flowery alpine meadows and steep gorges with roaring torrents, but sadly the native savages proved legendary, as did the great numbers of chamois and other game that were reputed by more recent travellers to have little knowledge of men. Neither did they have any trouble from outlaws; most of their difficulties and diversions on the journey being provided by the fickleness of their two guides, the truculence of their mules, and by the fact that at one stage they became badly lost. It would seem that the poor mules were pretty well justified in their demonstrations. At one point they were set to climb, with their baggage, an almost impossible slope, and presently when one of them slipped both mules rolled to the bottom, baggage and all. After that all the cases, tents, and bedrolls had to be hauled up by hand so that the mules could make the climb unladen, a process which did not please the guides, for one of them, as soon as the crest was reached, flung down his load to the ground and refused to go with them any further. Freshfield had become so infected with the Suanetian method of negotiation on a tricky point as to reach for his revolver, while his opponent reached for his dagger. The result – ridiculous deadlock. Neither had any intention of going further, or for that matter of backing down. It was left to Powell to sort the matter out. That night, as they camped in a deep dell among giant trees and ferns, the man came to Freshfield and made a flowery speech to the effect that, 'Englishmen and Suanetians are brothers,' and the rift was made good.

Their route varied between hard scrambling through thick forests, wading in the torrents, climbing through the prostrate limbs and trunks of fallen trees and steep climbs to high, grassy slopes where the going was easy. Here they met the occasional foresters and shepherds, who proved generally friendly, ready to sell milk, and on one occasion a live sheep. This transaction had a farcical sequel. The sheep was in the charge of Maurer, one of the alpine guides, when it gave him the slip and set off at a brisk trot in the direction of its flock. The guide set off in pursuit, and soon both of them, hunter and quarry, had vanished from sight, and there was nothing for it but that the others should sit and wait – though what prevented one or two others from rendering assistance is not clear. Three hours passed before captor and captive returned, both exhausted. By now there was only enough daylight left for them to seek out a suitable camping place, but there was no wood to make a fire on which to cook, so the wretched sheep was reprieved. In the morning the thought of having to look after the animal for a whole day was too much for Maurer, and when it started to get troublesome he let it go, so the whole party stood and ruefully watched their hopes of mutton chops scamper off. It was quite a serious loss, for throughout the rest of their stay in the forests they had nothing to live on but soup, and sour milk when they could get it.

At last they reached the second major pass that they were to cross since leaving Suanetia, and found themselves looking down over the wide, broad forests of the Kodor, with nowhere, as far as the eye could see, any sign of human habitation, only 'the rolling leagues of forest, the broad hills bright in the early sunbeams, the flashes of light in the depths; here a cliff, there a sinuous reach of river'.

A thousand feet below the pass, however, they came across three Abkhasian shepherds. From them they managed to extract the information that if they wished to reach the valley, then they must return to the ridge and follow along it for some considerable distance before a safe way down could be found. Freshfield offered one of them a knife if he would show them the way, and the offer was accepted. The man led them along the terrace and they followed, enjoying the glorious view, the sunshine, and the carpet of yellow crocuses and gentians on which they walked. After about two miles the shepherd led them down into the forest, where they found a pleasant glade by the river to have their lunch. Freshfield went off to have a bathe, and when he returned, their shepherd guide, having been paid in advance, had taken the opportunity to vanish, leaving them with no indication of the direction of a crossing place; their own guides had long since left the regions known to them.

Soon they were hopelessly lost. Freshfield plunged ahead up the banks of the river, through ever thicker forest, in the hopes of finding a crossing place. The Suanetians started to howl, and at each fresh outburst Freshfield would exclaim, 'Look, here is the road,' in a voice of confidence which he did not feel, until at last they were forced to give up at the foot of a sheer cliff. Understandably they had a bad night; worry and insects allowed little time for sleep.

In the morning someone had the bright idea of felling a tree across the river to form a bridge, and for an hour they laboured only to see the result of their handiwork swept away by the torrent. There was nothing for it but to return by the way they had come, in the hope of finding some kind of bridge lower down. 'In three hours we were back at the path. At first we searched in vain for any crossing amongst the labyrinth of water channels and islets; but after some time, guided by a clearing, which was probably an old track half overgrown, we came on a bridge formed of a single monstrous trunk concealed behind a thick grown island. How were the mules to get over? The Suanetians made a mad attempt to lead them over the trunk, but the wiser beasts declined, and secured with our alpine rope they swam the swift waters most pluckily.'

They now had to traverse country that alternated between groves of giant beeches, where the going was easy, and copses that were interlaced with fallen trunks made treacherous by loose stones. At last they crossed a meadow where shoulder high flowers were shaded by fruit and walnut trees, to find themselves standing on the brink of a truly formidable torrent, the Kluich. While they were discussing what to do a party of baggage horses came in sight on the far bank, in the charge of two picturesque natives. In response to their shouts one of the horsemen plunged into the river and swam his mount over to their side. Negotiations were opened on the subject of bringing over sufficient animals to transport the whole party to the far bank; but in a very short space of time the native took offence at some insult offered by the Suanetians, and shouting 'Suanetian asses!' in Russian over his shoulder, plunged into the river and started for his own bank. Freshfield had had enough. He plunged into the river, seized the man and concluded the arrangements, and in due course they were all safely transported to the other side.

Not unnaturally their unfortunate Suanetians were becoming more and more unhappy the further they were taken from the familiar country of their birth. 'We want to go home', was their constant cry, together with the loud voiced opinion that anyway the whole party was hopelessly lost. Their terror of the unknown was very real, and Freshfield showed considerable lack of perception by not realizing that, in spite of the fact that they now found themselves on a good track, the poor outlawed Suanetians were prepared to go to any lengths to get away. The track led them to Shkalta, where they had been led to expect that they would find Cossacks, 'post horses and good accommodation for man and beast'. As soon as the mules were unloaded the Suanetians struck. The single two roomed building that composed Shkalta proved to be occupied solely by a sick Georgian; there were no Cossacks, horses, or anything else by which the travellers could proceed. Freshfield pointed out to the Suanetians that they were engaged to go with his party until some alternative method of transport could be found. But their fright was too great. They were beyond all reasoning. Suddenly they seized their mules, and with howls of triumph galloped off into the forest. They were without food, they had not even waited to see if they could get their pay – they must have been very frightened indeed. How exactly Freshfield had imagined that these men, so far removed from their own ground, with rivers to cross, were ever going to get back, is hard to see.

But the position of the party was not as bad as at first thought. Leaving Maurer in charge of their stranded baggage, the others continued down the valley for about five hours, until they came to another station called Lata. Here they found that a party engaged on the new survey of the region had made their headquarters, and they were hospitably entertained while arrangements were made for the collection of their goods.

They were on the fringes of civilization once again, the real solitude of Abkhasia was behind them. Of the ancient race that had once inhabited the region there was no trace, their homes and graves had vanished, buried deep in the forests. Known to the ancient Greeks and famed for their athletic powers and good looks, they appear to have left no record of their existence, for they could not write and their language was never committed to paper. Their land became deserted of mankind; new settlers being almost nonexistent because the whole area had a bad reputation for fever. Only the forest flourished: wild beeches, firs, alder, fruit bearing plum trees and wild raspberries, all growing with many others in fertile profusion.

Eighteen miles from Sukhum they breasted a hazel covered slope and caught their first glimpse of the sea, and soon they were crossing fields that were farmed by a colony of Greeks, treading a well-made road between hedges. In time they reached the river Gumista, which had once, when in flood, prevented the city of Sukhum from being sacked by the Abkhasians. The bridge had been washed away but they crossed without difficulty. 'Ten minutes later we rode out on to a little quay and dismounted before the wide verandah of a bunga-low, where officers were still supping. I was hardly off my horse when I was addressed by name and asked to join the company. The evening ended among the luxuries of civilization, while the waves of the Euxine broke in phosphorescent foam at our feet.'

Within a day or two he was at sea, embarked for home, and as usual engaged in covering the whole story in letters. To his mother, a long description of the journey, starting at the eastern end of the Central Caucasus, which finished with a reference to Powell, now on his way to Tiflis: '... he will rather enjoy playing first fiddle and dining with the Archduke Michael and all that sort of thing, which he well deserves. Dent and I sent a formal report to D. K. the Gover-nor General which was duly published ... The Governor unluckily committed himself to the murder theory and seems consequently rather unhappy – at least he has in no way expressed satisfaction at our discovery. He tried to prove that one villager had a wound inflicted by an ice axe, but happily the Tartar proved an alibi ... This is the way to return from the Caucasus. The luxury of stepping straight from the roughness of travel into a well appointed deck cabin – salt water bath and hot water for washing – an airy deck house for sitting, and no boring fellow passengers – but for company an old sea dog who has seen half the world – is great.'

Much later he wrote his own epitaph on his young friend Donkin:

> White Soul in lands of purer light
> Who caught the secrets of the snow,
> For you no priest performed the rite,
> No hireling led the funeral show,
> Lost on the far Caucasian height,
> We know not how, content to know
> The guardian stars their watches keep,
> The mountain walls their ward extend,
> Where nature holds in quiet sleep
> Her own interpreter and friend.

What is fascinating about this whole episode, as described in Freshfield's book, is that it is the ultimate in camping tours. Spiced with the prospect of danger, in a temperate climate, surrounded by scenery as beautiful and unspoiled as fairyland, with a colourful native population not so civilized that they could not be looked upon with superiority, and used, and even abused, for the traveller's convenience. Freshfield and his companions were as unconcerned as to the future of their mule owning guides, even had they not run off in terror, as they were to accord honours to the natives who had so bravely made the first ascent of Elbruz with them.

Freshfield expressed the whole vivid Caucasian scene in his many writings throughout the rest of his life. The visions remained with him and he returned to them again and again, but seldom in conversation for he was never one to be a club bore in that respect. It is hard to tell whether the accumulated experience was expressed much later in the poem quoted below or if it was already in part completed during the final visit prompted by the search for his friends. It does appear to be a combination of sunset and dawn seen from the heights of Elbruz and a spiritual contact that the surroundings provoked within him as he contemplated the last bivouac. However it came about it was obviously the product of intense feelings which gives the lie to the coldness of which contemporaries sometimes accused him. He called it 'View and Vision'; one version appears in *A Tramp's Wallet* and another with slight amendments in *Unto the Hills*'published in 1914.

> I lay alone with the sunset, hard by the Caucasian snow,
> And gazed from my eagle's eyrie over infinite space below
> And infinite space above me, the lifeless wastes of the sky,
> And the fields where men as of old are born, grow weary and die:
> For Phoebus had stooped from the height and sunk to his nightly
>   rest
> Where the waves and sky were one in the far off Gates of the West,
> And the white-robed, soft-mist maidens, who spring from the salt
>   sea spray
> To dream on the hills at noontide, had quietly melted away;
> Bare, boundless,all-embracing, the vault of heaven outspread,
> While the face of the earth still glowed with the kiss of the day that
>   was dead,
> And the mountains shone transfigured, each hill and valley and
>   stream

Clothed round with light for raiment, and fair as a poet's dream:
A sudden star in the gloaming, a flash in a dusky space,
Shone Phasis, the ancient river, the pride of a vanished race,
At rest in the lap of the lowlands, where, girt in pomegranate close,
Aietes' city, Kyteia, looks up to the stainless snows.

At my feet lay the home of the outlaws, the vale of a thousand
    towers,
Where murder wades red-handed, knee deep in a garden of
    flowers,
Where glaciers in avalanche fall on a carpet of lily and rose,
And through leagues of glade and forest the fragrant azalea glows;
Where the snow-rhododendrons cluster on pastures unbitten by
    kine;
And above the quivering birch-grove the crests of the Stormpeak
    shine.

Then slowly o'er hill and valley were spread the wings of the night,
But the frosty summits about me shone forth as pillars of light,
And the ice-stairs all untrod, from Kaf's Temple of wingless peace
Stretched down towards golden Kolkhis, the Land of the Golden
    Fleece;
While over the earth's climbing shadow, unfurled on the field of
    blue,
Where the banners of fire once flickered the banner of day still flew,
Rose-red on the heights of Elbruz, on the domes that were built by
    Dis,
When the lava seethed and weltered where now roll billows of ice.

As high o'er Rome's Colosseum the purple valerium spread,
A shade to the proud patrician, a shade to the slave just dead,
So the face of the earth was full of beauty and story and strife,
While the dome of the sky stretched empty above the turmoil of
    life.

Then I watched till the chill before dawn, when the blood in the
    veins runs cold,
And the face of the earth was void, but crowded the heavenly fold;
The moonless vault was ablaze with the splendour of spheres
    unknown,
Suns upon suns in systems, each greater far than our own,
And the fragments of orbs in making were a causeway of living
    light,

As the star that heralds the morning sailed up on the skirts of the
    night;
And vain seemed all the beauty and all the strife of a world,
Blotted out in an instant's throb by the Vision of Space unfurled;
And Night grew greater then Day, and Life grew larger then Death,
And man's brief wrestle with Fate as an infant's battle for breath;
And the body was less than raiment, and our Earth as an inn on the
    road,
Where the traveller halts for an hour on his way to some far-off
    abode:
And the gods man makes in his image, the creatures of stock and
    stone
That led the nations to pillage, that fought each one for his own;
The creeds of saints and sages, who strove for a viewless goal,
Were as shadows athwart the ages from the depths of the human
    soul,
Dim shadows, feint and fleeting, yet born of that Infinite Day
In which on the Heights of Being all shadows must melt away;
For the shackles of flesh were loosed within the fetters of mortal
    fears,
And the walls of the sense fell down to the song of the circling
    spheres,

And the suns upon suns uncounted were forms of the living soul,
The law that abides in the Heavens to shepherds their flock to its
    goal,
And the Spirit spoke with Spirit, and the part was one with the
    whole.

Then again earth's memories found me, my school-fellow stood at
    my head,
And those we sought came round me, the living talked with the
    dead,
Till I woke on a world in sunshine, and void was the upper sky,
Had I seen – or dreamt – the vision? was it all or in part a lie?

CHAPTER 7

THE FRESHFIELD CHILDREN – DIMBOLA BECOMES THE FAMILY'S HOLIDAY HOME –
ELEANOR'S PASSION FOR LILIAN FOX – HAL'S DEATH FROM MENINGITIS – GRIEF AND
OUTRAGE – ESTRANGEMENT OF DOUGLAS AND GUSSIE – FRESHWATER NEVER THE
SAME AGAIN

The eldest of the Freshfield's five children was Eleanor. Born on 5 September 1870, it was very soon noticed by her mother that her looks seemed to owe more to the big-boned large nosed Crawfords, than to either the Freshfields or the Ritchies. She grew up into a long-shanked, healthy looking woman with a definite look of Jane Q about her; she was described as something between a Roman emperor and an alderman. But the looks belied the spirit, for her letters and diaries, both as a young girl and woman, show her to be much akin to her mother, somewhat intense, but with a dash of her father's commanding obstinacy. She was well read, as one would expect, and with her next sister, Janie, was fluent in French, and French literature, thought a good deal about God, and adored and admired her mother above all others. Second only to her mother, came her younger brother Hal.

Janie, the second child, was born five years later. She was softer and prettier, and in due course grew into a lively and attractive young woman much sought after as a partner at fashionable balls and parties. She was dominated somewhat by Eleanor but never seems to have resented it, shared her enthusiasm for things French, was not so troubled in early years by religious thoughts or doubts, had a lovely singing voice and played the piano reasonably well, neither accomplishment ever being mastered by Eleanor.

The third in this trio was the boy Henry, or Hal, born in 1877. Hal did not inherit his father's robust physique though that might have developed later. He enjoyed visiting the mountains with his parents and François, and when he was twelve and thirteen made several longer high level walks with the two men. But he did not have the same urge to climb every hill or explore remote corners in quite the same way. This did not affect either his father's or his mother's relationship with him, for although records of him make him out to be somewhat priggish, he was certainly a thoroughly nice boy, even if he did pull the chair from under a nursemaid causing her to take to her bed for several days in acute pain. He was more open as a schoolboy than his father had been, made friends more easily, and what he lacked in physical stamina he made up in other directions. He liked accompanying François on easy mountain walks, showing a keen interest in everything the old mountaineer had to tell him about the birds, trees and flowers they discovered.

He seems to have made a unique discovery when staying with his grandparents at Kidbrook, a discovery that was recorded with pride by his near relatives. He found the nest of a strange bird in the park. Consultation with an eminent expert at the British Museum confirmed that the bird was indeed a rare one, in fact it had never been known to nest south of the border with Scotland. But he had it in writing from the expert that he had found a pair of nesting ospreys in Sussex. On his next visit to Kidbrook he hurried off to see how the birds fared, taking Eleanor for company. As they approached the tree, keeping as quiet as possible, they found two boys in the process of robbing the nest. Hal waited until the boys made off with the eggs, and then gave chase, pursuing them far beyond the boundary of the park and into the forest, where he eventually tripped the thief with a stick, tackled him, recovered the egg and returned in triumph – shades of his father with his ice axe in Suanetia! It certainly shows that the son had inherited the same robustness of spirit, and the ability to take the offensive when roused.

When the Camerons finally abandoned Dimbola,[1] their home in Freshwater, in 1875, the increasingly eccentric Julia, now, according to Gussie, completely toothless, and her husband bed-ridden and only wishing to die in Ceylon, the Freshfields decided to take it over as their holiday home. The place had been sadly neglected after the departure of the Camerons, and visits were made to lay books and furnishings in the sunshine on the lawn to dry them out and get rid

---

[1] Dimbola is now a museum devoted to Julia Margaret Cameron and her work. It also contains a book shop mainly concerned with Mrs Cameron's life and relatives.

of the musty smells. In spite of the fact that Farringford had been abandoned as Tennyson's sole residence during the holidays, because of the crowds of visitors that would invade his private grounds, the ageing poet was still a regular visitor, with his family and now a nurse to keep him company and make sure that he did not collapse when he had one of his sickly spells. Tennyson had lost his son Lionel, and, with his increasing old age and loss of friends, Farringford was becoming a sad place.[1]

At Dimbola there were still childish fun and games in the Victorian manner – acting games, reading, walking and in the spring of 1891 there was riding. The children were in high spirits, and the shadow that had fallen over all their lives, and the fright it gave them when Hal had developed diphtheria while they were all staying in Italy the year before, seemed forgotten. Douglas had been particularly affected by this setback, which made him regretful of the formality of their relationship, even though they had become walking companions in the mountains in the company of François. After his son's fairly rapid recovery, he writes in the introduction of his first book of poems: 'We northerners for the most part live obscurely, after the fashion of our own skies, rolling up our true selves in a fog of false shame or modesty, fearing it would seem, nothing so much as to be open one to another, with something of southern frankness. That we should in company hide our woes, or even our average selves, is no doubt seemly. But our better selves – may we not show them?'

Also during the previous summer Eleanor had been suffering from a passionate affair of the heart, in that she had developed what might now be termed a 'crush' on a girl friend, Lilian Fox, to whom she ascribed the greatest beauty, finest feelings, and most wonderful

[1] In April 1888 on one of his many visits to Dimbola, this time with the composer Stanford, Tennyson was, according to Gussie, in 'Capital Spirits' although he remarked that Dimbola was full of ghosts for him. The relationship between the Tennysons and the Freshfields had become close, especially between Gussie and Lady Tennyson since the difficult situation between Gussie's brother Richmond, Aunt Annie's husband, and Mr Lionel Tennyson's young widow who had become involved in an affair on her return from India. The matter was eventually resolved by Richmond returning to Annie and soon after the widow re-married. At the time the matter caused considerable distress to the two families.

intelligence. They had been together to the passion play at Oberam-
magau, fallen in love with the player of Christ, and roused themselves to a state of seemly disgust at the appearance of Judas, both on
and off stage. They agreed that their spiritual relationship was
special, would endure all things, and was so strong that mere physical parting could not break the chord. Alas it was soon done! Just
before Christmas 1890 Lilian broke the news by letter that she was
to marry Herbert Trench.[1] However she was reassuring, saying that
nothing could interfere with their special relationship, that they had
long ago agreed that the feelings in a marriage could never equal the
spiritual accord that they had developed, and that Eleanor was to be
happy that this was so. Eleanor bore up bravely. But Christmas and
New Year passed and there was no letter from her beloved, until on
5 January she came up to town from Kidbrook, where in her state of
heartbreak and anxiety the '*éclats de rire*' of all the others had jarred
on her tenderest feelings, to find a three line hastily scribbled note
saying '...we are intensely happy.' 'Realized' wrote Eleanor in her
diary 'all of a sudden, as I was reading Lord Houghton, that the old
days and the old Lilian who belonged to me and I to her, could never
never be again. ... Read over with heartache some of her old letters
and came on this after reading Anna Karenina "My ideals of the
possibilities of love are too exalted ever to be realized on earth" –
and now her most exalted ideals are.'

The weeks passed with poor Eleanor suffering all the pangs of a
superseded lover. Longing to talk about or hear the name of the
beloved, at the same time she resented the mundane comments and
cries of glee the engagement aroused. She had come out into the
social world of London herself by this time, and filled her diaries
with a mixture of quoted philosophy and comments on concerts and
plays. There was some consolation. A shadowy figure dogged her
footsteps, and passed through the pages of the diaries of both
mother and daughter. Arthur Clough commiserated with her on the
loss of dearest friends through marriage.

But she did not pay him any particular attention as yet. So far as
her wounded heart was concerned Lilian could, but would not,

[1] H. F. Trench 1865–1923. Poet and playwright and one time artistic director of
the Haymarket Theatre.

Dimbola becomes the family's holiday home.

provide the salve. Eleanor first refused to be a bridesmaid, but changed her mind when a friend reported another as saying 'doesn't Eleanor even want to see you for the last time?' But little Katia, Eleanor's nine year old sister, was more pragmatic. 'Why, marrying isn't so very very awful, its only being with a gentleman.' Then one evening in March she attended a party, a very sophisticated party for such a young lady but the kind of occasion she had become quite used to under her mother's tutelage. Her Aunt Emily (Pinkie) who was now well known and accomplished as a concert pianist, was accompanying Joachim in Schumann romances, in the presence of Millais, Leighton, the du Mauriers, the Leslie Stephens, Fuller Maitland,[1] Lady Colville and her aunt Annie (Thackeray). Full of excitement at the thought of meeting Lilian at Paddington the next day, she was thrilled to hear from Lilian's own lips all the good things that had befallen her. But more mature handwriting appears at the foot of the page, making clear that even at the time she did not believe what she was being told. Lilian stayed a mere two days and poor Eleanor dashed off to see Aunt Annie with 'burning eyes' and filled her diary with passionate French, which she later scored over many times, and even tore out whole pages. The affair was almost over. Two days later on 28 March she arrived at Dimbola. 'The sight of Colonel Crozier on the Lymington pier made one feel one had never left it. Now for a nice time of reading, hero worshipping and primroseing ...'

The whole family were gathered, to throw off the effects of a long cold winter and the bad colds from which they had all been suffering. In a day or two Douglas took Hal to Ventnor to acquire horses on which they galloped home over the downs. The Island was filling up. Lady Colville walked in with Pippa Strachey[2] 'intending to take a great many meals with us and to be taken a great deal to Farringford by us!' wrote Eleanor, perhaps repeating a remark that could have been made by either parent. Eleanor went riding with Hal, but Gussie recorded the arrival and departure of Arthur Clough on his bicycle.

This was a holiday that was to be imprinted on their minds for ever; constantly recalled as if by so doing time could be put back and

[1] John Alexander Fuller Maitland, 1856–1936, musical critic and historian.

[2] Philippa Strachey, older sister to Lytton Strachey. Active supporter of women's education.

the current of events made to change course. Gussie and Douglas took Arthur Clough to Farringford; that sensitive shy charming man became speechless, quite overcome when asked to pace the ballroom with the Bard. Tennyson took him through to Lady Tennyson when he found he could not make the young man talk, saying to Gussie that he felt so afraid of young men. Clough[1] had indeed come in a very supercilious frame of mind. Douglas complained that there was too much talk about dentistry amongst the women, and later took himself off to hear Tennyson read him his great new poem 'Akbar'. But there was a break in the life of Dimbola. Their parents had arranged a rather more extended tour of southern Spain and North Africa, so, leaving the younger children, and taking Eleanor and Hal with them as far as Paris, they set off.

On 20 April Gussie wrote in her diary 'Hal, Eleanor left Paris at 1 from St Lazare Station where D and I saw them off.' On the evening of the 21st the young brother and sister arrived back at Dimbola, pleased with themselves at having accomplished the journey so smoothly. It was Hal's last evening at home before returning to Broadstairs and school. 'Oliver Strachey[2] to dinner – greatest fun –'

Hal was seen off, Eleanor and the others stayed on. Tennyson complained about 'a lot of women he did not care about coming to see him at Easter', and immensely excited Arthur Coleridge by showing him the manuscript of 'In Memoriam'. There were exciting letters from Seville and an exchange of telegrams with Hal as to the next address to send letters intended for their parents. Eleanor was in charge of her younger sisters, and took the responsibility seriously while enjoying the lovely spring and the beauties of Freshwater. But a cloud passed over the sun that had shone for so long on them all. There was a postcard from Hal to tell of the sudden illness of Mr James, a favourite young master at his school. Hal wrote, 'Is it not perfectly dreadful?' Gussie heard of it and wrote at once before going out, from her hotel, into the smart world of the Madrid races: 'Was haunted by the thought of Mr James killed in the flower of his manhood probably by some imprudence & overtrust in his strength

---

[1] A. H. Clough senior had in fact introduced his son to Tennyson when he was still a child.

[2] Oliver Strachey (1874–1960), brother to Lytton, at this time at Eton.

& youth. Anxious for sweet Hal in this first experience of death, so sudden, under the same roof.'

On Thursday, his family all unknowing, Hal took to his bed saying that he had the worst pain that he had ever had before. He felt guilty that he had not written often enough to his parents and asked for paper -

'Stone House 8 a.m.

'Dearest Mother,

You must indeed think me a dreadfully bad correspondent considering the quantity of letters you and Eleanor and Janie have sent to me and the very few I have sent to you. But it really is not my fault for I have been having dreadful bad neuralgia and never felt such pain and I can indeed now sympathize with you myself. I send my love and will write as soon as I am able.'

There was no relief from the pain of meningitis, mercifully the illness was short. On Saturday afternoon he said 'I should like to take all the pain in the world and make it into a big orchard, then cut down the trees and burn them. Don't you think that would be a good plan?' The death was an outrage to this family, who walked so serenely, so securely, with such splendid sureness through a world where others were afflicted and had to be supported in the bearing of the burdens of pain, suffering and bereavement. Their pride and dignity in the face of this tragedy was unquestioned; only God, in their secret hearts, came in for questioning. Eleanor quotes Carlyle in her diary, amidst a welter of French, 'Certainly if to be happy in this world was the reason for man being put here, the maker of it is a wretched blunderer.'

The shock, disillusionment and awe that surrounded Hal's death reverberated down the generations. Great-grandchildren of Douglas and Gussie were aware of it. Precious mementoes were preserved and frequently displayed. Eleanor in old age kept a little straw basket workbox with these sacred icons; letters about the ospreys, childish drawings and poems and, above all, lengthy writings done by the staff and boys at Stonehouse of Hal's last hours, every minute of them. The anniversary came to be known as 'Hal's Day', but even more painful was the recollection of that Friday, his last, when all the family were enjoying themselves in their different ways, totally unconscious of Hal's illness, pain, and suffering.

Douglas and Augusta, as was to be expected, behaved with absolute dignity. Douglas made the arrangements, acquired the peaceful plot at Brookwood that was reminiscent of some quiet glade in a wooded valley in the Alps or Caucasus, with its smell of pine and dark ilex. Augusta poured out her feelings in letters to her brothers and sisters, expressive, truthful and harrowing reading, but always controlled. Faith in their own personal God was destroyed. Each in their own way, Douglas, Augusta and Eleanor, had to find a way of living with what had happened. Douglas had never expressed any strong belief nor, unlike his parents, was he a conventional churchgoer; if the truth were known he probably regarded religion as unscientific mumbo jumbo. Not so Augusta or his daughters. Gussie started on the eternal quest to find some meaning in her son's death. She read books that argued for atheism as being the only logical belief, and was profoundly depressed by them, saying that she could not conceive of a life so barren, where love and goodness were without meaning. Eleanor was later to find comfort in the writings of Cardinal Newman, as did so many of whatever denomination. But it was the end of 'There's a friend for little children'; something more profound must take its place.

Brookwood cemetery lies a few miles to the south-west of Guildford in Surrey. It was new then, more a natural landscape of heath and woodland than a conventional necropolis. Wild deer wandered then, as now, shyly curious of intruders, grass snakes sunned themselves in the heather, and natural bird life abounded. The Freshfields decided on a family plot here; a low wrought iron fence was erected round it, and the memorial to Hal placed centrally at the back. It was an upright plinth, some eight feet high, of marble and bronze, with a decorated pedimented top. At its centre a carved portrait medallion was placed, surrounded by a frieze of birds; a thrush returning to her nest of eggs, small birds and animals worrying their way through a pattern of foliage, all appropriate to the memory they wanted so much to keep alive.

It was the end of the marriage, in the intimate sense, between the two parents. One has the feeling that he understood and condoned what had happened to her, and was ready, because he still loved her, to pander and support. But she needed her scapegoat. The old difference attained a new proportion. It was the travelling, the partings,

Sculptured head of 'Hal'.

that had caused the tragedy. Had they not been on their way to lay the foundations for yet another piece of travel writing on his part, then she might have been present and somehow, if not saved her son's life, at least been there with him in his terrible distress. Eleanor felt the same, and with more open hostility took her mother's side. Douglas became an outsider to their world, to be disparaged, not in an aggressive way, simply with coldness. Social differences were widened; intellectual and moral values made an impassable gulf. They felt he was incapable of genuine feelings, because he could not express them.

The two youngest girls, about to start school, were naturally the least affected. They would rebel eventually against, not so much their father, as against the luxury and extravagance of their parents' lives. But he retained one sympathetic ally. Janie had a softer core than her sisters; years and years later, with both her parents long since dead, she told how she felt that her father was underrated by his family, both as to his achievements and the understanding that he gave them all.

Although they still visited Freshwater several times every year, it was never to be the same again. True, Annie and her family were still living at the Porch,[1] and often Gussie's nephews or nieces, children of her sister Blanche, who had now become almost an institution in her own right at Eton, would stay. But as Gussie remarked, with old Mrs Brotherton, an unfortunate relative grumbling away in poverty and ill health on the one hand, and poor old Tennyson, now a toothless lion on the other, it was hardly an atmosphere that sparkled. It seemed so long since she had acted the part of Portia, sick with fright, in front of Tennyson, at the behest of Mrs Cameron, all those years ago, before the agony that every Friday seemed to bring whenever she stayed on the Island. The poet was kind to her now as he had not always been before, especially when her family's judgement had been called in question when Lionel's widow had become too closely involved with Richmond Ritchie, Annie's husband. Gussie tells how she and Tennyson walked the muddy lanes together and talked of the past, and their loss. It seems that the nurse no longer

---

[1] The Porch was a cottage close by Dimbola. During the Second World War it was demolished by a German bomb.

went with them, but he was afraid of dying, and deafness was a great trial to him. His old friend Jowett[1] was deaf too, and one evening stamped his feet with fury when neither of them could make the other understand what each was saying.

And what of Douglas himself in all this? He no longer seems to have wanted to visit Freshwater with his wife, and if he wept, he wept alone. Once he tried to write something of his feelings, but it is not a very good poem, contrived and a little mawkish, but there is genuine feeling in the last two lines.

> Before the dull earth closes
> Above our Darling, roses,
> Heap roses, spring's first roses,
>   On our beloved's bier;
> Since love, fond love, supposes
>   His spirit may be near.
>
> Primrose and violet shower
> Bluebells, the woodlands dower,
> Strip every hedgerow bower
> Of all he held most dear;
> Leave Spring without a flower
>   Since he, our spring, lies here.[2]

[1] Benjamin Jowett (1817–93), Master at Balliol College, Oxford. Regius professor of Greek etc.

[2] A second and possibly better poem was written much later by D.W.F. on this subject, part of which is quoted on pp. 282–3.

CHAPTER 8

Geography, and the affairs of the Royal Geographical Society, had been absorbing Freshfield's attention for some years, even though he had taken time off to visit the Caucasus. Within a year of his son's death he was directly involved in one of those great battles in which learned societies of the period loved to indulge.

During his time as editor of the *Alpine Journal* he had modernized and made the paper more attractive, and he was glad to see that the same was being done for the *Journal*, or *Proceedings of the Royal Geographical Society*. He saw no reason why the publication of a scientific body should be dry, uninteresting and too stodgy for general consumption. However, it was more than influencing the style and content of their publications during the next ten years that was to occupy his time, even though he was directly responsible for the *Proceedings*. His most important campaigns, which were of concern to the world outside the confines of the Society were, first, that the universities should recognize geography as a valid discipline, and second, that there should follow from this, with the advent of qualified university-trained young men, a much needed improvement in the quality of possible recruits available to the Ordnance Survey.

There is no doubt that his most important actions at the time of his Honorary Secretaryship were in connection with his ambition to improve the teaching of geography in this country, and to see geography accorded its proper place in the educational curriculum. He persuaded the Council to form a commission, under the chairmanship of Sir John Keltie, to enquire into the teaching of geography on the continent. When the commission reported, Freshfield became prime mover and advocate of the scheme which was eventually adopted, to subsidize the teaching of geography at Oxford, his old university. The plan bore fruit in 1888 and Cambridge was to follow in 1902. In order to carry through the work that the Council had started and stimulate continued improvement in geographical education, the Geographical Association was formed with Freshfield as its first chairman. In this way he became the father of geographical teaching in this country, and it was through his efforts that geography became an Honours subject, a fact that his own university was to recognize by granting him an Honorary D.C.L.

During nearly all the ten years he held the position of Honorary Secretary within the Council of the Society, his strong common-sense speeches carried the members along the path he had mapped. But there was trouble brewing in the ranks of the fellows. Not only had his various innovations themselves made him enemies, but so had his manner of putting them through. He had an air of knowing best what was right; energy that was disturbing to the fuddy-duddies, and, as the years passed, his naturally aloof, autocratic manner and his apparent imperviousness to criticism, caused resentment. He moved silently and purposefully in the shadows, eloquent only in Council, disdaining argument with the ill-informed except now and again to crush with withering witticism or lightning quip, on occasions delivered in Latin. There is little wonder that there were a number of fellows who were only waiting for him to show a chink in his armour. In particular there were those who saw the Royal Geographical Society as primarily a body dedicated to the active exploration of the world, and they resented the way in which funds were being diverted into Freshfield's particular, as they saw it, obsession with education.

It was his very dedication that was to give them the opportunity that they required. As he pushed ahead with his plans he little thought how he might be applying a light to the highly inflammable material that smouldered in the minds of the entrenched traditionalists, who saw in Freshfield a threat to what they regarded as the comfortable distinction that their fellowship conferred on them. He had long considered that there was every good reason why women should be admitted as fellows, which would bring the Royal Geographical Society into line with other similar learned societies.

In 1892 several applications were received from distinguished ladies to be admitted to the fellowship. At a meeting on 4 July the Council considered their applications, and decided there was nothing within the Laws of the Society to imply that there was any discrimination against ladies, and admitted them. There was an immediate reaction, which Freshfield himself described briefly: 'Their action was challenged by a number of malcontent fellows who styled themselves the "Associated Fellows". They were led by a person unknown to fame either as a geographer or a traveller – Mr Hicks of Bromley – aided by the Hon. G. N. Curzon[1] (Lord Curzon), several ungallant Admirals, one of whom, before any opposition broke out, himself seconded a lady candidate, and made themselves conspicuous in this sorry business, while Mr F. Galton (afterwards Sir F. Galton) played the part of an opportunist.'

The 'Battle of the Ladies' was joined. Freshfield disliked Curzon, whom he saw as flamboyant and dangerously irrational, and to some extent this may have affected his tactical judgement. Freshfield was to play a part in the battle that was decisive and, as far as he was concerned, disastrous. To start with all went well. When it first became known that the Council had allowed the applications of women, a letter from the alarmed fellows was sent to the Council, implying that they had no objection to the admission of women as such, but that they were of the opinion that the Council was out of order in accepting the applications; that they had in fact altered the Laws, and this they were not empowered to do, and they called for a Special General Meeting.

The meeting was presently held, and Freshfield was among those who spoke in favour of the ladies. The Admirals and other dissenters, in case the legal argument should fail them, had shifted their ground slightly and were now maintaining that there was little enough room for the fellows and their guests in the lecture hall, without lady fellows being admitted to take up still more. In his speech Freshfield took up this point. 'It reminds me' he said, 'of the story of the farmer who refused to subscribe to some church charities because the church was so crowded, and it was found on enquiry that he had only been twice in five years, and then by reason of

---

[1] Curzon was later to become an opponent of women's franchise.

church festivals. There have been only two such meetings here in the past five years.'

But there was more behind the opposition than a desire to see the Laws of the Society adhered to, or a desire to see that existing fellows were able to get seats for themselves at the more entertaining meetings. After the meeting, and the agreement to seek Council's opinion as to the legality of admitting women under the existing laws, Freshfield, as one of the Honorary Secretaries, and acting on behalf of the Council, first of all tried to appeal to them as fellows solely interested in the advancement of geography. But this was to no avail. The opposition had gained support and courage and they felt their case was a strong one. Unlike Freshfield they had nothing to lose. At each informal or friendly attempt to try to find some common ground for discussion, the opposition managed to become more formal and official in tone. While the Council went to Sir Frederick Pollock for an opinion, which turned out to be generally favourable to their cause, the opposition consulted no less a person than the Attorney General, and got an opinion that was generally in their favour.

It was fatal for Freshfield that, because the most vocal leaders of the opposition were neither geographers nor explorers, and in his opinion had never done anything to further the cause of the Society, he refused to regard them seriously. They sensed this, and it only goaded them into fresh efforts. He made no secret of the fact that he could not see any reason why anyone who had simply paid a subscription, nothing more, should regard it as some sort of distinction to put F.R.G.S. after his name.

> Should you ever get into a squabble
>> With men on whom argument fails
> The shortest way out of the hobble
>> Is to fasten some squibs to their tails.

There must have been moments when he wished he could do just that.

But feelings were running high, and there was danger of a sense of proportion being lost on both sides. Freshfield never lost sight of the main objects, declaring the Society was essentially a working one, it collected information about the geography of the world, and he could not see why half Her Majesty's subjects should be excluded from that work simply because they shared her sex. Although there was no question that the result should be in any way binding upon them, the Council decided to get the opinions of the mass of fellows by holding a postal referendum, for it was hard to gauge the opinions of the provincial and university fellows as to the course the Council should take. Freshfield, as Honorary Secretary was instructed to take the necessary steps to put this into effect.

It was then that he made his fatal mistake for, with the card on which the fellows were asked to record their vote, and entirely at his own instigation, he included the following letter.

'1 Savile Row.   1st June 1893

'Dear Sir, at the recent Anniversary Meeting of the Royal Geographical Society in the course of the discussion on the admission of Ladies to the Fellowship, it was suggested, and the suggestion met with the approval of the meeting and was accepted by the President, that the best course would be to obtain the opinion of the body of Fellows throughout the Country. General R. Strachey, acting in the absence of Mr Clements Markham – has consequently requested me to send you the accompanying note and post card. A general vote thus taken is not formally binding on the Society, but its results will, there is every reason to believe, be acquiest in, and confirmed at a General Meeting as a conclusion to the recent controversy.'

Had he stopped there all would have been well, and there is no reason to suppose that he would not have won the final round. But he went on: 'The admission of ladies is no new idea. It was accepted in principle both as a means of justice and expedience by the Council in 1887, and its application was deferred until a convenient occasion and that occasion arose when last year an eminent lady traveller, Mrs Bishop (Miss Bird), declined to furnish a paper to a Society that would not acknowledge her as a geographer. I need not catalogue the many other ladies, from our Gold Medallists, the late Mrs Somerville and Lady Franklin, to Miss Edwards and Miss North whose names are well known to all who are interested in literature and the results of travel.

'The ladies the Council particularly desire to see admitted as Fellows are in the first place travellers who contribute to geographical knowledge and also the ladies who have so warm an interest in geographical progress that they desire regularly to attend our meetings and use our library. Up to the present time such ladies, if widows or unaccompanied, have only been able to be present at such meetings by begging a ticket on each occasion from a fellow. The Society has refused their subscriptions, and they have been debarred from the privileges accorded to members. Is not such a state of things an anomaly at a date when ladies are already admitted as members of a large proportion of the more important scientific societies of the Metropolis, and of, I believe, all the Geographical Societies of the United Kingdom?'

He goes on to mention by name those distinguished and noble fellows who support the move, and to give the undertaking that on the question of seating at lectures provision will be made to accommodate fellows, ladies or gentlemen, before unqualified persons.

He winds up:

'The Council, deeply impressed by the importance of geographical knowledge to the coming generation of English people, and noticing every day how its absence is felt in questions of politics, commerce, and immigration, trust you will be able to agree with their view, and to answer the question submitted to you in the affirmative. I am yours faithfully. D.W.F. Hon.Sec.'

Confident that, as the Council had agreed to the admission of women to the fellowship, he was fully justified in expressing their views, and incidentally his own fervently held opinion, Freshfield also follows this circular letter with a further one to *The Times*, and even took the trouble to go round to the office of the latter to make sure it was printed before it should lose its topicality. He remembered a previous occasion when he had written a letter in connection with an election, and it had been published two weeks after it was all over. But this time all was well. By the time he had reached Oxford, where he had gone to see how the University fellows were preparing to use their votes, the letter had been published. From Oxford he wrote in triumph to Keltie, saying that all to whom he had spoken were using their vote in favour of the admission of women.

But retribution was swift and irrevocable. On 5 June a further circular letter was addressed to all fellows from the Royal Geographical Society. 'Sir, I am desired by the Council of the Royal Geographical Society to inform you that Mr Freshfield's letter of 1 June was written without their authority or knowledge, and that his action in so writing has been disavowed by them. The Council as a body have no wish to influence the judgement of any Fellow in the matter.'

Freshfield was shattered. He regarded this as a complete betrayal by the Council, not of himself, but of the cause of the advancement of geography. The Council had been absolutely unanimous in their decision to allow the admission of ladies – what then could be wrong with their putting their sincerely held view before the voters? It is curious how he could have allowed himself, with his legal training, to fall into this trap, and he never was able to see the reason for the Council's prompt action.

The result of the postal vote when it came in was strongly in favour of the admission of women, but nevertheless when the matter was again put to the vote at a meeting of the fellows, the idea was defeated. From the time of the Council's letter disclaiming his circular, Freshfield had remained silent. He delivered the first of the Children's Lectures, an innovation for which he himself had been responsible, and then, at the Annual General Meeting, resigned. He gave as his reason that he no longer wished to serve on a Council that had shown so little consistency in its policy.

Chief amongst his opponents in the matter of the Society's support for geographical education had been Sir Clements Markham, and the advocacy of lady fellows by Freshfield and his friends was regarded by Markham as dangerous, to the degree that he wrote 'objectionable woman' against the names of some of the candidates. He was immensely relieved by Freshfield's removal, describing him as 'one of those impossible people who always think they are right'.

But it was the members of the Council that Freshfield scorned, not the Royal Geographical Society, or the causes that it espoused. During his period of great influence he had achieved much, and it was only to be expected that he would bang a few heads on the way. He would retire into the background and wait for the course of time to remove the present incompetents from office. On leaving he wrote a few words for Keltie,[1] pointing out some of the lessons they must

---

[1] J. S. Keltie (later knighted) Secretary of the R.G.S. remained a friend and supporter of D.W.F. for the rest of his life. He died in 1927 aged 87.

learn from the recent battle, if the good of the Society was to remain uppermost in their minds. ...' The fellows of the Society desire to be directed, but they prefer to be consulted. Technical questions are better avoided, otherwise irrelevant prejudice may easily be imported into the consideration of material matters ...'

He remained extremely proud of his stand on the matter of ladies becoming fellows, never repented a single action, and in due course was to be fully vindicated. In light vein he expressed his opinion of the present Council:

> Our Council are birds of a feather,
> A feather that's whiter than chalk;
> They are very much cocks of the weather,
> But not at all cocks of the walk;
> Thirty-odd Geographical fogies,
> Their courage won't carry them far,
> They are dreadfully frightened of bogies,
> And dare not say 'Boo' to a tar!

On the matter of the admission of ladies he was prepared to wait, time was on his side.

> Yet the ladies will win in due season,
> And that as a matter of course;
> The laugh at the end is with reason,
> When folly has screamed herself hoarse.

But if the Council were in his opinion inconsistent in their policy, he at least would be fully consistent towards them. Even when the time came for him to make his preparations for his journey of exploration round Kanchenjunga, he refused to be placed under any obligation to them. An instance of this arose when he received a letter from Garwood, who was to accompany the expedition as surveyor, saying that he had been unable to procure a light plane table; Freshfield obtained one from the Society, but he makes it quite clear that it will be purchased – he wrote to the Secretary once again: 'I particularly desire that nothing may be loaned from the Royal Geographical Society which can in any way be thought to place me under any obligation to the present Council ...'

For in place of his work for the Royal Geographical Society, for the time being at least, Freshfield was finding other employment. First he became President of his old love The Alpine Club, and second there was work to be done to complete his great *Exploration of the Caucasus*, an ambitious combination of his and other expeditions to that date, illustrated mainly with V. Sella's unique photographs.

If he was being difficult as far as the Royal Geographical Society was concerned, as President of the Alpine Club it fell to him to have to deal with some of the most fractious members of that body, which had never been exactly noted for the harmoniousness of its affairs. One of the most famous of the sensitive 'prima donnas' of the peaks was the Rev. W. A. B. Coolidge, who, although living almost permanently in Switzerland, knew just how to make himself felt. At one point during Freshfield's presidency he took violent objection to the election to the committee of two members with whom he had quarrelled. As a consequence, he resigned from the Club and, in so doing said to Freshfield: 'Of course I must continue to correspond with you to wind up affairs, but apart from that I decline to have any further communication with you whatsoever. You have treated me in a way not only wholly unexpected by me but contrary to all the laws of friendship, and opposed to the interests of the Club of which you are head ...'

Strong words! But Freshfield who was adept at growling behind the fence, was equally adept at bringing this long exchange of correspondence back to normal friendly terms once again.

But he was not to be so easily wooed back into the active fold of the Royal Geographical Society. Although he had voluntarily abandoned the cause of the advancement of the science of geography through the Society, his exploration of Kanchenjunga in 1899 put him right back in the centre of the picture as one of the leading active explorers of the day and, as such, he certainly could not be ignored. It is possible that the Council were nervous of making a direct approach to him, for his reputation as a verbal chastiser had increased rather than diminished, with his aloof withdrawal from their active circles, for they instructed one of the Honorary Secretaries to write him a personal private note asking him if he would consider lecturing to the Society on his expedition.

But this did not do at all. In his reply he pointed out that all those years ago when he had returned, still a very young and junior explorer, from his first visit to the Caucasus, no less a person than their revered past President Sir Roderick Murchison had himself, personally, invited him to give a lecture. And now, when he was one of the Society,s most distinguished members, he was asked in this underhand way. He declined the invitation saying 'I shall not myself lecture again in London, but Garwood is at perfect liberty to do so.'

This placed the unfortunate Garwood in a very difficult situation. Freshfield was very much his senior, both in age and reputation; besides, Freshfield had been his leader on the expedition. He felt he could do nothing else but decline also.

But through all this Freshfield had remained on friendly terms with Keltie, and the latter seems to have acquired a certain amount of tact in dealing with him, for a few weeks later Freshfield was writing to him again: 'I have done my best to persuade Garwood to read a paper. I cannot force him; he expresses in the circumstances the strongest reluctance to do so. To avoid any further misunderstanding and trouble to yourself I may as well say categorically that I shall be ready to serve the Society whenever the Council sees fit to offer me the position to which I am entitled by my past services, that is to nominate me as a Vice President ... But I have no ambition to come back and shall be best pleased by being ignored. All I want to show is that the sulking is not on my side.' Keltie had the good sense to keep his own council on that one!

But on the publication in 1903 of his next great work, *Round Kanchenjunga* (somewhat delayed, Garwood having taken rather longer than expected to produce his map of the environs of the mountain) the Society awarded him their coveted Gold Medal, and he relented and delivered his lecture; and it was by no means his last.

The breach was healed, except perhaps there was one last echo of thunder when he wrote to Keltie in 1906 at the time when he was helping organize the expedition of Mumm and Longstaff to the Himalaya, half the expenses being paid by Lord Curzon in an effort to encourage the exploration of the region. Freshfield had been trying to find out if the Royal Geographical Society might find the other £3,000 that was wanted, but it was evident that had they done so they would have wanted to have a strong say in what the objects of the expedition were to be.

'Mumm and Longstaff will go with Bryce to the Himalayas, and will between them provide the £3,000 more if needful. Consequently in place of coming cap in hand to the Council, all that will be needed will be to get letters of introduction etc. If the Council insists on laying down conditions of a character, in my opinion, prejudicial to the success of a mountaineering party, I shall withdraw this request and run the thing through the Alpine Club. As the Alpine Club is going to pay, it must call the tune, and I cannot believe the Council will, at this time of day, fail to recognize climbing as a branch of geographical exploration, worthy of a good word if no more.'

CHAPTER 9

ARTHUR CLOUGH, THE BICYCLING VISITOR TO FRESHWATER – ENGAGED TO ELEANOR – NERVOUS BREAKDOWN – FRIENDSHIP WITH DOUGLAS – DOUGLAS REPORTS TO THE BOARD OF AGRICULTURE ON THE CONDITION OF THE ORDNANCE SURVEY – CLOUGH AND ELEANOR MARRY – CLOUGH'S ECCENTRIC BUSINESS ACTIVITIES – FINANCIAL RUIN – DEATH OF OLD MRS FRESHFIELD – JANIE ENGAGED TO EDMUND FISHER – FRESHFIELD RESENTS THE COMMERCIALIZATION OF MOUNTAINEERING – TURNS HIS ATTENTION TO MORE REMOTE REGIONS

If truth were told, in the years following the death of Hal, Douglas had many other concerns to occupy his time, quite apart from his problems with the Royal Geographical Society.

Arthur Clough, the bicycling visitor to Freshwater, and Eleanor's discrete shadow for many months had somehow attached himself almost unnoticed to their circle. He worked at the Education Office, where he was poorly paid, but, so he informed Eleanor, it was a good refuge for those who, like himself, wish to live retired, and look on as tired spectators at humanity and its struggles.

This seemingly languid young man was an interesting character, and somewhat unusual. He was the son of Arthur Hugh Clough,[1] the minor poet, chiefly famous for his friendship with Matthew Arnold and remembered today through his poem 'Say not the struggle naught availeth' quoted by Churchill in the Second World War. He also coined the couplet much quoted at present,

> Thou shalt not kill; but needst not strive
> Officiously to keep alive.

Arthur, the son, was clever, with an apparently timid personality, struggled with repressed homosexuality, and, surprisingly, was a brilliant shot and fly fisherman. His mother was Blanche Smith, cousin of

[1] A. H. Clough (1819–61) became secretary to Florence Nightingale whom he admired, and who took advantage of this fact as she did with others, working him nearly to death.

the redoubtable Florence Nightingale; his aunt, and father's sister, was the first Principal of Newnham College, Cambridge, and one of his sisters, Athena, was to hold that same position in the 1920s. Arthur was some years older than Eleanor, and in many ways his tastes and mental preferences were not unlike her father's though he showed little sign of interest in such athletic pursuits as climbing. He gave the appearance at that time of being modest and unsure of himself, but he had a way of insinuating himself into society, while professing to stand back and be somewhat disparaging.

But he suffered from terrible bouts of depression, and possibly he saw in Eleanor a strong support on which he could lean. His problem was to find the courage to take such a step. Eleanor was still, in the summer of 1892, never letting a day go by without thoughts of her dead brother, and remembered always what had been happening at the same time two years earlier. Her developing attachment to Arthur Clough seemed like a betrayal of the dead, and there were still lingering doubts as to her true feelings for another in the light of her mistaken passion for Lilian Trench, now a mother as well as a wife and rather more prosaic than the romantic glow of their teenage years. Things had progressed far enough that summer for Clough to be invited to spend some of a holiday that the family had planned in Scotland, fishing and walking in the hills, looking for a complete change of scene far from their usual haunts. It was a chance for them all to get to know the persistent young man.

Douglas, though he was delighted at Clough's sophisticated wit, as was Gussie at his learning, had doubts (as fathers do) about his financial situation. However when the couple declared that they intended to announce their engagement, he sent for Mr Trower, a notary who had started his career in Freshfields and to whom the family had transferred their private business, and arranged a settlement on his daughter, which would remain entirely hers in all circumstances. This was unusual in the days where the wife's property automatically became the husbands – Gussie complained often that she possessed nothing at all of her own. However it looked as though the whole plan might have to be abandoned, as shortly after the engagement Arthur had a nervous breakdown and vanished from the scene. Back in London, there was some distress as no one knew where he had gone, until eventually an intermediary made contact. The parents, including Arthur's mother were all very worried. Eleanor appeared to remain serene, sent messages of loyalty and devotion, and said that she would wait for him. He must have been in a very bad state. Those close to him decided that there was nothing for it but to take him for a short trip abroad to recover from lost sleep and find his mental equilibrium.

At his death in 1942 Arthur left instructions that his diaries, which were very full, should be destroyed, together with all his personal correspondence, so that it is only possible to surmise what was going on. We know that he was an agnostic who utterly rejected the established Church, and held the clergy and the episcopacy as a body in contempt. It is also a fact that he had homosexual leanings. Even in those days, homosexuality was more widely recognized, even accepted, among the educated rather more than popular imagination suspects. But at the same time it was considered an affliction, which had to be suffered in private by the afflicted. This was the case with poor Clough. He desperately needed the strong understanding presence of someone like Eleanor, but naturally in the circumstances the decision as to whether or not to marry was profoundly difficult.

But Eleanor herself seems to have had similar problems. She was already secretly doubting her own physical nature, and had been left in turmoil after the 'affair' with Lilian. She had lost the only male in her life, and was becoming increasingly attached to her mother and alienated from her father. At the same time she was a young woman of determination and knew her mind. She would not desert Arthur, whatever his problem, if he needed her.

Throughout this episode Douglas displayed a side to his character that might well have been unsuspected by those who knew him in other spheres. Rigid, as some would have called him, brought up in the attitudes of his mother, in matters such as this he was liberal. He liked Clough, they enjoyed each other's company and, above all, he was concerned for the happiness of his daughter. It was Douglas that ensured that contact between the couple was not lost, so that eventually they would have the chance to resolve their problems. Arthur and his father-in-law were to develop a rapprochement and friendship that was highly entertaining to themselves and to others. Douglas had found a conversational sparring partner worthy of his metal, and they were to become more like contemporaries than father and son-in-law.

On Clough's return the meeting was arranged; he and Eleanor had a long talk, and emerged ready to carry on with the marriage plans. It is easy to imagine what agreement the couple may have arrived at. There are many pointers including their childlessness, and Eleanor's devotion to her nephews and nieces when they were children.

While all this drama was taking place, there were also increasing worries about the old Freshfields at Kidbrook. As a memorial to their lost grandson the couple were building an attractive and elaborate village hall for the people of Forest Row. While they still held the reins of government firmly in their hands, Henry Ray was exceedingly deaf and somewhat out of touch, and Douglas was having to engage in tedious discussions on their business affairs. Not long after the village hall was completed it was burned to the ground, sadly on the very day of Henry Ray's funeral, and the whole thing had to be rebuilt. It still stands, and travellers passing through Forest Row on the main road northwards are confronted with its attractive facade with its pediment and Freshfield coat of arms.

Gussie worried too that one or other of the old couple would die first, and that the one left would be unable to cope. Although she still found the atmosphere and rigidity of Kidbrook as oppressive as ever, a note of fondness, if *in absentia*, crept into her jottings on the subject.

Douglas was also called upon that summer to give evidence before the Departmental Committee appointed by the Board of Agriculture to enquire into the present condition of the Ordnance Survey. He did this in his usual forthright manner, not sparing the feelings of civil servants, and boosting the work of the Royal Geographical Society which in its turn was regarded by the professionals as a bunch of amateurs. He told them that their maps failed in a number of respects, including the fact that they had no contour lines above 1,000 feet ('I am very fond of mountain tops'), the roads did not distinguish between carriage ways and cart tracks, the scale was too large, and the hill shading was inaccurate, remarking that he would not like to walk over a hill in a fog because of it. Some of his practical suggestions included the showing of roads in four separate ways, including footpaths; that the Ordnance Survey should sell maps on a normal trading basis on tough paper; that the date of the Survey and the printing should be shown on each copy, and a key printed in the margin; and that the depths of water in lakes should be shown. In spite of what they considered his personally high-handed manner, and their pointed references to the Government grant to the Royal Geographical Society, which they appeared to resent, most of his suggestions were implemented.

Arthur Clough and Eleanor were married on 9 February 1893. Douglas became somewhat involved in their affairs for the remainder of his life. For a short while the star of the young couple was truly in the ascendant. Arthur had been longing to leave the Education Office but had expressed no very clear idea as to what he would like to do. He had a sharp mind, his thought processes being amazingly fast, and, although untrained, he had an interest in architecture and building. At that time his mother had inherited Nightingale money and was building and furnishing a house known as Burley Hill, on the top of a ridge overlooking the village of Burley on one side and the open moors of the New Forest on the other. A certain amount of land went with the property, and it is presumed that some sort of a deal with this laid the foundations of their future. Whatever it was that he accomplished, within a short time Eleanor was writing in her diary that their fortune was made, although its foundation, like many things concerning the volatile Clough, remains a mystery.

Certainly he soon acquired a reputation in the Ritchie clan for being a clever businessman, and even Douglas Freshfield himself was prepared, with caution, to make further ventures possible, and over the succeeding years Clough was able to develop Freshfield land round Forest Row with his particular style of country cottages. Now that he had the security of his marriage to the redoubtable Eleanor, and some financial security as well, he blossomed. It seemed an ideal relationship. She had a huge sense of humour inherited from her mother, and from her father a manner of getting things organized and accomplished. She moved in an open way, high handed often, but was straightforward like her father, whereas Arthur moved secretly, and sometimes, it was to transpire, in a manner that some considered, at the least, furtive. In appearance he was pink cheeked, with walrus moustache, and his figure, while not stout, was bulky, especially when wearing the long tweed overcoat he favoured.

Through his mother he had acquired woodland and fields in the village of Burley, and he and Eleanor soon developed an affection for the New Forest. In about 1895 they decided that this was where they wished to settle, and chose a site in the middle of the old castle rings above Burley Street, with small paddocks and farmery, giant oaks and beeches, and the purple open moors to the west. Clough knew the type of house he wanted, and Eleanor, the setting, which would be its natural surroundings. The 'country house cottage' was popular at the time, under the influence of Ruskin and William Morris. It was a reversion to late Georgian, mellowed by the romantic vision of rambling cottage, but with wide windows and lightness, as opposed to the medieval dark of the previous generation. With this in mind, Arthur went off to consult a young newly qualified architect, Edmund Fisher, whose taste and style were like his own.

Thus it was that a new young man was drawn more directly into the Freshfield Ritchie orbit, and was destined to marry their next daughter Janie. Edmund Fisher was not however a complete stranger to the growing numbers of young people, cousins and their friends, that were drawn into the lives of the Freshfield girls in the richly furnished large new London home that Douglas and Gussie had acquired. His aunt on his mother's side was Julia, second wife of Leslie Stephen, and he was first cousin to their girls, Virginia and Vanessa. After the death of Julia Stephen contact between the Stephen children and their Fisher cousins was somewhat limited and strained, as, according to their biographers, Virginia and Vanessa could not stand their aunt, Mary Fisher, whom they considered an interfering snob. So far as Gussie was concerned however, the Fisher brothers and sisters were the nieces and nephews of Mrs Cameron, of those far off Dimbola days, and Mrs Princep of Little Holland House fame. The circle would widen, and the strands of connection would become more interwoven and extended. One of Gussie's nieces, daughter of Blanche, would marry Edmund Fisher's brother William, later Admiral Sir William, and the cousinship of the Fishers would draw in the Coleridges, also with Isle of Wight associations.

Edmund Fisher did not share the academic qualities of some of his brothers. He was a country lover and an excellent horseman, a skill he shared with all his brothers, perhaps inherited from a distant ancestor, the Chevalier de L'Etange. He was tall, thin faced and somewhat aesthetic in appearance and given to daydreaming. But he was an excellent architect, with a true originality and flare for creating atmosphere. The Clough's house at Burley seemed to have everything that a country and family house should – wide cool white panelled rooms, a dovecote, terraces and lawns. Before work started a mulberry tree was planted in the centre of what was to become their kitchen garden and grew to become the great shading tree that stands today. And all around, pervading everything, was the quiet remote Forest.

Soon after the house was finished Douglas and Gussie came to visit, and still in its raw state Gussie wrote of it: 'This sweet place is rather stormy, chilly, but very beautiful – the long line of the Isle of Wight vision-like above the trees, was a lovely greeting to the eyes out of my bedroom window this morning. The house inside is wonderfully pretty – their old Venetian furniture gives it great cachet – their flowers, bits of colour against the white colouring, the Morris papers which make it look larger and go well with the old English windows all make the finest, gayest habitation. And it has such character and dignity, that I think young Edmund must be something of a genius of an architect too. Outside things are still rather chaotic, but there is a promising low brick and stone wall at the end of their plateau, yew hedges ...'

Douglas was impressed too, not only by the house, but the evident pleasure and occupation that it was giving his daughter. It sowed in his mind the germ of an idea.

It might have been supposed that all was set fair for the Cloughs to live full and contented lives in their lovely home. Her father's organizational abilities that were Eleanor's too came to the fore. Castletop, a minor establishment by Freshfield standards, employed a cook, a parlour maid, cleaners, three gardeners, a coachman and a stable lad. They entertained regularly if frugally, and from the earliest days of motoring they kept a car and a chauffeur, for Arthur loved speed. All this was possible on a housekeeping allowance, coming from Eleanor's dowry of slightly less than £1,000 per annum! This left Arthur a free hand, as it were, to do his best, or as it turned out, worst with their capital. For the very nature of Arthur Clough's character and brilliance carried within it the seeds of their downfall.

However for a long time all was well at Castletop, and it quickly acquired the associations of a much used and loved family centre. Two generations of nephews and nieces looked upon it as an exciting playground, with benign Arthur slipping quietly in and out, absorbed in his business, expending his hours in sleepless nervous energy. When old Mrs Clough at Burley Hill next door was killed in an accident with her pony cart, there were Florence Nightingale relics to be divided between himself and his sister, who would keep the house, but her bed and writing table were moved to Castletop. From here Eleanor's cousin Molly Warr-Cornish married their friend Desmond MacCarthy, and years later their daughter Rachel would in turn marry Lord David Cecil and spend some time living in one of their cottages in the nearby village of Rockbourne.

Clough added to the village of Burley, building a whole row of worker's cottages, now called Clough Lane; building a village shop and a number of small farm cottages. Although Castletop had Eleanor's boudoir, as well as the usual drawing room and dining room, they always preferred that the servants should live in separate cottages a short distance away. The same applied to guests, and to this end they built a delightful miniature house they named Black Bush, on the opposite side of the hill. Gussie described it, and the whole neighbourhood in her vivid way. 'We are enjoying our family life here most particularly. I live out of doors, chiefly in their eight acres under a huge oak with impervious shade and a dream of a view. It is two minutes from the house on the north side of the ridge, the green hill falls to a wooded lane with thatched cottages, and rises again in a long stretch of moor where the cattle move about, and the edge of the forest crowns the hill with a long satisfying line. Impossible to see a more beautiful picture. It reminds me at all hours of the Rousseaus, Daubignys in line and colour – *la leisure de la forêt* – always enchanting to painters. The great wonderful view is to the west, over the sea, Christchurch tower to Badbury Rings. Arthur pointed it out to me yesterday, looking quite noble and purple, rising out of the blue expanse. Eleanor and Arthur's new cottage (Black Bush) is on a high green cape jutting out over the great moor. The wind whistles forever on the orchard, which makes a frame for the green-brown miles and miles. We have delightful long evenings, Eleanor, Douglas and I generally, while a happy cavalcade on horseback is exploring the Forest glades.'

While Eleanor looked after dogs, children and doves, and managed the village affairs through the first war, Arthur's business ventures grew wider and wider. He had become very interested in building, and in fact his designs for rural dwellings for agricultural use had won several prizes early in the century. All over the south, wherever he acquired land, farms or woods, he built new cottages and new farmsteads. He had estates and other ventures, including timber yards, as far afield as Melcombe Horsey and Mappowder in Dorset; Dibden, Burley, Rockbourne, Whitsbury and Wellow in Hampshire and Winterslow in Wiltshire. He also started an extensive building project at Forest Row on Kidbrook land belonging to his father-in-law, close by a timber business he had acquired.

It was during the First World War that things began to run away from him. Some of his schemes had an air of outright fantasy, others were managed by men who were not to be trusted, for he was an easy touch and naive in the ways of men. One scheme which had unfortunate results was to purchase large farms, split them up into smaller units, build a house and farm buildings, and then sell or rent them to returning servicemen at reasonable prices. In a few places the plan was a success, but the tide of economic events was turning against farmers and smallholders. All the nervous energy and mental versatility of Clough failed to stem the tide. The banks began to get restive, his now ageing father-in-law was prevailed upon to shore up the crumbling empire, and for a few years he staggered on, but dealing now in a less open way, sometimes playing one against another. There was still no proper system of control. There was an office in the yard at Castletop, and an accounts secretary, who was a broken reed at worst, and kept totally in the dark at best. The only contact in the field was Clough's own flying visits, never enough to keep either projects moving or costs under control. Eleanor began to sense, as his worries grew, that the storm clouds were gathering, and was concerned for his health. She persuaded him to employ an agent. Halford Vaughan was charming and good looking but an unfortunate choice. He was related to the Fishers, was intelligent and a trained land agent, but inexperienced and given to fits of despondency. He was totally unable to grasp the complicated twists and turns of events. He remembered later how he felt helpless with his responsibility, knowing that Eleanor looked to him to keep some sort of control over her

husband's alarmingly complicated affairs. Every morning the
famous car, with McDonald the chauffeur, familiar at almost every
town and village within seventy miles, was waiting at the front door.
The two muffled figures bundled into the back seat and Eleanor
would watch them swirl away, goodness knew where. They flew
along, enjoying the speed, (Clough claimed that he could do
Salisbury to Mappowder in half an hour), with Clough often scrib-
bling notes and memos to himself on his starched cuffs. Sometimes
they would pull up on a building site, sometimes in a farm yard, but
always the grey-coated fur-collared figure would become plunged in
earnest, low-pitched conversation with foreman or overseer, bailiff
or manager, only to climb back in and whirl away to the next port of
call. His little bit of lunch, a few Scotch oatcakes and cream cheese,
washed down with a tot of whisky, was taken in the back of the car or
in some farmhouse kitchen. But soon the eternal cigarette was back
between his fingers, and once more the mind would be endlessly cal-
culating, feverishly searching for a way forward.

Perhaps it was because he loved his wife that he kept trying so
desperately to keep her in the home she loved. But he had used
Castletop as security for loans, as he had his father-in-law's guaran-
tees, and his affairs had long since passed the point at which recovery was possible. The crash came finally in 1934 and in 1935 their
comfortable world tumbled about their ears. Castletop was sold,
their treasures and furniture went, the Nightingale bed and papers
went to America; only the settlement that was made on her by her
father all those years ago remained to Eleanor and, with a small
inheritance, she bought back a house at Winterslow from the
liquidators. Her courage and humour when the crash came, were
enormous, her descriptions of the bankruptcy proceedings hilarious.
The Chairman of Barclays Bank, who had actually called in the
Receiver, was one of the Fisher brothers, Edwin. On one occasion
they were called to the London Head Office, and were warned it
would be very awkward for the Chairman to have to recognize them
if he happened to pass. Eleanor described how they sat in a corridor
awaiting their summons, not daring to look above the pinstriped
knees that passed through their line of sight.

But for Eleanor worse was to come. The extent of Arthur's devi-
ousness came out. Not only had he begged money from her father to

keep the sinking business going, he had, without telling her, taken money from her sister Janie, persuading her, with his reputation still intact as far as she knew, that it would be a good investment for her. This was the saddest blow. She and Arthur were childless, and at least they had lived well, in a way which had given themselves and many others happiness. That they themselves should come to grief was of little account, but that they should involve her widowed sister was unforgivable. She could hardly bare the shame.

But much was yet to happen in the intervening years. Soon after the marriage of the Cloughs, on 2 February 1884 Henry Ray Freshfield died. Augusta confessed that she had grown fond of the kindly, serene, and universally respected, old gentleman who was her father-in-law. She hurried off to Kidbrook ready to console the widow, and if necessary take charge, and relieve her of some of the responsibilities of the estate. But she got a surprise – she described it to her sister: 'My great hope had always been that Mr and Mrs Freshfield would live on together, as I could not imagine one without the other. I thought that after fifty-five years of that closest companionship, a life of complete *égoïsme à deux* if ever there was one, she would lose heart entirely and not care to go on living. On the contrary it seems to have given her a new zest in life! The responsibility of Kidbrook and a large income (she talks most of the responsibility) seem to have stimulated her into new vigour, and enabled her to get through a bad attack of influenza last week.'

Mother and daughter-in-law still found it hard to understand one another. Augusta's unpunctuality, and lack of interest in household matters were a constant source of irritation to the old lady, and thus she was most reluctant to let the the reins of government pass to someone so incompetent. But, as time passed it became obvious that the strain was becoming too much for her and two years after her husband's death, she moved out, taking a villa near the sea. The Freshfields now had their large house, 1 Airlie Gardens, to which they had added considerably, and furnished with great richness, and in which they entertained their musical and artistic friends, and gave balls for the young. Gussie had become a noted hostess, Joachim lived next door and would often play for them and their guests, Pinkie accompanying. The ménage is described in Molly McCarthy's book *A Victorian Childhood* in kinder terms than those used by

Virginia Stephen, but all the same it must have been something of an Alladin's cave, done in a style that was warm, dark and rich, like the paintings by Burne-Jones that adorned the walls.

Now they set about transforming Kidbrook to their own taste. On flying visits they laid rugs from the east, hung pictures, and on one occasion rushed out and bought a quantity of coal scuttles. When at Kidbrook they entertained a good deal, but not in the 'county' manner reminiscent of Henbury; they preferred large houseparties of relations and close friends, with talk round the fire of art, love, history or travel, and games of charades or long walks into the forest. The tradition of physical exercise was a strong one in the family, and when in the country, long walks were the order of the day; partly perhaps, a leave-over from Leslie Stephen's Sunday tramps. They would walk over and inspect the alterations and decorations that Lord and Lady Bryce were making to their new home, and, more often than not, criticize them severely; or they would walk up the hill to a favourite picnic place on the side of a steep ravine amongst beeches, bracken and firs, called the Warren.

Even though Kidbrook was now theirs, and they had transferred from London many of the stored treasures that they had been collecting on their travels from all over the Continent and Asia, Augusta's feelings about the place remained unchanged. In 1892 she had been ill with phlebitis in a leg, and although she was able to resume all her activities, she now walked with a stick, and suffered a good deal from muscular pains. Everything about Kidbrook was wrong, from the head gardener laying out the beddings in a manner that did not suit, to the fact that it was a damp, airless and 'rheumaticky' place. She blamed all her sufferings on the house; even when they were abroad she would describe herself as feeling 'Kidbrooky'. Her frequent trips, collecting pictures and furniture, visiting favourite Italian artists, were as much an attempt to escape from this feeling of physical depression as anything else. Often the return was sad for her, filled with nostalgia for the warmth and clarity of the southern air.

'We have been back now for about ten days, but have not yet resigned ourselves to the murky sky and heavy air, and are still suffering from the nostalgia that seizes one so violently on one's return home. We are hurriedly giving two "At Homes" to distract us from the climate. Our villa really was in an Olympian situation – a plateau for the Gods rather than for Mortals. It would have been very convenient and delightful to have had wings, to have soared down like Minerva and Apollo across the Lombard Plain which stretched away to the horizon in front of us, to have visited the cities fair, and landed in the blue-green and purple sea – without the slow train and stoppages at junctions. Some days were so clear that one could make out the blue shadows of the buttresses, and the crystal of the glaciers of the Viso itself. And all about us, in between us and the Plain was that tumbled land of exquisite beauty which vines and chestnuts and campaniles make unique. Blanche was always quoting "O woman country wooed not wed" which Herbert [Trench – they were staying with Lilian outside Florence] declared improper. Our luxuriously furnished villa with its pond surrounded by elaborate grotto and aloes, on which floated two swans like enchanted princesses, was altogether like a fairy-tale.'

They were ageing of course. Douglas and Gussie both sported gold pince-nez on black ribbon; she with her stick and he now with fast forward-tilted shuffle-footed impatient progress, the hallmark of his later years. His voice had grown harsher, and the accents of both of them more rigidly fixed in the style of the young 'bloods' of the Crimea – 'orf' for off, 'corf' for cough and so forth. But her manner of conversation was colourful and expressive, children delighted in hearing her read, but the contempt for foolishness and intolerance of laxity was well marked. The coldness between them was being noticed by their oldest friends and relatives; there seemed so little direct communication, which Janie believed to be her mother's fault.

But their occupation of Kidbrook was to prove transitory. Old Mrs Freshfield did not care at all for being tucked away outside the family circle, without status or authority, and she missed the environment that had been hers for so many years. Douglas was persuaded to build her a dower house on the estate. As a start they selected a cottage, high up towards the ridge to the south of the park, bordering on the boundary of Ashdown Forest, and to the left of the main road. The place had been known to them all as Slacks in the past, and Edmund Fisher was asked to add to it and convert it into a suitable home for the old lady. In fact what transpired was a mansion. A delightful one it is true, larger than Castletop, more rambling, with open stone-pillared loggia, bay windows, and many gables and chimneys. It proved a great interest and distraction for both Douglas and Augusta. He was interested in the design and building of the house, and she made a new hobby of garden design and planting. At some period, while all this was going on, the idea was germinating that it might be a good thing one day to leave the old house in the hollow, that was so unsuited to Gussie, and build a new one for themselves, somewhere high up on their domain.

Alas, poor Mrs Freshfield was dead before the new house was finished. But the project had a number of outcomes; notably, after much meeting behind closed doors, while the ladies of the family awaited the outcome with baited breath, Janie became engaged to Edmund Fisher, and as a direct consequence serious consideration was given to the project that was one day to be Wych Cross Place.

With the alienation of his wife there was a loosening of Douglas's domestic ties; his quarrel with the Royal Geographical Society had relieved him of much work, and the Presidency of the Alpine Club was not onerous. Furthermore his major work, *The Exploration of the Caucasus*,[1] was now ready for publication. In spite of the fact that he was now into his fifties he felt in as good physical condition as ever and, probably spurred on by a sense of grievance against the R.G.S. and determined to show that he was still an explorer to be reckoned with, he began to make plans for a new expedition, entirely without the help of any official body.

In the year after Freshfield's final visit to the Caucasus, a new star in the field of mountain exploration emerged – William Martin Conway, later Lord Conway of Allington. Ever since Freshfield had first taken an interest in reports concerning what had come to be called Mount Everest, he had hoped that one day he might be able to visit the tremendous Himalayas for himself. He therefore was quick to accept when the Royal Society and the British Association offered to contribute to an expedition to be organized by Conway, Freshfield and another great mountaineer, Mummery. But the death of his son, followed by his wife's first serious illness, prevented Freshfield from

---

[1] V. de Sella had visited him in London to arrange for many of the pictures of the region to be produced in the book.

taking part. It was probably just as well, for by all accounts Conway was the sort of highly publicized explorer that Freshfield disliked, and this was confirmed, at least to some extent, when, after a trial run in the Alps, Conway and Mummery decided that their methods were so different it would be a mistake to undertake a major expedition together. As it was, the expedition turned out to be the most spectacular and successful that had yet been made to the Himalaya. Conway took his party into tremendous snowy regions never before surveyed or even seen by Europeans. He won widespread publicity and a knighthood as a result. He differed profoundly in his attitudes from Freshfield, and it seems likely that a joint expedition would have ended with rancour. Conway was a restless, heroic and openly ambitious character – Freshfield chides him and a fellow mountaineer when a bust of one and a portrait of the other are exhibited:

> Here's a cheer for the new mountaineer,
>   That very well advertised man;
> His methods are risky I fear,
>   But he "does" all the peaks that he can.
> And he anyhow gets his reward,
>   A pyramid proud for his bones,
> Or else to be "busted" by Ford,
>   Or drawn, as an angel, by Jones.

For the time being, while domestic matters were in the ascendant, he contented himself with the old chestnut of Hannibal's pass and tracing the paths once trod by de Saussure, researching the travels and writings of Placidus à Spescha, and using these as an excuse for further walks of his own, thus keeping him active and fit on the slopes and peaks.

But at the first opportunity he wanted to get away and repeat the more dramatic adventures of earlier years. Middle age made him resentful of the changes that the Swiss and Italians were making. Inevitable commercialization had rapidly followed the popularizing of the best known mountains as a playground, in which, incidentally, Freshfield had performed as prominent a part as any. The trouble was that what was considered 'popular' by Freshfield and all those like him, did not include the 'lower classes'. He was by no means alone in being fearful at the thought of city clerks, or shopkeepers and their families, invading the exclusive heights. Douglas and Augusta, in spite of more than usually liberal views, in her case towards the position of women, and in his in encouraging more general wide ranging education, held the deeply entrenched attitudes common to all classes that the existing hierarchy was the natural order of things. They paced sedately across their deeply polished floors, ignoring the existence of the army of polishers that had earlier vanished into the nether regions. Not that they were bad employers. The household accounts show many payments made, not only for attendance to the sick, even when the connection to the household was indirect. Old retainers were housed and pensioned. But the family lived on a magic carpet. If they went to Scotland, their own carriage, horses, coachman and footmen were waiting for them at the station. At Airlie Gardens there was a full complement of butler, footmen, cook and nursery staff. At Kidbrook and later at Wych Cross there was an outside staff of fourteen, not counting those on the farms. Yet almost without exception, in all the diaries and correspondence, there is never a name or a comment on all those who made such a lifestyle possible. Gussie had a lady's maid called English who was with her wherever she went, but she appears to receive no comment or consideration when the family life is written about. The next generation changed a little. Eleanor's diaries do tell who the families were that worked at Castletop, even when it was generally to note that they had failed in their duties or had even been found stealing! It was partly this, and the total detachment of their parents from the lives of the majority, that caused the two youngest girls in the family to rebel, though Katherine, through a sense of duty, felt unable to make a complete break.

Against that background, Freshfield could not tolerate the change of scene that was taking place in the Alps. He could not conceive that there were many who actually preferred to ride behind a smoking steam engine, or to find, when they reached some height, not the loneliness of an exclusive lofty view, but bar and restaurant. He wrote: 'Encircle a mountain with monster hotels; defile its valleys with the coal smoke of engines that drag a perpetual merry-go-round of crowded cars; sprinkle its skyline with huts or barracks capable at a pinch of holding a hundred guests; bind its crags in chains, and encourage suicide by marking out on them red tracks for guideless tourists and it loses much of its primitive charm. The temple is given over to the money changers.'

Many of the same battles are being fought today, even in our own towns and villages, but no one would dare to put their thoughts into such language.

> At Grindelwald the Eiger's peak
>   Is dimmed by wreaths of horrid smoke,
> Foul engines with their sooty reek
>   The vale of Lauterbrunnen choke.
> No more on Wengen's flowery height
>   The marmot sentinel we hear,
> A coarser whistle puts to flight
>   A crowd of cockneys swilling beer.

In the circumstances it is no wonder he turned his attention once again to more remote regions. Years before he had been a great admirer of Sir Joseph Hooker, the great exploring botanist and plant collector. He had met and talked with him of his adventures, and had been fascinated by his tales of the mountains and valleys of the Himalayan region. He had studied, in particular, the map of Hooker's travels in Nepal and Sikhim, now fifty years old, in which there was a huge gap signifying unexplored territory. This gap lay to the north-west of Kanchenjunga. But even had Freshfield considered the Everest region the natural choice, it was not open to him as the government of Nepal was not accepting visitors into their country on almost any pretext, so it was not unexpected that Freshfield's thoughts should have turned to the beauties of Sikhim and the environs of the mighty Kanchenjunga.

CHAPTER 10

Kanchenjunga, a most magnificent and dramatic mountain, third highest in the world,was then one of the best known and most often described of all the mountains of the Himalayas. Freshfield, who at fifty-four might fairly have considered his days for attempting such mighty peaks were over, was attracted by the reputed beauty of the area as well as a desire to make a useful reconnaissance. Interest in the region had recently been aroused in geographical circles in England because of a story told in an official report on the work of the Survey of India Department, about a journey made by Rinsing (Rinzin Nimgyat) a Bhutia native, and it was this that really decided Freshfield in which direction his expedition could best be employed. Like Kishen, Kinthrup, Nain Singh and Chandra Das, all of whose journeys can be described as 'epic', Rinsing was one of the well known native pundits. Unfortunately however, although he lacked none of the enterprise and daring associated with these explorers, his powers with the plane table and the accuracy of his reports left a good deal to be desired. There is no doubt of course that Rinsing crossed the Jonsong La, 'the loftiest and most difficult pass in this part of the Himalaya', but his resultant sketch map and report were misleading, and he was to become virtually lost on the return trip when acting as guide to Freshfield's party. After observing Rinsing at work in this occasion, Freshfield blames his deficiencies as a surveyor on a 'predilection to sitting in a snug tent', but perhaps he was being unfair, for later he gives a number of other reasons that might account for Rinsing's curious behaviour when his turn came to act as the expedition's chief guide. In a letter home from his camp, on the Zemu glacier, he describes Rinsing: 'in a black cap with a red band, a pig-tail and a chocolate coloured robe, he carries an ivory handled umbrella that would suit a bishop'.

He decided that he would aim to set out to explore the passes and glaciers in the whole region of the massive Kanchenjunga block, and to do this he would make a complete circuit of the mountain, so that particular attention could be paid to the north side, till then unseen by European eyes. He did not intend an attempt on the mountain itself, though there was a good chance that his mountaineering instincts would lead him up one of the lesser peaks in the area should the opportunity occur. Writing later in the *Scottish Geographical Magazine* he put the objectives in detail. 'Our object was to link the recent routes of Mr White, the Political Resident in independent Sikhim east of Kanchenjunga, with those of Sir Joseph Hooker in Nepal on the other side of the mountain in 1848. To effect this it was necessary to traverse the region left a blank on Hooker's map with the superscription "This country is said to present a very elevated, rugged tract of lofty mountains, sparingly snowed, uninhabited by man or domestic animals." Its delineation in the existing Government Survey Maps is, at least as far as the Nepalese territory is concerned, based rather on the imaginations than on the observations of the native explorers.'

The voyage out proved a mixed blessing. There was the imposing sight of Stromboli with a great stream of lava pouring down its side into the sea, there were three generals who never spoke to each other, and never to anyone else, there were ladies who 'undressed a good deal for dinner and air their shoulders on deck afterwards – very unattractive!'

The young played cricket when it was not too hot, with much appealing to the umpire and he held that the meals were excellent. The young doctors on their way to take up their posts in India were

Overleaf: Kanchenjunga. View of the left side of the Zemu glacier.   © Fondazione Sella and Instituto di Fotografia Alpina Vittorio Sella-Biella.

Towards Kanchenjunga.   The guide Rinsing.

intelligent but 'I can't say as much for the civil servants'. 'Nobody' he complains 'seems at all interesting. The Sellas', he notes to Eleanor, 'are the most quiet and gentlemanly companions but I wish we talked virtually a common tongue.'

After coaling they moved down the Suez Canal at six miles per hour, but at last they were in the gulf and a cool wind blew through the ship; there were shoals of flying fish and white waves. A few more passengers had joined at Brindisi where they saw Lord Kitchener 'land in a straw hat with no pomp at all'. 'Now doing sixteen miles an hour, a gilt cork on our masthead as a sign the *Caledonia* is the fastest ship that runs to India – cricket on deck has begun again.'

In Aden the temperature soared to above ninety in a grey windless air. He was 'disappointed with the sunsets and still more with the stars which have no Arabian brilliancy – A worthy missionary's voice comes up from the saloon, where he is preaching a sermon to I fear a small congregation.' A south-westerly swell caused the vessel to roll dreadfully. 'I was very nearly overcome last night' he wrote home 'but today I am recovering my sea legs – the ocean wave however is a bore. I cannot read a condensed Indian history in a seaquake – great weltering (peaks) of green, warm water tumble about without the purport like dignity of Atlantic billows – the ship rolls slowly and then pauses before she comes back again. It is the suspense of that pause which does it.'

At last the voyage was over. He landed at Calcutta and he then went out of his way to meet Gussie's brother, Gerald Ritchie, who was working for the Indian Civil and travelling up country. Gerald's wife and Freshfield's little niece were established in the hills away from the heat but planning to move herself and the child back to be with her husband. Freshfield interferes, writing to his brother-in-law suggesting it would be too dangerous to take little Peggy down to the plains and telling of a mutual friend who was willing to give her a temporary home. However his visit seems to have been a great success both in so far as he is able to travel with Gerald on his duty round as well as visit his little family. Margery wrote home to her sister-in-law Gussie 'how very much we enjoyed having Douglas and how grateful we are to him for having turned so much out of his way to come and see us. It seemed wonderfully natural to see him walking along the path to our little mountain where we met.' Fresh-field discussed joining them on a month's trip to Burma together with Garwood after his trip round Kanchenjunga; a plan which came to nothing, but one gets the impression that both sides took great comfort from the visit which did something to mitigate the home-sickness from which they all suffered.

Freshfield's first sight of the Himalaya must have fulfilled all expectations, and his own description of a travellers view from the train can hardly be bettered. 'Let him, if the skies are clear, endeav-our to be awake at earliest dawn. For with luck he may see a vision. As he looks out of the carriage window, he will at first observe only the dark plain and the dim, shadowy, rounded outlines of the foothills. But when he lifts his eyes he will be aware, if he lifts them high enough, far up, at an incredible height in the pale tremulous sky, a row of roseate flames. They are not clouds. While he gazes they harden from the phantoms of a dream into definite forms. They are the snow peaks of Sikhim, the giants of the Himalaya, the great-est mountains in the world, kindling with the remote dawn. ... The vision is brief, but ... it is one of those that can never be forgotten.'

After this, arrival in Darjeeling was an anticlimax, for, having heard so much about the view from this populous hill station, throughout their four day stay the snows remained obstinately shrouded in mist, and the magnificent view from Observatory Hill remained unrevealed until their return. All the same he was unable to resist giving one of his meticulous descriptions at this point in his book.

The team now prepared themselves for the serious side of the expe-dition. The team as assembled by Freshfield and equipped largely from the 'Army and Navy'[1] stores consisted of geologist Dr Edmund Garwood who was also an experienced alpinist who had travelled with Conway in Spitsbergen and was also an entomologist and pho-tographer; the celebrated photographer Vittorio Sella and his brother Erminio and a Piedmontese named Botta as photographic assistant; and finally a young Val Tournanche guide, Angelo Maquignaz.

---

[1] 'Our provisions came from the Army & Navy Stores, and were satisfactory in every respect. Careful packing is essential, particularly if the goods are to be placed at the mercy of the Peninsular and Oriental Company – in my experience the most reckless of carriers.' – D.W.F. footnote p. 7 *Round Kanchenjunga*.

Sella, Freshfield, Dover and Garwood.

The party had left Marseilles on 10 August 1899, and arrived in Darjeeling on 1 September. They left the hill station some four days later en route for Gangtok a seventy mile ride through the foothills; a shorter two day route could have been chosen but it was considered that, so soon after the rainy season, it would be prudent to avoid the lower steamy valleys for fear that some of the party might become ill before high altitudes were reached. Heavy showers accompanied their departure, and Freshfield seems to have been much impressed by the fact that the British soldiers once stationed in the now abandoned barracks under whose wall they cantered, used to be driven by boredom, and no doubt homesickness, to commit suicide.

The baggage coolies had gone ahead with their equipment, so the little party was able to proceed, only accompanied by their grooms – 'fine gentlemen', says Freshfield, 'who made a favour of carrying even so much as a field glass'. After about ten miles of tea gardens and forest they came to a clearing and got their first stunning view of the snows. First Kabru came into view, then, as they proceeded, the great bulk of Kanchenjunga itself stood revealed for the first time. 'The air was surcharged with moisture, sunset was at hand: blue and gold, blue hills and valleys, golden clouds and snows. Presently the gold turned to red and amber, laid in broad strips between the darkening green of the foothills and the azure pools of bare heaven.'

The journey was not comfortable. Three inches of rain fell that night, and throughout the following days they were plagued by heavy storms; the bungalows built by the government for travellers proved almost invariably to be leaking and rotten. But nothing could spoil his enjoyment and pleasure in the forest scene, even the raindrops sparkling on the lower shrubs called forth his admiration. He was especially intrigued by the people of the forests, the Lepchas, whom he likens to the inhabitants of Arcadia or the poet's Lotus-eaters, expressing the pious wish that the British officials will do something to preserve them, and prevent these mild, natural, forest people from being superseded by Tibetans and Nepalese.

Mr White, the Political Officer at Gangtok, which had recently become the home of the Sikhim Raja, was away, but they were met on the last slope that led to what was then a small scattered collection of houses, by his substitute Captain Le Mesurier, who had done much to make the explorer's journey easy for them so far. He had

Freshfield on the top of a gap above the Sayork-Chu.　© Fondazione Sella and Instituto di Fotografia Alpina Vittorio Sella-Biella.

commended to them by letter, when they were in Darjeeling, a Mr C.
Dover, who later became Road Inspector in Independent Sikhim, and
who proved himself of great value to the party, for not only had he
considerable experience of the people, and was able to help in orga-
nizing their porters, but also he had accompanied White on his travels throughout the region. It is hard to imagine how they would have
managed without him, a fact which Freshfield recognized, and he
was delighted to have him with them during the whole expedition.

Le Mesurier and his wife seem to have gone out of their way to
make Freshfield and his companions comfortable. White's charming
house with its surprisingly English garden was placed at their
disposal, and from here they were able to look out upon the distant
snows that were their goal. Much of their time here was spent in
making the final arrangements for the journey ahead into far
remoter regions, and an expedition of this kind was not without
major difficulties of organization. The justly famous Sherpas, who
accompany all modern climbers to the snows, were unknown then
behind the sealed frontiers of Nepal. Instead, Le Mesurier collected
numbers of volunteers from the surrounding Lepcha villages,
divided them into parties each with its own sirdar, to swell the
number of Bhutians that had acted as porters from Darjeeling. They
were also supplied with six Tibetans, possibly robbers, in the no
man's land beyond Kanchenjunga.

It was intended that as they climbed and used their supplies,
parties of porters should return down the route by which they had
come, so that only a minimum number of the most resilient would
have to tackle the highest part of the journey. For one thing the
natives of the lower regions regarded Kanchenjunga with superstitious awe, and there was a very real risk of the men deserting. It was
thanks to Dover that they were able to get any of the porters to
proceed further than the start of the Zemu glacier.

It was Freshfield himself who sought out and found the fearful
God of Kanchenjunga in the old Buddhist temple that stood high on
the spur above the valley. 'A very fearful and hungry spirit,' he says,
'riding on a white lion, to whom meat offerings must be presented by
the faithful.' To the native people upon whom the party were to
depend for porters the demon was a most vivid and real creature in
their lives, and there was little wonder that they should be in terror of

approaching so near to his awful lairs, and be so prone to desert at the slightest excuse. But there was an added difficulty. The natives were almost exclusively rice eaters, which automatically added to the numbers and unwieldiness of the baggage party – for rice is the bulkiest of diets and as such is the most impractical of foods for long-distance travel far from sources of supply. On an expedition designed to last three or four weeks, more than half of each man's load would have to consist of food for himself.

Edmund Garwood proved to be a companion very much more to Freshfield's taste than Tucker had been so many years before. Although there was a wide difference in their ages, they possessed the same teasing sense of humour, and the jokes were not always at Garwood's expense. He soon found that it was difficult to score off Freshfield on any matters of a literary nature, but there was one occasion when Freshfield's dislike of fatty food provided an opportunity. There was time on two successive days for an exchange of tea parties with the Rajah and Ranee. On the first occasion the couple came to the Residency – a picturesque and colourful little procession against the spectacular backdrop of the great mountains – Freshfield felt that he could have been assisting at the first night of a burlesque opera. The next day they returned the call by going to the small, temporary home of the Rajah (the Bengal Government was in the process of building him a new palace in the vicinity), and were introduced to the various local dignitaries and the young heir. The tea was the usual Tibetan variety, with lumps of rancid greasy butter floating on the surface. Garwood noticed his companion's struggles to look as though he was enjoying it, and when he was himself offered a second cup he begged to be excused as he said he wished to prepare his cameras to take a picture of the scene, 'but,' he added 'I know that Mr Freshfield would be delighted to have a second cup.'

There were other distractions too – an occasional picturesque pedlar 'giving Lhasa as his last resting place, provided with a trumpet made of human thighbones, or a pair of ornamental chopsticks, or a wide-brimmed, lacquered wide-awake, such as are said to be worn by noblemen of high birth and office in the sacred city'. But it was with such things as snow-spectacles and Whymper tents that they were mainly concerned. Each recruit to the coolie party had to be issued with food, boots, blankets and a tent; rations had to be unpacked, divided into daily parcels, even down to the salt, and re-wrapped separately. Most of Freshfield's London shopping, as done at the Army and Navy Stores, had been shipped out direct, and this was their first opportunity of checking it.

The next stage of the journey was to be a five day march over rough country, but still with well defined tracks and bridges, to Lachen, the last outpost before they would venture into the unknown. The Sella brothers, with Dover as guide, and half the coolies, set out forty-eight hours earlier than the rest of the party, as the traveller's rest houses along the route were too small to accommodate all of them; and it was also intended that the advance party should employ the extra time at Lachen in climbing neighbouring hills in order to take photographs.

On 13 September the main party set out on the next stage of the trek to the mountain. As the long arm of bureaucratic civilization, and the ties of home and family grew weaker, Freshfield's companions noticed a subtle change in him. He was back in his real element and loving every minute of it, quite undaunted still by physical labour, indifferent to discomfort, and impatient to be on the move for every available hour. Although he remained very much in charge, and his companions remained a trifle in awe, all the same there was a feeling that he had relaxed. His long experience made him an interesting companion, and he began to talk, and, in spite of his age, they felt confident that he could still be relied upon for all his old skills.

They set off once again in mist and rain, still in the company of Le Mesurier, who had asked to come with them as far as Lachen. At that time there were only occasional signs of native agriculture in Independent Sikhim, and for the first day their path led them up first gentle and then increasingly steep slopes, with glimpses down narrow misty gullies choked with tropical vegetation and flashes of tumbling waters at the bottom. But the relatively easy start to the day was misleading, soon they were to plunge down a 3,500 ft slope in not much more than four miles, into a jungle-choked valley, only to be confronted by great discomfort as they struggled upwards leading their ponies. The mist turned to a very heavy rain which later prevented them from calling at the Labrong monastery, though the monks blew the temple trumpets in greeting as they passed; for the intrepid explorers were anxious to reach the shelter of the official rest house.

Vittoria Sella, the brilliant mountain photographer, at Kanchenjunga in 1899. © Fondazione Sella and Instituto di Fotografia Alpina Vittorio Sella-Biella.

First Caucasus expedition with dragoman guard and guides. Paul, the interpreter, back row second from left; Devouassoud back row, second from right; D.W.F. seated centre; Tucker and Moor on the ground.

But they were destined to meet with further disappointment. In the past, White had devoted considerable energy to the establishment of these bungalows for the convenience of travellers to the remoter part of his domain. But slack native caretakers, lack of funds, and the steamy climate had played havoc. They were greeted with a leaking roof and broken beds, crockery and chairs. They complained bitterly that so much good work and so many good intentions on the part of the Political Officer should have come to nought, and on his return Freshfield did not hesitate to complain of the lack of funds available for the upkeep of the bungalows, in spite of the fact that he knew of, and was sensitive to, the unjust jibe that he was a mere, fastidious globetrotter rather than a real explorer.

Partly as a result of his strictures, during the next two or three years the roads and rest houses of Independent Sikhim were very much improved. As it was, because of the cheerlessness of their situation, they decided to return through the rain and call on the monastery after all.

In one of the conversations that Freshfield had had with White before he left London, the latter had expressed the rather gloomy opinion that it was highly probable that Freshfield would never get as far as the snows at all; and the next day for the first time Freshfield began to think that this prediction might well be true. It was bad enough for the first five miles in pouring rain, plodding wearily in the narrow muddy wake of eighty or so porters. But worse was in store. In a place previously described as 'a series of extremely bad slips, the rock consisting of friable mica and schist,' they were confronted by a moving muddy landslide caused by the continuous rain. Even Freshfield was constrained to admit later that 'there is a certain risk in such places,' though he hastens to add, 'but I would not exaggerate it'. Eventually they succeeded in negotiating the place and arrived at the crossing of the Rongrong river, 'a superb cataract rushing down a cloven ravine over which pale hydrangeas dripped, while the grey lichens on the nodding trees were shaken by the perpetual blast'. At last they reached the bungalow at Samatek and set about the miserable chore of drying their sodden clothes.

The following day they reached the deserted monastery of Chungthang. The weather had slightly improved, and at least they could now have the satisfaction of noting the changes of vegetation that were becoming apparent as they gained altitude. Gone were the spiraeas, begonias, and other more exotic plants of the sub-tropical regions below, to be replaced by rhododendrons and yews, and smaller plants of temperate climes. Taking advantage of the slightly improved weather on their arrival at Chungthang, Garwood set off through the meadows below in search of butterflies, and although he managed to collect some interesting species he was also severely attacked by leeches.

The next day it was decided to remain where they were to give the various gangs of porters time to collect, and as, for once, it turned out fine and pleasantly warm, Garwood and Freshfield set out together to explore the Lachung valley. Presently, after an energetic scramble, pulling themselves up with the aid of trailing vines, over a rock that blocked their path, poor Garwood, suffering from his leech bites, elected to remain at the spot where they had eaten their lunch. On his return from a solitary ramble Freshfield teased his companion for pursuing his geological studies by searching for a stone soft enough to make a pillow. Next day, though mist and drizzle had returned, they climbed on through forests of rhododendrons up to forty feet high, in a narrow V-shaped ravine, cut by tumbling waters from the snows above, into a land of larches, hazels and other familiar trees. They were becoming conscious too that it was autumn, deciduous trees lent brilliant flashes of colour to the otherwise sombre scene. At last the party emerged into wide alpine meadows studded with firs and larches, with their goal, Lemteng, visible only a short distance ahead. They had reached an altitude of nearly 9,000 feet.

From Lamteng it was intended to plunge into the thick forest of the Zemu Glen and climb to the snout of the mighty Zemu glacier itself, which would then lead them westwards directly to the base of Kanchenjunga. They were on the verge of real mountaineering country; but, alas, rain and mist persisted. Freshfield wrote that 'our readiness to quit paths and roofs in order to plunge into the wilderness was not abated, but the exhilaration ordinarily felt on leaving a horse track and becoming a free biped ... was sensibly diminished. Morally as well as physically we were, for the moment, somewhat damped.' But the most difficult and arduous four days of their whole approach to the glacier, lay ahead. It was this section of thick rhododendron forest that had stopped the intrepid Joseph Hooker many years before and, knowing this, Freshfield had sent a party of Gurkha pioneers ahead to cut a track. The Sellas offered to remain at Lachen for a time, not only as a means of forwarding supplies and letters for as long as practicable, but also to act as an effective deterrent to porters contemplating slipping away back to their homes. The first day out from Lachen, singularly wet and gloomy, struggling and slipping up the dark gorge, they reached a terrace, which Freshfield calculated was the site of Hooker's highest camp, and found their own pioneer party encamped in the long grass of an open glade. At least their tents were dry 'and by no means uncomfortable'.

Although the tents may have been a pleasant change from the leaking, draughty accommodation they were forced to accept below, they were no compensation for the miseries of the following night. As they climbed, the glen became still rougher, and a good deal of time was spent scrambling miserably and somewhat aimlessly amidst treacherous roots, boulders and eternal mud, until, the porters thoroughly exhausted, they were forced to camp uncomfortably amongst the rocks. But in spite of all this Freshfield still found time to be delighted at every view revealed by the parting veils of mist: glimpses of towering rock precipices streaked by romantic waterfalls: 'ripening seeds and withering leaves stained the slopes with reds and browns of autumn. The rocks were everywhere clothed with grey lichens and mosses. Even in the leaves of the rhododendrons there was much variety. ... Under the dull canopy of the sky the wet colours had a singular depth and transparency. There was opportunity for a painter!'

In spite of the fact that the rain was still with them, the following day proved different. The trees and shrubs grew progressively more stunted, and at last vanished altogether. They found themselves struggling upwards through long boulder-strewn grass. Then 'at last we arrived at the bend in the valley and saw before us close at hand, a most exciting and suggestive, if by no means beautiful, object: the snout of a glacier, foul with moraine'. Almost as if it was some living thing they approached the ice of Kanchenjunga.

They made camp that night on the Southern side of the glacier at a height of 13,910 feet. Freshfield must have been entitled to allow himself some small degree of satisfaction for having brought his unwieldy party through such a difficult preliminary stage. Although there had been some mist and a little drizzle during part of the day, a few hours more of climbing would see them well above the level of dreary rain that had plagued them so far. When he came to write up his notes that night he was able to recall with amusement an incident that took place during the day. At one point it had become necessary to cross the Zemu river on to the glacier itself, but there was some difficulty in finding a suitable crossing place. At last, however, they found a natural bridge in the form of two giant boulders, one on either bank; they leaned over the river so that they almost touched. The crossing was not very difficult, but it was awkward for the heavily laden porters; the operation took some time, and Freshfield withdrew to watch the scene. Rinsing, the native surveyor, dressed in chinese costume, stood on a pinnacle directing operations, while Dover, dressed in white flannels, bustled about helping with loads. The men, as Freshfield had earlier described them, looking like 'animated fire screens' with their wicker protective shields on top of their loads, teetering uncertainly before climbing precariously down from the rock. If Freshfield was himself still wearing the cutaway tail coat which he was reputed to have been wearing when he parted from Le Mesurier, then the picture must have been complete.

In the morning it looked as though their luck must have changed. At first light when Freshfield thrust his head from his tent he could see blue sky in the direction of the head of the glacier. Jamming on his boots in great excitement he scrambled up the embankment of loose moraine and out onto the ice. He found a suitable vantage point, but to his disappointment Kanchenjunga was still out of sight round the corner. But in spite of this he had a good view of the mountains to the north of the peak, and that, coupled with a first glimpse of the sun for a long time, sent him back to camp very much elated.

Because the guides were reluctant to cross to the north side of the glacier, where the going would have proved easier, progress that day was not very good. However they made some three miles in an easterly direction, and finally crossed over the ice, which was at that point about two miles wide. Here the main party made camp and a consultation was held. It was decided that Dover would establish a base camp at this point, as the first sight of ice, and glimpses of the awful panorama ahead, was already having its effect on the porters, some of whom were showing increasing reluctance to proceed. The rest of the party, with a dozen picked men, moved on to higher ground to establish an advanced camp from which to reconnoitre. They had now reached the limits of Political Officer White's exploration, which he had described to Freshfield in London; and it would be necessary for them to search out the passes which they hoped would take them round the Kanchenjunga massif.

Another day brought a repetition of the misty conditions, and the smaller party made good progress using the trench formed between the high embankment of moraine to their left and the sides of the mountains. It was with pleasure that they found edelweiss and gentians, and enjoyed the keen mountain air after their long toil through steamy tropical forest. They camped at 15,130 feet, and during the remaining daylight Garwood attempted to bag one of a herd of mountain goat that they had seen on the hillside, but possibly because he had been feeling unwell for the past two days he was unsuccessful.

The following day dawned fine, and although the spot on which they had chosen to pitch their tents did not afford a very good view, they were face to face with Kanchenjunga for the first time. Freshfield was anxious to be off. Garwood, who was still indisposed, elected to stay behind and perhaps shoot something for the pot, while the Sella brothers sought some vantage point from which to photograph the mountain. So Freshfield and Angelo Maquignaz set out together.

It was Freshfield's intention that day to get as far up the glacier as possible and find a suitable place for a still higher camp, from which to put his main plan for the next few days into operation. This plan was to assault one of the lesser peaks, of about 20,000 to 22,000 feet, in order to find out if 'first, the 21,000 foot gap leading into Nepal north of Kanchenjunga was accessible to coolies from this side; second, if any practicable line of ascent existed to the snow plateau lying west of the northern ridge of Kanchenjunga; and finally if the Zemu side of the 19,000 foot gap at the eastern base of Kanchenjunga was accessible'.

In high spirits the two set out, Freshfield noting the alpine flowers growing in the shelter of the rocks, and promising himself that he would collect some of them on his way back to camp. They passed the shores of a pleasant lake, which he thought a most suitable spot for a future alpine hut, then launched out over the ice to cross the mouth of a tributary glacier that joined the Zemu from the north-

One of the few pictures of D.W.F. climbing Kanchenjunga.   © Fondazione Sella and
Instituto di Fotografia Alpina Vittorio Sella-Biella.

Porters' Camp, Kanchenjunga.

The Bhutanese royal family.

west. Once across, they paused for ten minutes to absorb the scene around them. For all the reasons – geographical, geological, scientific – that Freshfield and other members of the Alpine Club might give to justify their passion, at a moment like this Freshfield must have felt confirmed in his belief that the real reason for climbing mountains was for the views. Kanchenjunga stood three miles off, towering another 13,000 feet above their heads, its mighty cliffs hopelessly inaccessible.

They pushed on until they reached a point in the middle of the glacier that came down from the ridge which ran almost due north from the main summit to a lesser double peak which they christened 'The Twins'. Here, at an altitude of 17,000 feet and about four hours from their camp, they ate lunch. The weather had become very oppressive, and Maquignaz fell asleep, while Freshfield, contrary to all his instincts as an experienced mountaineer, could not resist the opportunity for one of his solitary rambles. 'A virgin solitude – a scene that since the world began no human eyes have ever rested on – moves us most of all. ...'

Presently, as he sat some distance off, contemplating the aloof grandeur of the great peaks, he noticed a change taking place, 'the heaven was troubled; a thin veil of mist blurred, but did not at first hide the mountain outlines'. This was the advance guard of a storm that would soon cause terrible havoc and loss round Darjeeling, and acquire worldwide notoriety.

For the moment Freshfield was not unduly worried but, realizing that some change for the worse was imminent, made haste to rejoin his companion and together they hurried off towards camp. By the time that they had reached the shores of the lake it had turned suddenly cold, snow had begun to fall, and visibility was failing. But by then they were able to follow the stream as guide. Presently they heard shouts, and were met by their native servant with umbrellas! Later, white with snow and utterly exhausted they flung themselves down in their tents – it was very difficult having to hurry in that rarefied atmosphere.

They went to their sleeping bags that night quite unconcerned. The tents were snug, keeping out the drifting snow efficiently, and they had no reason to suppose that they were experiencing anything other than an untimely shower. The next morning did not reveal any change for the better, but everyone remained cheerful, occupying the time in clearing paths between the tents, clearing snow from roofs, and preparing provisions. At noon a party got through from the lower camp bringing mail forwarded by Le Mesurier, and newspaper reports of the Dreyfus trial, which kept them occupied during the afternoon while heavy snow continued.

In the evening they were forced to give serious consideration to their position when, after considerable difficulty, a further party from below got through to them with the news that some of the porters who were supposed to have arrived at base from the upper camp the night before had not turned up. It was dark and still snowing, so Freshfield was forced to decide that it would be useless to risk further lives in making an attempt to find them before daylight. This was a decision that he did not at all like making, and he lay awake most of the night, worrying about their own position and that of the missing porters. If the snow did not cease by morning it would be imperative that they should all try to get down to base, otherwise the task might become almost impossible.

That night Darjeeling took the worst brunt of that terrible storm. In several places the hillsides collapsed, washed down by torrential rain. Over 27 inches had fallen in 38 hours. Bungalows, houses and roads were swept away; about 400 lives were lost, including a family of English children. Newspapers all over the world carried the story and there was a good deal of speculation as to what might have happened to Freshfield and his party; some of it rather wild. A number of avalanches were supposed to have been observed from a distance of forty miles, in which, it was claimed, the party had certainly perished.

It was still snowing hard in the morning, and they packed as best they could in preparation for their attempt to get through to base. Once started they made very slow progress, floundering often to their waists in soft snow, unable to see where they were placing their feet on the treacherous ground.

Again Freshfield's own words are best to describe what happened next. 'Presently the gloom grew less opaque, the dark fog turned into shining mist. Then of a sudden the veil before our eyes was rent. The giants of the Himalaya glared down, incredibly vast and strangely transfigured, on the train of miserable ants crawling at their feet. We found ourselves scorched and blinded in a world of dazzling, unbroken and unmitigated brightness. The blaze of the vertical sunshine reflected from the myriad facets of the newly fallen snow, and enhanced by the shining particles of floating mist, was terrific. Nowhere have I felt such intolerable heat as in this frozen wilderness.'

This sudden onslaught of heat was very nearly too much for Garwood, who was in imminent danger of collapse, and had to rest until, in a short while, the mist again reduced the power of the sun. But by the time they reached their destination they were all in pretty bad shape; it took Garwood several days to get well, while Freshfield's face and lips were so badly blistered and burned, that, with the intense cold they were to suffer later, it was a long time before he was able to eat in comfort.

There was at least one piece of good news to greet them when they finally struggled into the lower camp; the missing coolies had turned up that morning, having passed the night sheltering in the rocks. There was a sudden drop in temperature that evening, and Freshfield and the party from the advanced camp went to their sleeping bags, now bitterly cold and suffering from sore throats and violent headaches.

Next morning the one bright spark in a situation of considerable gloom was the way in which Dover had managed to maintain discipline and cheerfulness amongst the natives. As for their plans and hopes it now looked as though they would have to abandon the greater part of their programme, as it would clearly be impossible to take heavily laden porters over the high passes. Freshfield announced that he had decided to take half the porters northwards, over a series of easier yak passes towards Tibet and then turn east over the Jonsong La, due north of Kanchenjunga and which was supposed to have been crossed by Rinsing on his previous visit. He suggested that the two Sellas with Dover should take the rest of the party back by a lower route to a convenient spot to await his arrival from the other side of the mountain. However the whole expedition preferred to remain with him and share his fortunes.

Two further days were spent at this camp while a programme of surveying and photography was carried out by the team, and runners despatched to Le Mesurier to inform him of their change of plans and advising him that further communication would be impossible once they had crossed the ridges into Lhonak.

The yak path they were taking should not normally have given them any difficulty, but the soft snow made progress very slow and they were hardly started when Garwood broke down completely and the whole expedition was forced to stop for a further day to allow him to recover. They were late in starting the next morning, and Freshfield, impatient even of necessary delay, pushed on alone to the first pass where he watched the approach of their army, 'headed by Rinsing in his silk jacket and round cap, using his umbrella as a sunshade, and closed by Mr Dover in his white flannels.' Amused he repeated the performance the following day, going ahead to a point near the summit of the next pass, but this time remaining concealed as the train approached. 'The procession advanced, chattering cheerfully so long as they were unconscious of my presence. Suddenly they caught sight of me: their cheerfulness disappeared as if by magic. Some fell on all fours, some fell flat on the ground under their burdens, all groaned piteously. Then I laughed outright, and several of them joined in, like children found out in a game.' There had been a somewhat similar scene that morning when Freshfield had done his camp inspection, many managing to produce real tears in their pretended agony. However a small number were in genuine distress through having ignored the boots or snow spectacles with which they had been issued, and a small band had to be sent home. It was due to Mr Dover's energy and skill in dealing with the porters so far out of their normal realm, that the expedition was able to proceed at all.

Two days' trek from their enforced stop due to Garwood's illness, they waded through soft snow down into the Lhonak valley and 'lunched luxuriously on a hillock carpeted with exquisite light blue gentians'. They were now in a wide, gravelly bottom which, to the west, led to a series of high peaks and passes into Tibet on the northern side, and Nepal on the other; their camp that night, in the centre of the valley, was about twenty miles, as the crow flies, north-east of Kanchenjunga.

At that time the government in Lhasa, not without reason,

Overleaf: Crossing the Jonsong La at 6,300 metres. This was the head of the glacier which Freshfield later realised gave him the confidence to proceed against all advice.
© Fondazione Sella and Instituto di Fotografia Alpina Vittorio Sella-Biella.

displayed a similar disregard for treaties and established frontiers as have the Chinese in more recent years. On the understandable grounds that the agreed frontier, which follows the watershed from Kanchenjunga northwards round the valley in which they were now encamped, did not include, on the Tibetan side, the settlements and pastures habitually used and grazed by Tibetans, they now laid claim to the Lhonak. When the frontiers were originally drawn up, and virtually imposed by Delhi, little attention, if any, was paid to local custom in matters of grazing, for it was fairly obvious that the area was of no use to the people of Sikhim, cut of as they were by the difficult gorges through which Freshfield and his expedition had climbed so laboriously. However, reasonable as the Tibetan claim might have been, lethargy in Delhi encouraged the Tibetans to still further demands and it was quite possible that Freshfield might have run into bands of armed Tibetan irregulars. Fortunately they had by now been removed to the permanent villages further north.

Being a visitor, and often the recipient of kindness at the hands of local officials, never deterred Freshfield from making his opinions on local matters known when he got home, even when they were at variance with the opinions held by men on the ground. The fact that he was, more often than not, at least partly right did not make his strictures any the less wounding. Some years later he discussed this very point with Keltie, Hon. Secretary of the Royal Geographical Society when, on his return from Ruwenzori, his published opinions about various matters concerning local administration out there caused offence. 'How far,' he asks, 'should a traveller be induced to hold his tongue as to the misdeeds of foreign officials (in that case the Belgian Congo) by their personal civility to himself?' So it was that in his book *Round Kankchenjunga* Freshfield came to complain that officials like White, who had done wonderful work in exploring and visiting all parts of their difficult territories, should nevertheless have thought fit to keep much of the geographical knowledge they had acquired to themselves. Freshfield had much to say of the then recent border dispute with Tibet. The 1959 dispute between the Republic of China and India over the Tibetan border areas was based on grievances of long standing, and even if by default not commission, the British must bear part of the blame. White, in the course of his journeys as Political Officer, had been as far as Lhonak, and had made several other remarkable and certainly arduous expeditions. It was unfortunate that he did not share Freshfield's passion for geography, but possibly Freshfield gave him little credit for the fact that his travels were accomplished with other, somewhat different, objectives in view.

They were delayed in their journey westwards the next afternoon by the slaughter of an apparently unresisting yak, surprised amongst the rocks; and camped once again just above the snowline. The following day, while the porters carried on to a suitable place from which to make an assault on the high Jonsong pass, it was decided to follow a suggestion of Rinsing's, who, now they were entering the region of his previous exploration, had assumed the role of chief guide.

Freshfield and Sella agreed to accompany Rinsing on a visit to the Chortenima La, a great pass supposed to lead north from Lhonak to Tibet, and which Rinsing had visited on his previous journey. The main party was to continue its westerly advance in the direction of the base of the Lhonak glacier, while Rinsing led his two companions to a small valley leading northwards, which, according to a rough sketch map made by White, was called Sayok Chu. They had a number of their Gurkha police with them, who had proved themselves keen and energetic climbers, and being free from the worry of porters made a brisk climb in brilliant sunshine over fairly difficult country. Freshfield was already having doubts as to whether they were in fact on the path that was supposed to lead to a pass of fair importance; but when they finally reached the summit he was even more mystified, for the descent on the far side looked virtually impossible. However Rinsing insisted that this was in fact the Chortenima La, and Freshfield sat in the sun trying to make the country revealed to their view correspond with what he knew lay north of the pass. Eventually he had to admit defeat, especially as the river below was flowing in exactly the opposite direction to that expected.

In fact they were not standing on the watershed at all, but very nearly five miles to the east of the true position of the pass and a good mile south of the main ridge, looking down on part of Lhonak. They returned to the valley still puzzled, not realizing the true nature of Rinsing's mistake until some months later.

But the unfortunate guide's confusion did not end there. The next day proved to be one of the most trying; for not only was progress difficult, alternately wading through icy water or slithering amongst boulders in soft snow; but there was also anxiety about the route they were taking. As they approached the end of the Lhonak glacier in the morning, Rinsing had pointed to a distant depression in the ridge saying that it was their route to the Jonsong La. Freshfield at once pointed out that this was a different route to that which Rinsing had indicated when standing on the Chortenima La the previous day. A discussion ensued between Rinsing and Dover, and while it continued Freshfield identified to his own satisfaction the Jonsong Peak and what he believed must be the direction of the pass, and accordingly ordered the party forward.

Freshfield, in taking a course dictated by his own experience as a mountaineer, would have been less than human if he had not continued to feel anxious at having entrusted his whole party to a route opposed to that pointed out by their guide, the only man there who had been over the same ground before. This, coupled with the trying ground and the hot sun, combined to make him very bad tempered. 'I never felt so much disposed to abandon mountaineering as a pastime!' he says. They camped that night in deep snow, all somewhat depressed.

If the going was but little better next day, there were distractions. In the first place there was the view over their shoulder. As they climbed steadily upwards, so the great peaks and ranges of Tibet were revealed. 'Some of them perhaps were within the horizon of Lhasa itself: the imagination leapt, using them as stepping stones to the golden terraces of Potala, the palace of the Dalai Lama.' Then there was the enchanted grotto, an ice pool perfectly reflecting the blue and glittering snow cliffs that encircled it: to Freshfield the perfect antithesis to the ' fairy dells of Sikhim where the brimming streams dash down dells choked with flowers and ferns'.

Camp that night proved a less happy affair. In spite of the encouragement and example of Dover and the Gurkhas the party had become strung out during the afternoon so that some of the men were very late getting to camp; and a number of them having thrown away their stoves were destined to spend a cold night.

Apart from the 'excessive quantity and villainous quality of the new snow' progress was not quite such a labour during the early part of the following morning. But as they approached the immediate vicinity of the pass they encountered a steep slope of deep snow overlaid on hard névé. The position was hardly made easier by the knowledge that later expeditions would no doubt 'run over flowers where we waded in snowdrifts, and find our great pass a very ordinary pass'. That is if they should be more fortunate in their weather.

Rinsing who, if his qualities as a surveyor had been called in question, was at the very least a capital walker, was one of the first to breach the final snow cliff and reach the summit. Freshfield had paused a few feet below when Rinsing called down to him that they were after all on the wrong pass. Freshfield very forcefully told him to hold his tongue, for should the fickle porters have heard such news there would have been an end to the whole expedition.

Freshfield hastened to join the guide. Rinsing had told them that from the head of the pass they would have a view of all eastern Nepal, and in the distance the highest mountain in the world dominating the range. The view that met Freshfield's gaze when he reached the gap was utterly different. Instead of the wide golden plains stretching away below the foothills there was only the grimmest glacier-filled trough, surrounded by frowning black cliffs, and apparently completely blocked at the far end by the dramatic bulk of Kanchenjunga itself. A less promising direction in which to find some way out of the mountains it would be hard to imagine. Freshfield's immediate reaction was to wonder if he had chosen the wrong route, and that Rinsing had been following a correct instinct when he had tried to take them to the north of the Jonsong Peak. But logic and his own highly developed sense of direction and mountain topography convinced him on reflection that he must be right and that the correct route lay before them, down the slope into the midst of the jumble of mighty peaks where to all appearances there was no way out.

But the Sella brothers, when they heard that it was his intention to forge ahead against the advice of their native guide, were utterly appalled. They were convinced that Freshfield was obstinately trying to prove his point out of vanity and at the risk of all their lives. But he was not prepared to argue. He told them to take half the porters, Rinsing, and supplies, and return the way they had come – he and Garwood would press on. Without further ado he strode off down the slope and, after a moment's hesitation, the others all followed, glad to get out of the biting cold wind that swept through the narrow gap. While they had been discussing, Garwood's hat had blown away beyond recovery. 'I was able to give him half my double wide-awake,' said Freshfield – that faithful companion of earlier Caucasian days was not altogether an object to inspire gratitude, but Garwood seems to have accepted it without complaint – the wind must have been very cold.

In a few minutes the others all followed, perhaps convinced, at least to some extent, by Freshfield's confident attitude. He himself was soon distracted by the fascinating view of Kanchenjunga's north-west face, never before seen by European eyes. As soon as they were out of the wind the Sellas stopped to take photographs, at that time the highest ever taken. But as they forced their way downwards the shadows were rapidly growing longer, some of the porters still showed as dots high on the pass behind, and camp was made in the shelter of some glittering snow castles. 'Soon the shadows deepened; the light faded from the sky; the cold became intense. Planets, brighter and nearer it seemed than their wont, hung in the blue vault like tiny solid balls. We seemed to stand on the verge of interplane-tary space in a region where organic life had ceased and there was no room or death,' They were at nearly 20,000 feet, and the temper-ature that night showed 27 degrees of frost inside Freshfield's tent. Even the coolies were hushed, awed by the magnificent night, so that the only sound was the distant boom of an occasional avalanche, rumbling and echoing like a salute.

Their anxieties about the route they were following were relieved the next morning. The lower they had trudged down the narrow valley, the higher and more forbidding the great mass of Kanchen-junga had become. The weird shapes and upheavals of the glacier became more violent; black frowning cliffs rose on either side down which tumbled frozen cataracts of ice and snow. Examining the curtain of rock ahead for some vestige of a way out Freshfield suddenly noticed a tiny wisp of cloud float into view low down, from between two cliffs that he had thought connected.

His decision to push on from the Jonsong La was in fact neither arrogant nor foolhardy; but based on a practical certainty. He was then at his zenith in terms of practical mountaineering experience, and the most unlikely person to have forced the party forward in a forlorn attempt to prove his point. When he stood on the pass examining the terrain ahead, everything indicated that they were standing at the source of a moving glacier, and since they already knew that it could not drain into the Green Lake area, or the Zemu, there was only one possibility; that it must turn westwards from the Kanchenjunga range and drain into Nepal.

But what of poor Rinsing? Freshfield makes several suggestions as to the cause of his actions both on the Jonsong La and the Chortenima La, including the theory that it was a deliberate attempt to prevent them from entering Nepal for superstitious reasons. But it seems certain that, excellent walker though he was, his first exploration had been conducted almost entirely by guesswork and he had never entered Lhonak by the Jonsong La at all, but by a route somewhere to the north-west of the Jonsong Peak – in fact at the place that he had indicated when he tried to make the party advance up the Lhonak glacier. The reason why he did not recognize the spectacular view from the Jonsong La, which could surely never be forgotten even by a confused native, was that he had never seen it before, and what he was expecting was a combination of what he had actually seen from the ridge to the north-west and the Chunjerma La.

However once the small, cloud messenger from the valleys of Nepal, settled the question of their way out of the rock prison, Freshfield's other anxiety returned. The porters were becoming more difficult to keep in any semblance of an organized baggage train. That morning it had been discovered that some had never arrived in camp the night before, and a Gurkha was sent back to see if there was any sign of them camping on the other side of the pass. Freshfield, watching the man nearing the summit through field-glasses, was amazed to see him running; a tremendous feat at that height. Great difficulty was experienced in getting the rest of the party to strike camp and shoulder their loads; some of them in fact refused to move at all. On inspection it was found that, through their refusal to wear the boots provided, they had developed frostbite. But eventually after their feet had been bound, and a 'stimulant' issued all round, they were persuaded to make a start. But they had already spent a far longer period in snow and difficult conditions than had ever been expected, and Freshfield was anxious to get them to more friendly regions, where there would be wood for fuel and the possibility of replenishing supplies.

A prolonged halt was made for a late breakfast; the gurkha and the rearguard were seen approaching and counted; and having, as he thought, accounted for the whole party, Freshfield once again pushed ahead into the increasingly jumbled and turbulent formations of the glacier. 'Its surface was as tormented as an angry sea. The frozen waves rose from fifty to a hundred feet high. We wandered circuitously along their crests, which were divided by hollows modelled into blue grottos, or filled with pools of steel grey water. We were never brought altogether to a standstill, but we seemed to go round as in a labyrinth.' That night they camped once again on ice, but at least they were pretty certain of turf and fuel on the morrow.

And so it proved. First through a fantastic moonscape of spires and pinnacles of glittering ice; then a splash through the many surface streams that flowed down the glacier, picking their way amongst boulders and debris; till at last a sharp westward turn round a spur, into the main stream. There Rinsing, sure of himself once again, hurried forward to lead them up a steep bank onto turf, where patches of melting snow mixed with fading flowers.

They had passed the previous six nights embedded in snow, and during the days had ascended the 20,207 foot Jonsong La, and descended the Jonsong glacier to the 17,000 foot level, in conditions rendered far more difficult than might have been expected owing to the heavy September snow fall. As the groups of porters arrived at the site chosen for the camp, known as Pangperma, they became immediately cheerful, dropping with their loads the memory of their previous troubles.

From this vantage point Freshfield was able to give his full attention to the previously unknown face that Kanchenjunga presented. Although he would have liked, had supplies been adequate, to explore further the approaches to the mountain, he subjected all he could see to a meticulous inspection and made a full mountaineer's report on the prospects and advantages of the possible routes. His summary, together with Sella's photographs, were a complete justification for the tour, and his assessment an invaluable source of background information for any party making an attempt on the mountain.

It was not until 1930 that a full-scale attempt was mounted on the basis of the survey and advice given by Freshfield. This was the expedition mounted by Professor Dyhrenfurth in which Frank Smythe took part. Their first view of the mountain from very nearly the same spot somewhat appalled them, prepared, though they were. Afterwards, writing in his book *Kanchenjunga Adventure* Smythe says, 'One thing was very clearly impressed upon us at the start, and that was that if such an experienced mountaineer as Mr Freshfield considered that Kanchenjunga offered the greatest chance of attack from this side, it must indeed be a formidable mountain.' Freshfield was obviously pessimistic about the outcome of any assault but he gives the impression that he feels that if any attempt at all were ever to be successful, then that attempt could be made from this side, even though, as he says, 'so skillfully is each comparatively weak spot raked by ice and rock batteries'. The fate of his friend Mummery could have been in his mind. As it turned out he was wrong, partly because of the limited knowledge of the effects of great heights on climbers current at the time, but more especially because a portion of the saddle between Kanchenjunga and the Twins, along which he says mountaineers should be able to find a route, was invisible to him. Had he been able to see that particular section of the route he was suggesting, he certainly would have realized the problems it presented.

The history of the conquest of Kanchenjunga has been a long tale of tremendous endeavour and sudden violent tragedy. In 1905 the first attempt was made under the leadership of Alaister Crowley. They chose to attack the face visible from Darjeeling via the Yalung glacier and actually managed to establish a camp at over 20,000 feet. But they seem to have courted disaster when six of the party traversed a steep snow slope in the heat of the day, starting an avalanche which killed four of them. In 1929 E. F. Farmer, an American, was exploring the same Yalung glacier, and climbing towards the Yalung saddle. He left his porters at one point, while he climbed higher to obtain photographs, and was never seen again.

But it was Dr Paul Bauer's 1929 expedition that constituted the first really determined effort. They attacked the mountain from the Zemu glacier on a route that Freshfield did not even consider, so formidable did it appear to him. They suffered terribly, and were finally routed by a series of tremendous storms which followed them the whole way back to Lachen. The 1930 team on Freshfield's suggested route on the Kangchen glacier fared even worse. With the fate of Mummery still in his mind Freshfield had warned of the danger of avalanches on the north-west face. The 1930 expedition experienced one of the most terrible examples of ice avalanche that can ever have been witnessed by man; had the party been in its path they would have been wiped out in an instant. As it was a Sherpa porter lost his life, and the rest of the party were so stunned by the experience that it is to their great credit that they were able to continue their determined assault until convinced of its impossibility; and even then to go on up the Jonsong La and finally climb the Jonsong Peak.

In 1931 Bauer was again attacking that terrible north-east spur and this time, although they managed to reach the ridge at the top of the spur, they lost two of their party, one European and a porter, who fell roped together some four thousand feet to the glacier below. It was impossible in the days of Freshfield's expedition to have any conception of the difficulties of climbing at the great height of a Himalayan summit, and men were yet destined to learn the hardest way.

To quote Smythe again. 'The Alps are the playground of Europe, the Himalayas the playground of the Gods ... There is nothing friendly about a Himalayan peak. You feel that it is coldly hostile, that it resents intrusion. It allows no latitude, it seizes upon the slightest mistake. It will kill you if it can.'

But even from such a comparatively modest affair as Freshfield's reconnaissance, Kanchenjunga was to demand its toll of human life. In the more cheerful atmosphere of the camp at Pangperma Freshfield was once again informed that all his party were accounted for. Half an hour of fairly flat walking over pasture land at the side of the Kangchen glacier brought them to a small cluster of deserted huts, the summer grazing station of the villagers of Kangbachen; from now on they were once again on a distinct man-made path. As they descended, crossing and recrossing the Kangchen river the glacier itself became completely obscured by rubbish and debris, so that only an expert eye could tell that there was ice hidden beneath it. But a mile above the pastoral hamlet of Kangbachen they left the glacier for good.

Kangbachen was also deserted, and they pitched their tents among the stone sheds. Thirty years later when the next expedition passed on its way to Kanchenjunga by this path, Kangbachen appears to have grown to a more considerable place, and the sturdy hill people proved excellent guides. But this time Freshfield was not unhappy that their meeting with the people of Nepal was postponed; for they were in a land forbidden to Europeans, and there was no telling what form of opposition they might have met.

In fact they made their first contact with the people of the valley the very next day, when they approached a village and were given a friendly but shy reception. There was no sign of any official person who might try to prevent their further progress or forbid them to obtain fresh provisions. However Freshfield, remembering a less fortunate occurrence in the Caucasus, led his party through the village, which was called Khunza, and ordered a halt on the far side having secured their line of retreat.

Obviously the appearance of so large a party from such a totally unexpected direction shocked the villagers into supplying some of their needs, though what they were able to produce proved somewhat meagre, and led to the local customs official, when he finally showed up, agreeing to their future progress; obviously glad to be relieved of such a responsibility.

Deep in its sheltered, pastoral valley, Khunza was out of sight of its great grim neighbours. After the snowy wastes above they were especially charmed by its sparkling rivers. Freshfield felt he had entered a natural, wild garden; dwarf junipers crept over the boulders, variegated rhododendrons grew through the crevices. Perhaps he wondered if he could make part of his garden at home echo a few square yards of remote Nepal. But pleasure at this change of scene was to give way to a feeling of disappointment and regret when they made camp that night. The news was brought to him that one of the Sikhim coolies, on the day after they had crossed the Jonsong La, had told his companions that he was quite unable to proceed any further and requested that he be left to die. His companions had taken this request entirely as a matter of course; received his instructions regarding his property, covered his face and left him. They had regarded the incident as of so little importance that they had never thought to tell either Dover or any of the others. Freshfield blamed himself bitterly that he had not made certain that all the party were accounted for, but on several occasions in crossing the snows they had become so separated that this was virtually impossible. But there was little doubt that the prolonged stay in the snows had been a severe trial for the coolies, in spite of the fact that care was taken to distribute loads as fairly as possible, and a Gurkha party had acted as rearguard charged with the task of rounding up stragglers. However without Dover their losses might well have been very much greater.

Almost everyone prepared to leave Khunza with regret the following morning; the coolies because of the hospitable quarters they had found with many of the villagers; the Europeans because of the pleasant scenery and air of the place. For this reason, and because there were dues to be paid for supplies received, they were doubly late in making a start. But in a very short time they were forced to stop again because of uncertainty about the correct path, and they had to send for a villager to guide them. Finally, however, they were led on a long, dull, and somewhat airless climb under dense rhododendrons, which gave way at the first crest to an area of rough pasture. Mist filled the valleys below, and low cloud shrouded the mountains above, so that the great Himalayas were 'thus reduced to the scale of a Scottish landscape'. Perhaps the dullness, and lack of any dramatic view to distract the walkers made them more conscious of their general weariness; Freshfield complained of a lack of enthusiasm and a 'weariness of the thighs'. But for a spell at least this was to be forgotten the next day.

They camped 1,000 feet below a pass called Chunjerma, from which, if earlier reports were reliable, they would be given a special treat. It had snowed a little during the night, and for once the morning was fine and clear. Fearful lest the mists should return Freshfield chivvied his photographers ahead, anxious not to miss such an opportunity. 'Half an hour's uphill run,' he writes, 'the slackness of the day before forgotten, and a few inches of snow on the path no impediment – brought me in advance of my companions and the coolies, to the loose stone-men and the waving prayer flags that crowned the ridge.' Once there, he turned and looked back over the heads of his struggling companions, northwards, past the shining mass of Jannu, over the jumbled, tortured intervening ridges – to the highest mountain in the world. Even the much travelled Sir Joseph Hooker, the only European to stand on this spot before Freshfield, had declared this the 'most magnificent spectacle I ever beheld'. But to a connoisseur of mountains it was the magnificent snowy pyramid of Jannu that demanded his immediate attention, and he was soon lost in speculation as to the relative merits, for sheer spectacle, of Jannu and the Matterhorn.

Having absorbed the full impact of Jannu, he turned his attention to the whole prospect. Afterwards he wrote: 'If I could not, as in the most famous panorama ever imagined, see all the kingdoms of the world and the glory of them, yet all its zones and all its seasons, arctic frost and equatorial glow, winter and autumn, spring and summer, seemed to have met together within the range of mortal vision. I was perched at an altitude Kanchenjunga Group, the snows of which I, as it were, touched. On one side rose its majestic walls and towers of rock and ice; on the other I overlooked all Eastern Nepal ... and the southern borderland of Tibet. Beneath the deep blue vault of heaven, the giant mountains of Nepal stretched in a wide curve, extending all along the line of the northern horizon from a point nearly due west to the base of Jannu. Some, the more distant, were tinged as with pale gold, others shone in silvery light. Wherever the nearer range dropped, fresh peaks and horns shot up over its unknown and untrodden passes. Below the bright belt of new fallen snow on which I stood, the great spurs of the mountains were spread out range beyond range, clothed in the brown and amber of autumnal woods and pastures, or the duller hues of pines and junipers. Lower still lay the tropical forests of the foothills, a fair broad carpet of perpetual green, broken here and there in the blue depths of the valleys by the flash of running waters, while far, far away to the south, a vague sea of pale sunlight and diaphanous, rainbow-tinted haze indicated the position of the Plains of Bengal.'

Certainly Freshfield and others like him loved the mountains they explored, and were most anxious to convey to their less fortunate friends every detail of each new and exciting prospect. In our own hurried times, when we are so impatient with the descriptive passage, and shy away from the 'purple', it is as well to remember the less fortunate mountaineers who, passionately interested in the unfolding world, could, through writers like Freshfield and Conway, sit at home and build, detail by detail, a grand panorama seen through other eyes. Such detail had to be scrupulously accurate; any future visitor to the same spot should be able to recognize every feature as an old friend. Freshfield may have been more tolerant than others in this respect, as we shall see in respect to W.W. Graham's Kabru claim.

Freshfield applied several times for permission to visit Everest, but as it turned out this was the only view that he would ever be vouchsafed of the peak. Through the clear upper air that day it stood some seventy miles off as the crow flies. At the time it was known that Everest was the highest peak discovered so far, but it was thought that there might be a peak still higher elsewhere in the distant ranges of Tibet; certainly native travellers had confirmed that there were mighty rivals as yet unseen by Europeans.

He had a strong prejudice against the calling of mountains by the names of explorers and climbers, and had objected strongly when certain mountains in Canada had been named after past presidents of the Alpine Club. The naming of the highest mountain in the world after a surveyor, however meritorious, when it possessed an ancient native name, struck him as presumptuous, and a bad precedent; he continued to refer to the greatest peak of all as Chomokankar, which means 'The Lord of the Snows'. It is to be regretted that Everest is so much easier for Europeans to say and remember, and that the native name should be almost unknown to most people. As usual Freshfield's writings on this matter got him into trouble. In September 1904 he wrote in the *Geographical Journal*: 'To call the highest mountain in the world after one of its late chiefs may seem natural to a department: but it will hardly persuade – and it has not succeeded in persuading – the world to share its view.'

The result of such an outburst might have been expected, and in January of the following year Freshfield wrote to Keltie at the R.G.S.: 'You tell me that the present head of the survey is very angry at my letter in the September *Journal* – I have read it again and see nothing to regret or modify in it: I regard it as a very temperate reply to a memorandum in which my previous articles were most unwarrantably misrepresented and specific statements I had made (which would be endorsed by every European orographer), described as absurd. An officer, formerly of the Indian Survey, took occasion, when reading a paper on another subject to the British Association at Cambridge, to drag in the memorandum and emphasize a passage reflecting on climbers without giving notice to me, being chairman, of his intentions.'

But this was another battle that he was to lose.

For a long time he and his party stood on the pass, identifying and pointing out to each other the mighty peaks, until at last the time came to push on, down the vale below the Yalung glacier. Where the path dipped finally below the ridge they looked back for a last glimpse of the magnificent scene with Garwood's figure, busily absorbed with his plane table, a dark cutout against the brilliant skyline, and the distant Everest. Then they were in the mist again, which spoiled any view they would certainly have had of the Yalung glacier and the summit of Kabru on the far side. They finally, however, came below the clouds and were able to look down into the wooded glen of the Yalung river, and to see the mounds of earth that were the frontal moraines of the glacier. Ahead, over a number of smaller intervening ridges, was the Kang La, the frontier between Nepal and Sikhim, a dip in a long crest that climbs up to the summit of Kabru.

At the end of the nineteenth, and during the early part of the last century, indefatigable and scholarly historians like Coolidge worked with passionate intensity cataloguing the great peaks and their first conquerors. From this distance in time it is not so much the individual feats that catch our attention as the whole amazing phenomena of adventurous exploration that gripped so many of the Victorian upper classes. It seems a very great pity that what might well have been one of the really great exploits of the whole of the era of great mountaineers was marred by argument and suspicion. In 1883 W.W. Graham had led a mountaineering party over the Kang La from Sikhim into the valley of the Yalung. From here he claimed that he and his companion Emil Boss climbed to the summit of the 24,000 foot Kabru, the highest peak ever climbed by man, and if the claim were true it remained a record until 1930. However many people thought that the vagueness of Graham's description of the ascent signified that he was mistaken, and had in fact climbed some lesser summit in the area; and there were others who thought that it was quite impossible to reach such a height in a comparatively short time, because of the rarefied air. Freshfield was more generous. He had always been of the opinion that far too much was made of the difficulties that would be experienced at great heights and he knew Graham as a good mountaineer of what he would regard as the right school and with the right motives. Graham's exploits had always been far reaching and bold, but, as Freshfield pointed out, it was well known that he did not bring the same careful accuracy to his writings that others were accustomed to. It was a great disappointment to his coolies that, because of the urgent need for stores, he was unable to remain in the region of the Kang La long enough to make an attempt to climb in Graham's footsteps.

So it would be left to others to explore the Yalung glacier and the snow face of Kanchenjunga that feeds it; for a few years more the paradise of Nepalese belief, which was supposed to be in its recesses, would remain undisturbed. The following day the party crossed the Kang La, which proved disappointing from a scenic point of view. They made a very long march through bitter cold with sleet, and over rough uneven ground, but in spite of this the coolies were anxious to keep moving ahead, realizing with mounting eagerness that they were at last going in the direction of their homes. The Sellas remained in the vicinity of the pass that night in the hope of getting a view of the Yalung glacier before leaving in the morning, but they were forced to catch up with the main party next day, having spent a fruitless and uncomfortable vigil. Yet another hard day followed, a drop down a deep gorge, with the river tumbling and cascading beside them, and magnificent rhododendrons overhead, followed by a 2,000 foot climb over a further pass on to 'a wide upland, a true alpine pasture. After we had crossed a brook and a hollow, two stone huts suddenly loomed through the dismal drizzle, and – a welcome vision – a white pavilion of the comparatively lordly dimensions affected by officials on tour. We were at Jongri, and our friends at Darjeeling had sent out a relief party to meet us'.

Here they got their first news of the outside world; of the outbreak of the Boer War; of the terrible storm in Darjeeling; of their own deaths in an avalanche, and enough mail, Freshfield said, to occupy them the whole of a wet day. They were destined for a disturbed rest that night however. A herd of yaks, scornful of ice axe assaults, insisted on trying to push down and eat their tents. Freshfield dreamed that he was about to be buried in an avalanche of white yaks.

The village of Ushkul, one of a number in Suanetia where the first expedition received a hostile reception. © Fondazione Sella and Instituto di Fotografia Alpina Vittorio Sella-Biella.

In the morning the wide pasturage in which they were camped reminded Freshfield of some of the well known climbing resorts in the Alps, and it occurred to him that the place would be a fine site for development; a curious thought, considering that he preferred the lonely heights and untrodden paths to more populous places. What would he have had to say if the 'monster hotels' and defiling 'coal smoke engines' of his nightmare had invaded the Himalaya?

In order to complete the full tour of the mountain, and to inspect all sides of it, one further task remained. Selecting a party of the fittest of the coolies, and leaving the others to recuperate, they set out in a more or less northerly direction for the Guicha La, almost two days away, from which they could examine the Yalung glacier, and the south side of the mountain.

The morning's climb, partly through scrubby country, partly over stony ditches and streams in the direction of the base of Pandim, took them past a ruined hut at a place named Alukthang. As Fresh-field pointed out, it was a last point on the most direct approach to Kanchenjunga from the inhabited parts of Sikhim which could be reached without venturing on to ice, and as such it had acquired a special significance. Every year a party of monks climb to this point to offer a week's prayers to the demon of Kanchenjunga, for from this position the lower summit of the mountain appears as a single great peak rather than the massive summit which it presents from almost every other point. At night they saw a very good reason for the worship of Kanchenjunga. A full moon rose behind the summit of Jobonu, remaining for a long time invisible to the watchers; but the snows and ice of the peak became a floating 'silver shrine' far above their heads.

In due course they visited their pass and Freshfield examined the surrounding peaks with his usual care for possible routes to their summits, but the whole of this valley had been fairly well explored by Graham, White, and others, and there was very little that was new or startling for him to report. He admitted that he was some-what disappointed with the scenery of the valley, as though, after the great climax of the Chunjerama pass their eyes had become used to the merely magnificent. But their time was running short, for next day dawned a winter's day. Garwood made an early start and shot a muskdeer on Pandim while Freshfield continued his examination of the heights with the aid of field glasses until it was time to pack up and return to Jongri.

Their time in the high snows was drawing to a close. Already there were feelings of regret, now that the difficulties of the tour were behind them. Had they made the best use of their time? Was there not still time to climb one of the greater peaks, and so, as it were, put a mountaineer's seal of success on the story of the whole expedition? But it was obvious, on a little reflection, that the season was too far gone for any such ambitious scheme. They consoled themselves with a day spent on Kabur, a very minor summit on the ridge to the north-west of Jongri, but at least it entailed some rock climbing with the use of the rope.

'On our return to Jongri that night we lit a blazing bonfire and sat round it under the brilliant stars ... Our blaze had a quite unintentional success as a beacon. A servant at the 'Shrubbery', the Lieutenant Governor of Bengal's residence at Darjeeling, ran to Sir John Woodburn with the news that there was a new star on Kanchenjunga. A telescope revealed the terrestrial nature of the phenomenon and gave the first news that we had successfully accomplished our enterprise, and got round Kanchenjunga.'

The return journey to Darjeeling was on the whole a considerably more pleasant affair than the outward one. It seemed as though Kanchenjunga, an insult avenged by the great storm, was now showing them a smiling face. When they returned they found that native opinion was divided as to what had actually stirred the God to such a display of wrath. Some said it was the expedition's intrusion, others that it was military manoeuvres that had taken place in a sacred spot near Darjeeling.

During their last days Freshfield rose early each morning and his tall solitary figure could be seen silent and motionless on Observatory Hill watching the dawn illuminate the great mountain. Stoic that he was, he was probably unaware that his weight had dropped to not much more than ten stone.[1]

This was the climax of his climbing and exploring career. If the last expedition to the Caucasus had been something of a wonderful

---

[1] In the *Scottish Geographical Magazine* D.W.F. said of the indomitable Dover 'who suffered only from increased appetite and gained several pounds in weight'.

camping expedition, the Himalayas were something different. He was used to seeing a new mountain, and finding a way to reach the summit – but he was conscious of the Spirit of Kanchenjunga, and his awareness creeps through in his writings. This mountain was alive, and it was malevolent, just as the natives believed.

Round Kanchenjunga was his best book. His descriptive powers were at their height, he was impressed and excited in a way he had not been for a long time by the presence of the Himalayas, and an element of humanity creeps into the pages that did not do so in the Caucasus writings. It was to be published by Arnold and only a few copies had been distributed when a fire destroyed their warehouse and it was not thought possible to reprint. However there are enough copies in libraries for the work not to have been completely lost and the story is there for those who seek it out for themselves.

D.W.F. on Table Mountain.

CHAPTER 11

Douglas arrived home, with a bad cold and lips still scarred, to a somewhat cool reception from some of the family. Almost all of them had been staying in Scotland with a number of young friends of the children, following Janie's wedding in July, and it had been from there that Douglas had parted from them to start for India. During the holiday Gussie had begun to suffer a good deal from her leg once again and, only two days before he left, Eleanor had noted ominously in her diary that a short walk that afternoon to sit in the heather was the last of any distance that she would make for some time. When Douglas arrived back he found Gussie was in Brighton recovering from the problem with her leg which had eventually necessitated a special invalid carriage on the train down from Scotland. Eleanor had devoted a good deal of time to nursing her mother, and *The Times* report that Douglas's expedition might have been wiped out by an avalanche did not help matters. On top of all this, the war in South Africa was rageing, friends and the relatives of friends had been killed or wounded, and a pall hung over their lives that no amount of jingoism could remove.

But the new house at Slacks, to be called Ashdown Place, was nearly completed for Mrs Freshfield, and was impressive. Edmund Fisher was pleased with it, and Janie was going to have a baby, the first of Douglas and Gussie's grandchildren, while Gussie herself, having caught the idea of gardening from Eleanor's enthusiasm for Castletop, had transformed Kidbrook, and was turning her attention to the layout and planting at the new house.

However within a few days of Douglas's return, the flags were out on Brighton pier, Ladysmith had been relieved, and in spite of painful legs Gussie was wheeled out to see the celebrations. But she improved enough that summer to take a prolonged trip to Switzerland and Italy while Douglas walked in the mountains. She was joined by various members of the family, including, for a long period, Desmond and Molly McCarthy. Desmond was great company, for since Gussie's first illness she had read more and more omnivorously, and she found conversation with a young person of Desmond's talents stimulating.

The building of Ashdown Place, combined with her illness, had decided Gussie that she did not want to live at Kidbrook any longer, and gradually the idea grew up that they would build a house that was high up out of the valley, where there were views and the air was clear, and her 'Kidbrooky' pains would trouble her no more. On the southern side of the steep-wooded slope that lay to the south of Kidbrook, there were large beech and pine trees, standing amidst bracken and gorse. Here the family in the past would often picnic; the children to play amongst the warrens, the adults to admire the view over a steep valley, completely wild, to a further ridge with the blue outline of the South Downs beyond. Here the pungent, mixed scents of pine needles, gorse, heather and bracken mingled in the dry warm air to give an atmosphere very different from the mist-shrouded Kidbrook far below.

The place was officially called Prestridge Warren, but it was more often locally known as Shelley Warren, after the family that had once owned it, who had sold it to the Prime Minster from whom in turn Henry Ray had purchased it to add to his land at Kidbrook. It had always been pretty inaccessible, the road south from Forest Row to Lewes having been pronounced unsuitable for a gentleman's carriage not many years before. Such track as there was crossed the ridge 600 feet up, a lonely crossroads, just below which stood the infamous Roebuck Inn. This was Wych Cross, and it was here that a private track led into the beech woods on the right, to the favourite picnic place. In the past the Roebuck had had the most villainous reputation, a smuggler's haunt where murder and woundings had been common in the previous century under the barbarous rule of the 'Fair Traders', who had, in considerable number, been at open war with the authorities, and frequently ended up being hanged in their dozens.

The idea, once mooted, seemed to take on a progression of its own. It was a winter of concerts, parties and hosting at Airlie Gardens,[1] and weekends at Kidbrook. In spite of her leg Gussie was as ever surrounded by discussion and argument. There was Ralph Vaughan Williams, who was married to Edmund's sister, telling her that he had never hated any music quite so much as Arthur Sullivan's to Tennyson's *Maud*; there was Henry James giving them a great shock by appearing at dinner without his beard. But there was still time, one November day, to take the carriage and drive up to Shelley, the name they had almost decided to give the place, with Arthur Clough and Richmond and all to agree totally as to the site.

Edmund was to design the new house, and after talking privately with his father-in-law, he went away and sketched out his plans. Richmond seems to have taken a rather proprietorial attitude to what was intended, and when Edmund's plans were discussed for the first time he upset his sister by abusing them, saying nothing would do but a French chateau like Fontainebleau. Clough joined the argument as well and the discussion seems to have become quite acrimonious.

But Douglas and his architect stuck firmly to their own ideas; it was Douglas's idea that the south windows should be rounded bows which was arguably not in keeping, but he thought the sunset views would be much enhanced from them. By the next day, on a further visit to the site, the angle and position of a dignified English 'E' shaped house was agreed. And then, within a couple of months two totally inconceivable events took place. In January the Queen died, and not long after so did old Jane Q. They hurried down to Kidbrook, where the old lady was lying in state, looking, they all agreed, very noble. They buried her at Forest Row, in a howling, freezing gale, her old retainers from her Kidbrook days carrying the coffin and laid her with Henry Ray, near Hal's memorial, and less than a hundred yards from the rebuilt village hall.

It was the end of Kidbrook. They decided to shut up the house,

---

[1] Augusta's niece, Molly MacCarthy (Ware Cornish, in her book *A Nineteenth Century Childhood*), gives a brilliant description of a ball at 1 Arlie Gardens. Gussie, thinly disguised as Mrs Tallboys, is described amongst her friends and relations against the background of the London house with great colour. The book was published in 1924 by William Heinemann Ltd. See Chapter 1.

use it as a store for all their treasures, and to move temporarily to Ashdown Place, higher, and therefore surely healthier, for Gussie, while the new house at Wych Cross was built.

Rancour over the new design was soon forgotten. Even Richmond, after an afternoon with his sister at the site with Edmund, discussing the steep slope of the ground and the south-east aspect which would cause great building difficulties, had a final and amicable discussion with the architect, plans laid over the piano that evening.

'*Folie de grandeur*' or simply a rich man's attempt to placate his estranged and ailing wife, call it what you will, Wych Cross Place, as originally designed and built, was a remarkable house. Gussie was now one of the leading Edwardian hostesses of the literary and artistic world. Aunt Annie, a successful novelist and biographer, together with du Maurier, Henry James and the Sidgewicks perhaps represented the core of her literary circle; musically there was her old friend Joachim who would often play accompanied by Pinkie in the music room at Airlie Gardens; there were some of Douglas's friends from the climbing as well as the legal world, amongst whom were Lord Bryce, the Pollocks, and of course, Mr Tucker. There were many more enjoyed her table, the conversation and the ambience created by their pictures and furniture, their porcelain and their tapestries. A new generation would see all this as an arid and selfish exercise in the display of wealth and arrogant intellectual superiority, but at the time it did not seem so. The house was to have everything: wide, sunny windows through which soothing breezes could enter to caress Gussie's aching limbs; a long gallery, where all their treasures could be displayed in glorious profusion of colour and detail and terraces and fountains in the Italian style. There was a stable block with a clock tower in the English style; azaleas and rhododendrons tumbling down steep ravines like some Caucasian foothill; even the giant rhubarb by a pond, as at the camp in Abkhasia, and a long truly English yew walk. But, above all, there was the view, where the sunsets could come clear and uninterrupted; a new sense of light and space – a fairy palace.

Meanwhile, as a distraction and a kind of rehearsal, there was a garden at Ashdown Place to be created. It is still there. The house, now divided, is essentially the same and possesses the singular charm and grace that Edmund Fisher seems to have been able to create. The trees have grown and it is not visible now from any distance as it once was, but the family would have no difficulty in pointing out the features of the place where they spent several happy summers before the final move. Later it was sold to the Cavendish family; Lady Dorothy, later Lady Dorothy Macmillan spent some of her early youth there.

Douglas liked his women to be intelligent and attractive, it is true, but he had the conventional Victorian attitude to the position of women in society. He was not much enamoured of the the lives of ladies like 'Thena Clough with their powerful intellectual desire to change the status of women through education'. He wrote another of his rhymes about his wife and daughter's new found passion for creating gardens which did not go down too well, especially, one imagines, the last verse.

> Mother Eve contrived, we read,
> Mankind of paradise to cozen;
> Her daughters to repair the deed
> Make paradises by the dozen.
>
> In the fair gardens you create
> No cruel ambushes lie hidden,
> No belted angel bars the gate,
> No serpent rustles in, unbidden.
>
> Within each flowery fragrant space
> You fashion for some happy master
> Old Satan finds no lurking place,
> No lure to lead us to disaster.
>
> Here, ladies, lies your proper sphere,
> Not cloistered in a woman's college;
> The tree of life to all is dear,
> Will do without the tree of knowledge.

The new century and the new reign brought many changes so far as the Freshfields were concerned. Freshwater and Dimbola were no longer visited after 1900, though the house was to remain the property of Douglas until 1924. Up to 1892, when Tennyson died, once or twice every year some or all of the family would stay there and Gussie would record their hours with the old poet now somewhat pathetically dependant on his few remaining contacts with the old

Part of the south front, Wych Cross Place.

days. Annie's cottage for herself and Richmond at Freshwater, the Porch, which was situated almost opposite Dimbola, served as a haven for them both and later for Annie in her widowhood. But now Tennyson was dead and Douglas paid one or two more visits to the Island to arrange for the erection of the now familiar Ionic Cross on the down above Farringford and the sea where the poet had loved to walk. He wrote an epitaph for the old Laureate, but not one that would find favour in today's climate.

Arthur Clough's mother had died as the result of her second bad accident driving her pony cart through the lanes on the edge of Cranborne Chase, and Gussie began to complain of a new and still more alarming pain, this time in her arm. In the early years of the century other familiar faces were lost to their circle. A letter from Gerald Duckworth tells Gussie of the fading last days of Douglas's friend and alpine enthusiast, Leslie Stephen.

But none of this dampened the excitement caused by the completion of the great house at Wych Cross in 1904. Briefly it stood empty awaiting occupation, a beautiful shell to be brought to life. With snow drifts of white ceilings, honey-coloured waxed floors, stairs and panelling, it seemed to one observer to catch and store every ray of sunshine that fell in the beautifully proportioned rooms. Edmund Fisher was so excited on the first night he stayed there he never went to bed, but wandered around, appreciating the vistas and detail, the spaces and openings that his imagination had created. Sadly his promise was never fully realized. In the next ten years there would be a few houses in the Home Counties for which he was responsible, an extension to the buildings at Newnham College, Cambridge, and Somerville and New College Oxford. Perhaps the Anglican church in Rome was his most important public building, but Wych Cross, while it stood, was his masterpiece. He was to die from peritonitis, which he contracted while serving in Flanders during the First World War, leaving his widow, Janie, with seven children.

It is hard to analyse just how the special character of Wych Cross was brought about. It was not the same as many other large Edwardian houses that were built at around that time. Was it the plaster ceilings designed by Blankart, the gardens by Mawson,[1] the Morris

[1] Thomas Mawson, landscape gardener and author of 'Life & Work of an English Landscape Architect'.

papers and the rich antique Persian rugs, the golden, locally quarried stone or the extraordinary richness of the contents, displayed with imagination and put to use if use there was for them? There was a barrel-vaulted dining room with painted ceiling, while the walls of Douglas's study were lined with richly coloured and embossed Spanish leather. Gussie's bedroom was hung with Chinese silk, and even the nurseries on the top floor, which would one day house grandchildren and great-grandchildren, were beautifully thought out, even if they were a trifle hot when the sun shone in midsummer. The steepness of the slope upon which it was set posed great problems. A large excavation was necessary so that the main south terrace and front of the house could be supported, but the resultant views across the valley to the hills beyond was all that both Gussie and Douglas could have dreamed.

It was often filled with guests, both family and friends, some of whom have left sharply etched pictures of the house and the life within it. To quote Virginia Stephen (Woolf): 'I have just come back from the Freshfields, where I talked for long stretches about Tolstoy. Mrs F. has lost the use of her right arm; and has a good deal of pain, but she seems to me a valiant woman who keeps afloat, and strews her bed with the last French review, and the last English memoir. "So convenient for my daughters that I can read: they can leave me alone".'

But writing on the same subject to Lytton Strachey a few days later: 'We stayed with the Freshfields a week ago. Nature and art did their best; it was sumptuous; but they were like waxworks, slightly running in the sun, except for Gussie, who has the spirit of a Roman empress. I daresay she is a hard woman. We sat in a little summer house and discussed the immortality of the soul, and mid-Victorian scandal. I never saw anything so remote as she and poor Douglas. He seems to have stiffened all over, and is now practically jointless.'

Gussie's fatal and painful illness was to last for ten years, with increasing severity. It began in May 1901, when she was told that 'measures must be taken to meet the danger', and shortly after underwent an operation, which might have proved dangerous. As she drove home with the faithful Eleanor from the surgeons she said how much worse it was for her daughter, as she had lived with the fear for so long. Eleanor arranged for a second opinion and Sir

Thomas Smith was called to the house. Douglas and Eleanor were in the library when he came down and gravely delivered his verdict of confirmation. A few minutes later Gussie entered with 'a wonderful look on her face that brought before me with strange vividness the vision of a stag, its head raised, listening to the first faint baying of the hounds. I believe that in those few seconds her spirit faced and accepted all that lay before her.'[1]

That evening she attended Douglas's lecture to the Alpine Club on Kanchenjunga, and as they drove there she said to Eleanor 'I do hope you will build the house in the Warren, whatever happens to me.' But although she was to suffer pain of increasing severity for ten years more, this time the operation was a success. She spent the afternoon before at a Joachim concert, perhaps the most favourite of all her diversions. She spent a happy day talking over old times with Annie and Richmond, and was operated upon in her own home, to recover in Brighton once again. But the arm was now useless and the pain in her leg was never entirely absent.

After the building and the move into the new house, which had entailed the joyous unpacking of Kidbrook and the rediscovery and display of old treasures, which Gussie found exhausting but very enjoyable, there was the great interest in the gardens. Apart from the general formation of terraces, walks, streams and ponds, the gardens were almost entirely the work of Gussie. She planned the transition from the extreme formality round the house which faded naturally without barrier into seemingly unplanned wilderness; the severe terraces blending into the Sussex hillside. The lake at the foot of the steep slope surrounded by trees and shrubs, with a wide smooth path leading down to it, looked perfect when seen from across the upper terrace with lily pond and fountain just below. The soil was not good, and there was considerable trouble getting the vast, walled kitchen garden productive, but the head-gardener, one of the few to win mention and praise from his employer, known affectionately as the 'professor' because of his familiarity with the Latin names, won even this struggle. And soon the walls were clad in espaliered fruit trees, and the hot houses were well on the way to producing grapes and nectarines.

Years later, when Douglas Freshfield was dead, but before the

[1] Eleanor Clough's diary 1901, unpublished.

house was partially pulled down and the rest altered almost beyond recognition, Beverly Nicholls was to describe it as a 'creation of genius'.

To one faithful old friend Douglas wrote a letter describing his new home, for it was some time since François had been well enough to visit England; and François wrote back in his round handwriting to express his admiration for the *'nouveau chateau'*.

But it was almost the last letter that Douglas was to receive from the little house under the shade of Mont Blanc, for a few months later in 1905 François died. Verses written by Douglas for his friend concluded:

> Let the frosts bite; they cannot chill the glow
> Lit by the memories of other years;
> Embers through which shines the far Syrian snow,
> Or Caucasus its conquered peaks uprears;
> Smoke wreaths that frame old friends – young faces too
> For old and young find guide and friend in you.

At home, within his great house, with its large gardens and woods, it was perfectly possible to live in distant proximity with his estranged wife without open disagreement. 'Remote' as Virginia had described their relationship, no one would have considered them ripe for separation. They agreed and cooperated over the planning of Wych Cross, on its contents and the continued acquisition of antiques and pictures, including, to celebrate their arrival, another Corot. One has the feeling he was trying to please her, and at the same time withdrawing for fear of rebuff – not an unusual situation. He had his responsibilities, both new and old; he had patched up his quarrel with the Royal Geographical Society, and had been honoured by them with their coveted Gold Medal. He had his friends, boring as some of them might have been to the rest of the family, for Garwood and Tucker were frequent visitors, as was Lord Bryce, a near neighbour and writer with many of the same interests as himself.

But Douglas had not given up his desire to climb, and still in his heart there lurked the urge to find some new place to open up and explore for himself. In the meantime there were many trips abroad to familiar and well-loved haunts, with now and again the opening up of new prospects in less familiar lands like Norway.

But there was one particular hope which he had by no means abandoned, which was that an expedition should approach the highest mountain in the world, as he had Kanchenjunga, and examine it with a potential climbing expedition in mind. It is not certain when he finally gave up the idea of leading such an expedition himself, but he had certainly had Dr Longstaff in mind as a possible companion, if not eventual leader for such a scheme. He continued to try every way possible to persuade the government of Nepal to lift their ban on foreign travellers just for this instance. But even with the influence wielded by his brother-in-law Richmond Ritchie, now the Political Secretary to the India Office; the good offices of Lord Curzon who had offered to fund part of the expenses; the support of the British Association and the Royal Geographical Society – all were to no avail.

It was possibly his very next attempt at a summit expedition in entirely new mountaineering regions that finally convinced him that his serious active days were over. For in the meantime, in 1905, he was invited to accompany a party of scientists and lecturers of the British Association on a tour of South Africa, the Rhodesias, Kenya, Uganda, Tanganyika and Portuguese East Africa, which would include their attending the official opening of the new railway bridge over the gorge below the Victoria Falls. At the same time he arranged with Arnold Mumm that they would meet after the official junketings were concluded, and together make a serious attempt to climb Ruwenzori, a mountain formation that had attracted his attention several times in the past, in particular in connection with Joseph Thomson's visit to the Kilimanjaro region at the time when Freshfield was Secretary of the Royal Geographical Society.

He had little enthusiasm for the journey, or at least that is the impression he gives when writing to Gussie. One gets the feeling that he was trying to make amends at last for the past desertions that she so resented, though they were few and far enough between; there were explorers who never displayed as he did such consideration for their domestic encumbrances. His last letter from Airlie Gardens to his wife at Wych Cross before his departure speaks of his depression in a way he would not have found it possible to do in direct speech. After telling of certain financial arrangements that he had made to take care of his expenses while away, and also incidentally arranging to pay £200 for a Watts they had decided to acquire, he added 'I am very low at going. I am getting too old and time is too short to leave what one cares for most. Long journeys are for the young, and one misses more than one gets.'

For long journeys he had always preferred rail travel. At sea he was sometimes sick, often bored, and disliked the chummy 'fun and games' atmosphere of long ship-bound life. But if he had to be at sea he preferred the weather to be cold, so that he could retreat quietly to his stateroom. At least this time, unlike in the Indian Ocean, the ship did not roll, and the temperature was never intolerable. All the same there is an air of flat resignation in his letters home during the voyage to Cape Town, from whence they intended to begin the long journey north overland, which is only relieved a little on arrival. 'Thursday 17th. August. I have today energetically climbed Table Mountain 3,600 feet. I had to do it as a party of the Cape Town Mountaineering Club had prepared the exercise for me. It is a wonderful little mountain and a hard rock climb all the way I had to go up, which (this for Bryce) is called the Table Face Rosete – the top is guarded by a range of cliffs, in many places tremendous precipices with fantastic crags, and of course, abundant vegetation; on the top the anemonies and fields of tall yellow daisies, in the gorges ferns and great shrubs.'

He left Cape Town after an official reception held in their honour, and dinner with the Governor, to travel overland to Durban, Ladysmith, and Pretoria, and then a foot trek to Bulawayo and Victoria Falls. The journey thus far was interesting to him as his first taste of African travel, and he seems to have stood up to the strain very well. On arrival at Bulawayo there was a gala reception. Part of a long letter which he wrote home describing the progress of the British Association gives an insight into the travelling and squabbling habits of the learned ladies and gentlemen. It is addressed from Mozambique Channel on 18 September. 'I only sent off some PCs. last week, for in the scrimmage at Bulawayo after our return from the falls it was not easy to write. Today the weary are at rest – some of the party have slept twelve nights running in the train, I five out of the last six, the last three in a compartment with Sir R. Jebb,[1] who bore up beau-

[1] Sir Richard Jebb (1841–1905). Another friend of Tennyson. Greek scholar and professor of ancient history, published his edition of Sophocles in 7 volumes, 1883–96.

tifully, almost to the last moment. You will know, or you might know, our general doings as *The Times* reporter tells me he sends off daily despatches. Our little excursion to the falls meant 560 miles by train; I have done 5,500 in all in Africa! We had two days there, they are wonderfully picturesque. One's first feeling is there is not a mass of water expected, but in time one realizes what a scale the whole thing is on. And when the river is high after the rains the falls themselves are said to be hardly visible through the spray. The Zambezi comes down a lake-like bed a mile broad and then goes over five chief falls into the cleft, the opposite bank is level with the top of the falls so that you see them magnificently, the surrounding forest is tropical. In the fierce noon we steamed over the new bridge in the first train (this was the opening ceremony), then went down into the gorge, then crossed to the island between the falls. Here Jebb and Lord Ross (sic)[1] were nearly upset, left to cling to a rock among crocodiles, there we found lunch laid out by Sir C. Metcalf on the bank. Then we marched through the rain forest where in the perpetual dew of the falls all sorts of ferns and flowers grow. Lastly I went to see the falls by full moon, where I encountered Mrs Hopkins who talked about her husband and how he was to have gone out with Rhodes, and discussed utilizing the force of the water. Then a most unquiet night in a room next a bar where the railway men were celebrating the completion of the bridge. Early next morning I secured a boat with three others and was paddled upstream five miles to a settlement – a delightful voyage. The Darwins[2] came up in another boat. In the afternoon we started back to Bulawayo.

'I have passed over our visit to Rhodes's grave. It is a most strange and impressive landscape, a labyrinth of low hills rising 500 to 1,000 feet above the rest of the country, grey and brown granite bluffs weathered into most fantastic shapes, isolated blocks of pinnacles. On top of a bare dome stand a dozen great boulders and in the centre is a plain slab over Rhodes's grave. An immense landscape of height and hollow spreads on all sides, the colouring is rich, the

---

[1] This must have been the 4th Earl of Rosse, Laurence Parsons (1840–1908), researcher into astrophysics. One cannot help remarking how some of the elderly distinguished failed to survive for long after this expedition.

[2] Sir George Darwin, at this time President of British Association. Son of Charles Darwin, he was chiefly known as a mathematician and astronomer.

foliage having an autumn tint. They say the funeral was a wonderful sight, people coming from all parts in a stream to pay homage to the Great Chief. One feels at every turn what a force he was, and also what an intelligence. Fifteen years ago the region we went through was an unknown savage wilderness – of course things are still very unfinished but what has been done in bad times, with the Boer War, cattle disease and horse sickness to fight against, is wonderful. Bulawayo and Salisbury have laid themselves out and built a considerable number of substantial houses and offices.

'Everywhere there have been official lunches and speeches and at Beric we found a magnificent banquet spread. After returning to the steamer for a much needed wash and change we assembled here and were refreshed by the choicest champagnes and a flow of eloquence from our "Ancient Allies" – the feast was on such a grand scale that it is presumed that the King of Portugal must have ordered it. The British Assn. returned on board quite hilarious and departed wildly cheering and cheered through Portuguese tugs and gunboats; this morning they are slumbering in deck chairs lulled by the ocean swell, and many are more or less ill ... Still it has been a most arduous journey for women and professors. I believe in the trains there have been grumbles and quarrels, but the circle in which my acquaintance with the Darwins and Jebb landed me has been very harmonious. Jebb talked beautifully until the last moment when he sighed "Our sorrows are over" and quarrelled violently with a waiter – I did my best to help him fasten up his things and get his meals. Darwin has got through his business efficiently, he is not exactly a sympathetic speaker and his tact is not infallible, he is not up to Jebb's standard, but that is a high one – I am afraid to write anything about our Professor, he makes his friends anxious! I have not made out any charming ladies beyond pretty Mrs Fox, though the photograph taken yesterday makes the party look quite smart and may make O. . . . (daughter Olivia) regretful. She will not be if she realizes the uneasy nights, and the morning struggle for one washing basin. I have kept quite well and one way and another got enough exercise to make me hope I shall be ready to cope with Arnold Mumm and his emergence from the Red Sea.'

He arrived at Entebbe a day or two before the appointed time for his meeting with Mumm, so he rode out to Kampala, the old capital of Uganda. He compared it with Rome because it stands on a number of hills, and reflected how in the old days when Royal Geographical explorers Burton and Speke were searching for the source of the Nile, it was the scene of so many atrocities under King Mwanga; with the royal wives so fat they could not stand and the endless executions at the King's whim. But now it was the residence of the old tyrant's grandson, a boy of thirteen, who had an English tutor 'to teach him lawn tennis and football, and to hack his subjects shins instead of cutting off their ears and noses. So quickly does the old order change in Darkest Africa.'

Mumm having arrived and all their arrangements completed, the party set out on their first long stage to the mountains, a 200 mile trek to Fort Portal. Douglas did not seem to have any qualms about setting out on such a trip at his age or, if he did so, he blamed it all on homesickness, and claimed that he was pretty fit and acclimatized, and anyway had been fortunate enough to hire a couple of mules to carry both himself and Mumm. And for a start all did go well; not even the lions that were said to make the route dangerous gave them any cause for alarm. It was rather one of their domestic animals that was the cause of the great misfortune. Freshfield described his plight in a letter from Fort Portal: 'The post goes off from here by runners eight days to Entebbe, tomorrow. But when will it reach London and will it find you in the middle of your Joachim whirl, when all else is forgotten? I am sending you a telegram at the same time which will prepare you for our return being delayed – in the wilds there is no certainty of travel and one depends on a dozen chances. I must let Mumm have his fair shot at the mountain which we are now face to face with. I am sitting in the verandah of the house of a local magistrate. He is away himself but we met him on the round and he has put his house at our disposal. We made our journey in a fortnight from the lake very easily, no hitches of any sort. We found a nice young South African to act as interpreter, and two mules and rode and walked at pleasure for the first week. Then my mule, which had been only too much of a sheep, suddenly made a very bad shy, and threw me heavily. I cut my cheek and got a severe bruise on the lips which was quite incapacitating for four days. After a day's rest I got carried on a litter (a common way of travel here) and now, the tenth day, I can walk three miles and am convalescent. The Doctor here says I shall be perfectly restored in a few days. Luckily I was very well at the time and had no feverishness or complications. But for the first twenty-four hours poor old Mumm was much frightened and wanted to take me home at once. I know K. and O. will say that this is only what I deserve for careless riding, but Mumm will bear me out, we neither of us had any reason to suspect our beasts of such diabolical tricks. There was no excuse whatever, not even a lion in the bush. One day I did count the prints of five lions within a mile, when walking in front one morning.'

It was as much as he dared tell about the accident, which was in fact a severe one for a man of his age; Mumm said afterwards that he was very concerned about his companion, not only at this, but at several later stages of their adventures.

Interesting as it was at the time, this was neither a successful nor a happy trip for Freshfield; one gets the feeling all the time that he was suppressing a strong desire to give up. Even the mountain that he had come so far to find left him unmoved; there are none of his grand, descriptive passages, merely the opinion that its appearance was more fascinating than sublime – and he liked his mountains to be sublime. It was a very poor substitute for the greatest Monarch of all, the Everest that he had fondly hoped would be the goal of his most important, and perhaps his last, expedition.

For all that, Fort Portal was situated in a remarkable position, on a spur of the mountain range itself, and only a few miles from a fine view from the escarpment over the valley of the western Nile. They stayed resting at Fort Portal for four days, using the time, for the most part, in questioning the local native chiefs and a missionary, Mr Maddox, about the slopes that lay ahead. Maddox, in particular, was useful as he had experience of both the paths and the climate, having himself climbed as high as the glaciers. They were assured that midwinter was one of the two dry seasons on Ruwenzori.

The problems that were to beset this ill-starred expedition started almost at once. Each day they were treated to a violent thunderstorm which made the twisting switchback paths slippery and difficult for the native porters. On the second day Freshfield and the alpine guide, who formed the advance party, crossed a swollen torrent and a mile or so further on sat down to await the others. No sooner had they done so than a storm of unusual violence broke, and Freshfield described himself and guide[1] as sitting under their umbrella like 'moist toadstools' waiting in misery for several hours. Eventually the remainder of the army arrived, and accounted for the delay with the further bad news that one of the porters had fallen into the torrent, losing his load, which consisted of vital climbing gear, their boots and rope. The latter had eventually been retrieved, but it was not a very encouraging start.

There was no time to make any further progress that night and the following day they were delayed still more, as most of the crossing places over the rivers were unusable because of the floods and they were forced to use ropes.

At the village, Bihunga, they dismissed their Entebbe carriers, who had proved themselves pretty inefficient. But there was doubt at first about their substitutes, for there were rumours that some of the tribes of the mountainous regions were still cannibals. But all was well, in spite of all the other difficulties that awaited them; at least they were spared hungry maneaters or lazy feckless followers. In this they were lucky, for one traveller had reported that he had been led to wander in circles through the bush, losing all his goods in the process.

The weather was determined to do all it could against them. It delayed their start, and when they did finally leave the village it was in pouring rain; in his written description of the climb he said gloomily at this point, 'Henceforth I only mention the weather when it is fine.' Mentioned or not, it was the weather, water and mud, that dominated the whole story. 'Mudlarking' he called it, but there was very little of the 'lark'. Their first camp was unfortunate, for, in spite of the deluge, there was no water available for cooking. The two men who were sent to find some were benighted, and spent the hours of darkness shivering in the bush, in terror of leopards.

'Next morning it still rained. Before long the path, hitherto fair, entered at once the upper glen and the bamboo zone, and became

---

[1] The guide was Moritz Inderbinnen of Zermatt, who looked after the damaged D.W.F. with great care throughout the difficult trek and climb, and to whom Freshfield paid tribute in the *Alpine Journal*.

execrable. Frequent halts had to be made while our men opened the track between the dripping stems of the bamboos. At each halt a fire was lighted, and we clustered round it, shabby Europeans and shivering natives, a sorry spectacle. The track got worse and worse – it was an alternation of almost perpendicular sodden banks and deep bogs. We either sank up to our knees and were held fast in black sludge or stumbled over stumps and stems.'

It is perhaps here on the dripping sides of Ruwenzori that we come closest to this man whose whole life is visible to us in his copious writings, both published and private, yet who so seldom revealed his humanity. We can see him, squatting on his haunches under an umbrella, staring at the misty prospect, the rain dripping from his wide-awake, from his grey moustache, seeping down his neck, and creeping into his stiffening bones. As always he was a stoic. But now, for the first time perhaps, he was full of regrets. There was the regret that he had left it too late; too late to make the kind of outstanding contribution to the knowledge of the mountain world he loved, as Conway or Longstaff had done; too late to be the first man to explore the close approaches to Everest. His serious exploring career had been too short in terms of actual time given over to it, but it was enough to sacrifice the happiness and understanding he shared with his wife. He wanted now to make it up with her, a sick woman whom he still admired and loved. His letters home are full of a poignant, understated appeal for sympathy, for some recognition that he was growing old and lonely and would like her encouragement at last. Janie sensed this for she, with her growing family, and the kind of domestic situation that neither her father nor her mother ever had to contend with, was perhaps closer to the realities of personal relationships than either of them, for all her mother's philosophical and emotional intellectualism. Janie had a strong sense that her father was underestimated at home, and the possibility that he had feelings was ignored. The letters her mother received touched and worried her. Douglas had already been given the honours that meant most to him and there were more to come. But this man, so confident in his familiar home surroundings, was vulnerable here, and Mumm too felt it, and worried as to the responsibility that it put on his shoulders.

But the mountaineer who had conquered the difficulties of Kanchenjunga was not going to give up, even though their camps were no refuge from the eternal damp and drip; their next was a crude rock shelter which oozed perpetually, and not even the cheerful blaze of a fire could cheer him. Poor Mumm's attempts at levity depressed him still more. The next day the effects of their height gain became apparent in the vegetation, for they were now over 11,000 feet, The flowers and trees took on a new and grotesque form, like nothing he had seen before in all his travels, except that here and there the familiar violets and blackberries seemed to have wandered in from another world.

The next serious obstacle was a forest of great trees that had all been uprooted by a hurricane and now represented a giant heap of spillikins: 'The logs are hard, slippery and covered with moss, which peels off under the boot. The actual soil lies six or eight feet below, and great care is needed to avoid the horrid pitfalls which gape at every other step, and threaten danger to limb if not to life.'

They purposely delayed over the next stage of the climb, taking a day to cover the ground that could perfectly well have been traversed in an hour, all in the hope that the weather might so far improve as to make their successful attempt on the mountain more likely. From their highest camp, Bujongolo at 12,500 feet, a position that was, if possible, still less comfortable or attractive than the last, Freshfield and his two climbing companions set out on a short survey expedition, to try to discern what might be ahead of them on the actual slopes of the mountain. For there was certainly nothing to keep them in the camp, where it was impossible to stroll a yard in any direction without getting into water up to the knees, or falling among hopeless entanglements of rocks and trees.

They pushed on up the rapidly narrowing glen, until they reached a level marshy piece of ground, The snout of the glacier came into view, thrusting downwards between rocky precipitous hillsides decorated with grey lichen draped tree-heaths that resembled the 'vegetable ghosts of a vanished world'. One and a half hours from camp they reached a level with the glacier, at about 13,000 feet, where they lit a small fire and ate their lunch, and discussed the advantages of establishing an advanced camp at this spot. The continual damp coupled with the effects of his fall from the mule two weeks previously were having their physical effects on Freshfield, and when the heavy rain clouds lifted temporarily and the others thought it best to push on a bit further up the glacier, he decided not to follow, having received their assurance that they intended nothing more than a reconnaissance. So he remained nursing the fire and 'contemplating the glacial sources of the Nile, which vindicated so triumphantly Ptolemy against his critics, and reflecting what a very odd corner of the world I had got to'. Because of the mist and cloudy conditions the true strangeness of the landscape was never revealed to the climbers while they were in the immediate proximity of the mountain. Perhaps if they had been Freshfield would have been able to write of it in more impressive terms. Only once, a day or two later, when they were already in full retreat were they vouchsafed a fleeting glimpse of what they had come so far to find and failed to conquer.

His companions returned to report that there was no very great difficulty ahead; the cliff that had stopped all previous explorers did not turn out to be so very formidable, and they had succeeded in reaching the top of the icefall with a certain amount of step cutting. There they had found themselves at the foot of a gently sloping snowfield, but mist and sleet prevented them from going further. There was little doubt that given a couple of days of good weather, there would have been nothing to stop them reaching their goal.

But good weather they were not to have, not even a couple of hours. At last, 'The continual gloom and damp affected our muscles and our morals; there was nothing dry in camp, and it was impossible to dry anything. When the order to retreat was given no one protested; we were almost glad of it.'

The return was rapid; and what had taken three days of arduous climbing, slipping back one pace in three, took them only one day to cover in reverse. And two days from their highest camp they had bidden farewell to their faithful hill porters, and had established themselves for a day of rest and recuperation in the open valley.

It seemed that they had left the mountain just in time, for the rainstorm that had followed their departure must have been worse than anything they had experienced, and many of the mountain torrents had become quite impassable. They were now camped by the Mubuku, which they were informed was usually an ordinary trout stream; but while they were there it 'came down in sudden spate, filling its channel from bank to bank, rearing in yellow waves six feet high against every obstacle, and tearing the tall reeds in bundles out of the shallows'. It was an impressive sight, but one to make them glad to be out of harm's way. It was from here that they had their only true sight of the mountain: 'On the following morning we were hastily summoned by the porters. When we came out of our tents we found them gazing with wonder at a most extraordinary sight. The sky was generally overcast, but low on the eastern horizon a narrow belt was clear. Into this belt the sun had just climbed over the hills of Ankole. The peaks of Ruwenzori were visible against a leaden vault. The sun's rays as they struck the snows, painted them not an "awful rose" but a deep blood red. The lower rocks and woods – this was an effect I have never seen elsewhere – were turned into a rich purple or strawberry colour. In the circumstances there seemed a demoniacal mockery in this farewell appearance of the mountain. In five minutes the spectacle was over and a curtain of mists speedily fell on the snows.'

But Freshfield's troubles were not yet over. Considering he had tackled the mountain while little more than convalescent from his fall, the way in which he had stood up to the strain of continual soakings and chillings was remarkable. He had always been impatient of physical limitations, and as he grew older the more pronounced this characteristic became. But this time even he had to admit defeat. Many others would have judged similar experiences as those which he suffered on the slopes of Ruwenzori at least with some measure of pride, But Freshfield always looked upon this episode with some shame as a major failure. The trouble was he was getting old, and would not admit it.

The next immediate stage was a source of pleasure. Wandering ahead of the caravan, a practice he always enjoyed for it gave him the opportunity of seeing the wild life undisturbed by chattering followers, he came upon a round lake where hippopotamus bathed, and almost every conceivable type of water fowl and bird was represented. To his great delight he was able to witness the almost legendary dance of the golden crested cranes. He was not a naturalist, and had few leanings in that direction; he knew the Darwins, father and sons, and had all his life subscribed to the evolutionary theory, but that was almost as far as it went. In all his books on travel and mountaineering there is scarcely a mention of fauna. He was in an area teeming with elephant and game of all kinds; he might have seen

gorilla on the mountain slopes had he looked out for them, but neither his letters nor articles pay any attention to them except to mention the abundant herds seen from the train. Of flora there is plenty,
mainly as adjunct to scenery. He would identify trees and plants that
grew at different altitudes. He loved the flowers that decorate the high
alpine meadows and he would use them to give intelligible descriptions of different regions. It is strange that in all his writings there is
hardly a mention of bears. There must have been times when he was
in close contact with them, for they were still abundant in parts of the
Alps and the Caucasus, but he does not mention even the possibility
of such an encounter. One reason for this may have been that he never
had any desire to become a sportsman. Going out after game, even for
the pot, did not appeal to him. At Kidbrook and Wych Cross his own
children, his sons-in-law and his wife's relations all made use of the
sporting facilities, and the two youngest girls as well as Edmund
Fisher hunted. But the necessary slaughter of the unfortunate yak
behind Kanchenjunga had filled him with disgust, as did the killing
and instant cooking of sheep in remote mountain regions. Now, here
on the shores of Lake Edward, in an area teeming with game, at a time
when most others would have desired to 'bag a trophy' as a memento
of the visit, the idea just did not enter his head. This lack of the sporting instinct may have been the reason for his fundamental lack of
interest in wild life; those who stalk game learn and understand their
ways, and through this will often develop a real interest in their study.
But here, with all kinds of natural life, human, bird and mammal, he
could hardly fail to have been moved. He noticed dark ladies bathing
in the waters of this crocodile-free lake (did his letter revive the old
worries at home?) who 'managed their blue gowns with at least as
much decorum as Parisians at a French seaside resort'. There were
pelicans, geese, and the dancing cranes; and if there were no lions, at
least there was the skull of a man, lying in the road, who had been
eaten a few days before, caught napping under a tree.

However his next letter home, despatched by runner to Entebbe,
retains some cheerful stoicism, for he was anxious not to cause
undue worries as to his condition – perhaps he was afraid of opposition to any further plans he might raise for the Himalayas: ' perpetual cloud and rainstorms made it impossible to get to the top. The
travellers who have been before us have never taken the trouble to

find out the right season ... The walking was detestable, the scenery weird, romantic, stupendous, the vegetation extraordinary, it made one look for pre-amite monsters; heaths feet high with lichens, trees like gigantic Brussels sprouts.'

'We saw the highest source of the Nile, coming, in a clear, little stream one could jump across, from the ice at 13,000 feet. We were four days going up, two coming down ... To venture on an unknown glacier in weather of this sort would have been foolhardy. If a party missed their way back and got into the wrong valley it would probably mean starvation, as the forest is practically impenetrable.'

He concludes: 'Mumm is bearing his disappointment well. He still dreams of shooting something large, but not a quadruped will venture near him ... I am looking forward to our return to civilization, African travel is far too slow for my liking. I want no more wilderness for ever and ever.'

They had been provided with an escort of two or three Nubian soldiers, for they were now about to enter into a region where certain tribes had been known to cause trouble. Only the previous year a District Collector had been 'speared through the heart while he sat reading in the verandah of a rest house'. Shortly after passing the skull of the man eaten by lions their escort arrested a man who was carrying a spear, contrary to the law. When, the next day, they found themselves in an attractive area of hills and hollows, lakes and dense vegetation, the prisoner made an attempt to escape. However, much to Freshfield's regret, as the prisoner made a dash into the thickets, he tripped and a pursuing Nubian was able to rearrest him.

But there was trouble ahead. Late that evening a party of villagers who were bringing food to Freshfield's porters, were attacked by the men of another village, and one of the carrier party was badly wounded. One Nubian, having a gun, was able to capture three of the attackers whose intention had apparently been to prevent the supplying of the white men. So alpine rope, which had been carried so far to no avail on the mountain, at last found a use as fetters for the prisoners. That afternoon they passed through a thunderstorm, which made them all nervous as the lightning struck the ground all around, and caused them to wonder what might be struck next.

That night was very uneasy. It was an unpleasant low spot, and their escorts did not improve matters by assuring them that the surrounding hilltops were thick with spearmen, invisibly keeping watch on their every move. Certainly when they began to break camp in the morning there were shouts from the bush, which were interpreted by the escort as meaning, 'The white men are starting'. It was possibly the men from the village to which their prisoners belonged were hoping for an opportunity to make a rescue bid. 'We were too strong a party to be assaulted in the open. Their only chance would have lain in a rush out of the copses that frequently overhung the zig-zags of the path. There was an opportunity, however, for a display of martial ardour; we kept close order, and Mumm, as commander-in-chief, bristled with cartridges.' But suddenly there was a short distraction, Ruwenzori revealed one glistening white spear, thrust upwards into the blue. Immediately ardour was turned from martial to photographic; hollow square was formed round Mumm, who carefully adjusted his camera – but alas the picture never came out.'

They had no more difficulties with the natives, which was just as well for Freshfield was becoming increasingly sick. All his life he had been impatient of illness or any incapacity caused by chance accident; he pitied others who so suffered but never for an instant considered any misfortune to himself. He would only notice that he was ill, or had been hurt, when it became sufficiently bad to impede his progress, and then it annoyed him intensely, which in turn gave his companions cause for worry. In middle age his short, shuffling steps carried him along at an extraordinary speed, many younger men found it hard to keep pace, and he seemed impervious to stubbed toes, twisted ankles, strains or bruises, or anything else that might affect a more cautious walker. A new generation of climbers, especially foreign, was finding its way up new paths in the Alps wearing special gear such as crampons; but Freshfield, coat tails flapping, sometimes with a bootlace undone, would rush past them, apparently unseeing, intent only on solving some scenic problem of his own. But the strain of his fall followed by the appaling conditions on Ruwenzori, had taken their toll at last, and on returning to Entebbe he collapsed, and was taken to hospital where he remained for two weeks.

He would not have mentioned this in his letters home, except that he was afraid that his emaciated appearance might frighten the family if he arrived without warning them.

CHAPTER 12

The comforts of his London home, his clubs and Wych Cross, and the familiar routines of his various honorary appointments must have been more welcome to him than ever before; there was no nostalgic dreaming of his wanderings in Africa as there had been after previous long journeys. It was his friend the Duke of the Abruzzi, who, the year after his own visit to the Ruwenzori mountains, did for them what Freshfield had hoped to do. As Freshfield wrote in the *Geographical Journal*: 'His Royal Highness the Duke of the Abruzzi, who has paid a visit to London since his return from Africa, has promised to offer a paper to the Society on his recent ascents on the Ruwenzori Range, of which he has made a complete conquest, having climbed the twelve highest snow peaks, which all stand in a close cluster within a radius of a few miles; none of these he tells me, exceeds 17,000 feet.'

He was quite ready, in this case, to grant the honours to another. The Duke presently arrived with his paper, but written in Italian. Although he could read it in English he did not feel competent to do the translation. Freshfield translated, and rewrote the lecture for him in a single day.

While slipping and stumbling amongst the treacherous tree roots and mud of Ruwenzori, Freshfield had nostalgically pictured to himself his wife in the midst of what he called her 'Joachim whirl'. It seems that in spite of her illness and pain her life was as full as ever; in fact while he was away in Africa she writes in her diary not of the blessed relief from pain but of the blessed relief of solitude after weeks and weeks of a full house. But the very next day it started to fill once more. As Virginia Stephen indicated, and Aunt Annie often mentioned, she was certainly a woman with a very special kind of

courage. In the morning she would wake in the silk-hung great bedroom at Wych Cross, where breakfast, papers and letters were
brought to her, as well as a half bottle of Champagne, which she
maintained was the only way to cope with the pain that would return
with waking, although the newly invented Aspirin was proving a
helpful alternative. On the day that Douglas's telegram had arrived
to say that he was at the foot of Ruwenzori she was dining with Lady
de la Ware and Rudyard Kipling, before returning to an evening dinner party of her own. Most of the great at whose feet she had sat as a
young woman were now dead, but she had, as it were, become a
channel not only for anecdotes to pass on to the young, who then, as
now, were not always much impressed, but also for criticism, based
on her wide reading and experience, of their developing talents.

Pinkie had now formed a lasting friendship, and had chosen to
live with Edith Sitchell, biographer of the period of the French Revolution and a poet. It was not unusual for an evening to include Pinkie
at the piano, and Janie singing perhaps one of Ralph Vaughan
Williams's new songs for the composer who had dedicated his song
Lynden Lee to Janie. Desmond MacCarthy would sit with her in the
cool of the evening in the summer house at the end of a terrace and
talk of his future and the novel he hoped to write. His mother had
been to see Gussie as she was worried about his future and his lack
of progress. Perhaps it was Gussie that set him on the path that
would eventually lead to his becoming one of the leading literary
critics of his day. Her dinner table lists are peppered with the names
of the new as well as the old generation of her family and their
friends. Leslie Stephen's two daughters, Hallam Tennyson, Lytton
Strachey, Edith Sitchell, Sydney Colvin, her favourite brother Richmond, with sometimes his wife Annie, a true link with the great past
– they came to talk, dance, or simply play dumb-cramb. Janie, with
the cool eye of the next generation and now a wife and mother, remi-
nisced years later on this period, saying that when they were young
they had met many famous people 'who seemed quite ordinary at the
time, and some of them were not very nice'.

Gussie did not suffer fools gladly, was terribly formidable to the
shy and intolerant of the gauche, but those who could hold their
own were sure of permanent interest and support. However her
affection seems to have been reserved for her own family and the

increasing number of nephews and nieces, and the descendants of the old friends of her youth.

There was a growing number of grandchildren too, with whom she could be stern when behaviour got out of hand, but at the same time there were special evenings when they were brought down to the library or to sit on her bed while she read to them. When they were small a special favourite was the 'Dicky' Doyle Fairy Book, written and illustrated by Doyle when she had known him many years before when her own children were small. There were the golliwog books, old rhymes illustrated by Cruikshank, and of course Kate Greenaway. As soon as they were old enough there were tears to be shed over the opening chapters of David Copperfield.

'Remote' as she and Douglas seemed to be from one another, there were still civilized shared interests. There was no question of separation in those days, and no need for it in their circumstances. There were no arguments, just ways that had parted, and there was plenty of room for that in their great houses. If deep in his heart he felt that his chances of becoming one of the great explorers of all time had been spoiled by insistence on domestic priorities, neither did she openly blame him for the death of their son brought about by their absence following his desire to travel. But they would still share a sunset from the windows at Wych Cross, and he would still buy for her whatever pictures she expressed a longing to own.

Douglas's arrival home just after Christmas was followed by a round of dinner parties, chiefly concerned with the election to Parliament of Herbert Paul, married to her younger sister Nelly (Eleanor). Gussie was so disgusted with Paul's speeches she would not have him sit at her end of the table, and sat with George Trevelyan and Clough-Williams-Ellis.[1]

As the almond blossom at Wych Cross was bravely opening against the winter sleet, Douglas and Augusta set off for Italy to rest and recover in sunshine, for he had suffered a return of the fever just as the doctor in Entebbe had predicted. As usual the organization of the trip was perfect, for, whatever the reason for travelling, he delighted in arranging every connection and night's stay to follow

---

[1] Clough-Williams-Ellis – architect, best known for his romantic village Port Merion, N. Wales.

with a smoothness that was belied by the crossing on this occasion: 'an awful crossing', wrote Gussie, '– groaning and convulsed ladies who were told by the exasperated stewardess they MUST use their basins at once, as she had not enough for all.'

And in a few days they were renewing acquaintance with their favourite city, for she had revised her opinion of Rome since the days of their honeymoon: 'Yesterday we woke up in Frascati to a sky swept clean of every cloud by a cold tramontana, the snow (which in Italy is golden not white) thick on Mnte. Sinnaro. We drove off in our two little carriages to the most poetical and most decayed of all the great Villas – the Torlonia. Noble effects of light under the huge ilexes, on the green terraces, on the rivers of clear water pouring over the mossy stone cups into wider and wider basins. The size and the design of all these Roman things strike one more and more, whether the avenues of ilexes or the flights of steps or the arches of the basilicas or the figures on the roof of the Sistine. The drive past the magnificent Aldo Brandini facade through the stately little town of Frascati to the great Mandrazone was pure rapture. The ground is covered with shining purple anemones under the olives and the stone pines on the way, but flowers are almost a superfluous detail in the glory of the whole. The view from Mandrazone is magnificent indeed; Rome a pink patch on the pale blues and greens of the Campagna, St Peter's a white bubble in the morning light – still finer in the afternoon when it is dark with the light behind it. The little boys of the best families in Rome play about under the care of the Jesuit Fathers. We drove to Albano, Annicca Nemi in the afternoon – our old haunts not much changed or spoilt. Only the lovely arched gate of Albano through which the mules and oxen and country people streamed with the miles of view behind them, has been done away with for the tramcars. The new museum and all the statue museums are an immense enjoyment with the guidance of the German book, which at last makes one grasp the different styles and periods. Plydytus and Lsippus, Scippius, Praxitiles ...'

From Rome they went to Florence, from Florence back to Paris and home, bearing in triumph a new Corot for the gallery at Wych Cross, 'Fontainbleu – Chateaux and Pond'.

But Augusta's health was deteriorating, and in the autumn she was advised, after their return from a stay in Scotland, that she must undergo a further operation for cancer. They spent the worst of the winter of 1907 in the south of France, but she was suffering a good deal, her arm giving her sleepless nights. They returned to Wych Cross in April – she was glad to be back: 'April 26th. Pitch dark. Pouring rain. Went home nevertheless to Wych Cross. Comfort to get out of murky smoke fog, but rain went on for the rest of the day. Young trees, larch and birch exquisite as we drove up in smelly old brougham. Carriage drive exciting with blossom. Found house full of flowers – schizanthus, pink and purple cineraria, stallata, gardenias in full supply, three gorgeous malmaisons in my room, last of the lilies of the valley, Empress daffodils, red amaryllis ... Enjoyed the cherry trees, red pyrus, japonica and judas tree, all my own planting, all in lovely blossom.'

That year Douglas took his last solitary ramble through mountains for some time, visiting the Dinaric Alps, exploring the mountains of Dante, collecting material for an article, but his own inclinations for the present kept him increasingly at home, content, geographically at least, to work in the shadows. On his return from Africa he had written his customary articles for the Alpine Club and the Royal Geographical Society, as well as a further article for the latter on the subject of the frontier line between Uganda and the Congo. His lectures to the British Association had begun to attract a certain amount of attention when they were published overseas, and one in particular, 'On Mountains and Mankind', was republished in America by the Smithsonian Institute, which resulted in his being invited to the United States and Canada, an invitation which he postponed for the time being. Many of his earlier climbing companions and some of his rivals were now dead, Moor had died as long ago as 1887, but Tucker was still very much in evidence. Douglas remained faithful, while Gussie was unable to restrain her comments. 'There has taken place a great emptying of the house by the 10.15 ... finally Douglas and Mr Tucker who Douglas rather unluckily captured for that dreadful Pageant Masque on Saturday. Well poor Mr Tucker, always a bore has now become a perfect phenomenon – or rather the archetype of the bore who always empties rooms – who brings on illness of exhaustion and impatience. The first evening the exuberance of the Masque attenders succeeded in talking him down, but last night no one stood up to him. Dear

Gerald went off to bed at 9! Arthur to sleep on the sofa, Douglas to his book, and the ladies were left listening to the recital of the last Niebelungin Legend, mistakenly not used by Wagner! However it was only at meals and in the evening that he was allowed to appear at all.'

In the late winter of 1908 they visited Florence once again. Gussie's pain was more frequent and alarming, but she kept up with all the normal round of family life. When pressed not to put too great a strain on herself she merely said that so long as she could help it she did not want to be 'entirely laid by'. She had earlier told Eleanor that all her life she had regarded illness in herself as a definite progression, something you came through stage by stage and then got well again, but ever since her operation in 1907 she knew that this was not what was going to happen.

So one evening in December 1910, as she went up to bed in Airlie Gardens, having entertained friends to dinner she said to herself 'Now no more. I am too ill'. A few days later she was driven down to Wych Cross in the motor that they had recently acquired. She went directly to her bed and never came downstairs again, nor did Eleanor ever leave her side.

But it was not quite the end. Though the pain dulled her senses the mind's activity seemed as vital as ever. Every evening after tea her three eldest grandchildren came to her room to be read to by their Aunt Eleanor; lying about her bed, eating the special treats of the sickroom, they shared amongst other thrills, Dr Jekyll and Mr Hyde.

In the middle of February there seemed to be a turn for the better. The pain in the arm grew fiercer and fiercer by night and by day, though the doctors said they could find no trace of actual disease. Still she managed to read Arthur Clough's friend Walter Raleigh's[1] book on Johnson, Madam Bovary for the third time with increasing admiration, Aylmer Maude's *Tolstoi* and Stevenson's letters, which she liked so much that she dreaded coming to their end.

But the respite was short, and the remaining weeks were an agony for her and those who looked after her. She was in terror of losing control of herself, and believed at each stage that if the next was

---

[1] Sir Walter Raleigh 1861–1922. Author and lecturer in English Literature – fellow of Merton etc.

worse it would be unbearable; but always she had to return to the task of making her suffering bearable to the others. When at last at the end of April she was told that her illness was indeed mortal her spirits rose, knowing that there would soon be an end to the weariness of the pain. There was one terrible moment, when the Victorian manner of dealing with death, generally more open and acceptable than that of later generations, went too far. Her eldest grandson, but ten years old, back from school, was taken to say a final goodbye to her, and she told him that she would soon be dead, and that she was happy to go. For a ten-year-old this was a devastating piece of news, and he maintained that the horror of it never left him for the rest of his life.

As the flowers of spring burst into life around the great house, she died. All through the long illness Eleanor kept copious notes of her mother's visitors, her sayings, and her medical treatment. The comings and goings to and from the sickroom are all there, but there is no mention of her father. Eleanor's guardianship of her mother, and her possessiveness were plain to see, but it must have been that she did not care to mention her father's contacts with his wife, rather than that he never came, or was not wanted.

He had allowed his desire to travel far afield to be restricted over a good many years by her dislike of being left during the earlier years of their marriage, and she made sure that his conscience was unquiet when he was already far away. Once, many years before, while he was working on 'Murray' and they were staying in Devon, he wrote:

'Sunday morning Turin.

My Dearest. I got last night, late, your dejected note of Wednesday. It is no use going back a week, and I have torn up my first answer. I am sure that by the time that this gets to Woodey Bay you will have entered into a new phase. I fear that it is Blanche's slow recovery that has brought you all so low. Your account is certainly most dismal, and your rheumatism makes me unhappy – why do you always suffer from damp directly I cross the Channel? Is it a reckless indulgence in drafts when the check of my chilliness is removed? Has sea bathing become impossible? The Woodey Bay of your description does not seem the same place that I left ten days ago. I trust it has reverted to its former and better state. It may console you that the sky is clouded again this morning ... But I wish

I could have gone on thinking of you and the children enjoying your-
selves, instead of in such a poor plight.'

Throughout their engagement the love letters had flown to and fro
like little birds. It was time for a realization of a great romance in her
life, living in the environment she did – the elopement of the Brownings exactly fitted the romantic ideals of the young inexperienced
girls of Victorian England. Her ideal was not, in the end sustained;
he believed his was, or could have been.

But now it was all over; they would not share any more sunsets
together, and in many respects Wych Cross was to lose its generative
power. The only comment Douglas is recorded as having made was
that he had no desire to grow old, and he hoped he would soon
follow her. They piled the bed with her favourite Florentine irises, so
that the fresh, waxy flowers filled the room with their scent, and the
children made posies of primroses, and once again the whole family
found themselves standing inside the wrought iron fence under the
pines of Brookwood. Now was added the deeply carved sarcophagus of Carrara marble, to the centre of the square before the memorial to her son.

All his life Douglas enjoyed the company of women who were
intelligent, especially if they were beautiful as well. Gussie had been
beautiful, was intelligent and courageous, and by Douglas's actions
if not by his words we know that he loved her. It was a great pity that
the affection that she was able to inspire from others towards herself
did not enable her to give her husband the love he craved.

Aunt Annie, now Lady Ritchie, wrote from beloved Freshwater to
Pinkie: 'I am glad you wrote. Last night in my dreams I was crying
and crying about death. Now that I am awake, I wonder what I cried
for and why I minded so much, and now here is the daylight and the
green fields and the sea from my window, and the wind-blown
Freshwater trees. I keep saying to myself about death what the Lieutenant on board the Titanic said, "It doesn't matter very much."
Thank God we have lived – and lived about the same time. But my
heart aches for you and for all of them.'

Douglas went abroad. He visited Canada and the United States,
fulfilling the engagements he had postponed a year or two previously, but wandering alone through the Rockies. A snap-shot taken
of him, with his battered portmanteau and famous cut-away coat,

standing on the railway lines of some Canadian outpost, has about it a touch of pathos in the circumstances. But he was equipped to deal with solitude, and he was not a man ever to be distracted by considerations of self.

The next year, 1912, he went no further than the Pyrenees, enjoying their small scale as he had enjoyed the larger scale of Canada; he wrote to Keltie: 'One can be content with mountain architecture without spires and towers, only gables.'

But he had not yet admitted defeat in the sphere of large scale mountain exploration. At the age of sixty-eight he started to plan and make arrangements to carry out an expedition into the unknown mountainous regions of Chinese Turkestan. It was probably fortunate that the Great War was to intervene and he was forced to abandon the idea. But having set the planning of the expedition in motion, he set off on his travels once again. This time he crossed Siberia by the famous new railway, visited China, and then crossed to Japan. On the Trans-Siberian Railway he met by chance Mrs Carruthers (Miss Markham) and they formed a friendship that was to endure, to their mutual comfort and the dismay of Eleanor, until his death.

His powers as a mountaineer may have begun to fade, but he was still an extremely formidable walker, something he proved conclusively on a three day tramp into the Japanese Alps. He was only prevented from attempting to climb to the peaks by the lateness of the season, and in fact a party of British naval officers had found the higher slopes impossible because of the ice. After his walk he wrote for the *Alpine Journal*: 'My plan was to cross from Shimashima the Tokugo-toge (Toge – pass) to the headwaters of the Adzusa-gawa, and then descend through its long gorges in two days, returning to the same spot.'

He made up a small party for the expedition, which included Eric de Bunsen of the British Consular Service, a Japanese courier, and a small band of porters. But on waking in their comfortable little inn on the morning they were due to start, it looked as though they were to have the kind of luck that had dogged him on Kanchenjunga and Ruwenzori, for a tremendous rain-storm was raging. He described the walk in *Below The Snowline*:

'We waited till 9 o'clock and then, encouraged by our porters, braved the weather. We had the reward we deserved; after a time the rain subsided, grew intermittent and finally left off. Nothing could have been more beautiful than the first part of the walk. It was early in November. The well-made modern path gave us leisure to use our eyes. The precipitous walls of the gorge afforded a feast of the most brilliant autumn colours, reds and yellows. Firs stood out upon the crags with a regard for artistic effect they show only in Japan and Italy. Every corner displayed a vignette that surpassed the last.'

His freshness of approach continued. He still managed to see each new scene in isolation, and appreciated its specialness, unlike other well-travelled writers of the time who were more inclined to compare the view of the moment with the memory of grander scenes. His simple pleasure in natural mountain country never deserted him, whether in the familiar Alps or the magnificent peaks of the New World. They climbed a 7,000 foot pass that day, and spent the night, after an eight hour walk, in an isolated wooden inn, that was not unlike a Swiss chalet, but where they were expected to provide their own provisions. In the morning they set off over frost covered ground and plunged into the steep-twisting gorge. The nearness of snow peaks was a great temptation, but Freshfield had to be content with the chosen path. One evening he met with an acquaintance, the Reverend Walter Weston, and apparently on this occasion Freshfield most untypically laid bare his heart. More than twenty years later when Douglas Freshfield lay dying, Weston wrote to Katherine, 'for I long had a deep regard for him as I have had the privilege of becoming growingly intimate with him. I shall always cherish all he told me of his deepest personal sorrows one night when we were alone together in a secluded Japanese inn in the mountains – an unexpected self-revelation which I should have almost suspected would be nearly impossible'. It may be he had talked of his lost son, who was surely still often in his mind, for in 1914 he published a sonnet which shows surer touch than the earlier poem.

> The May returns, but He returns no more;
> The sylvan choristers from over-sea
> Find their old chauntries in each hedge and tree;
> For us no voice rings through the open door;
> The slow sad waves that sob along the shore,
> The cliffs, the downs, the copses whisper: 'He
> Returns no more, whom best we loved to see,

Has gone from hence, gone home for evermore.'
What if this World to that for which we yearn,
Some larger life that lies beyond the tomb,
Be but the pictured page that children turn
'Shadowing great histories in little room,'
And souls too bright to dwell with shadows here
Must onward, where realities appear?

But happily there were a number of sights which attracted him while in Japan. One night on their walk they were housed in a comfortable bath house, and enjoyed the comforts of a 'social bath'. Afterwards while sitting on the step lacing his boots he was intrigued by the sight of 'three damsels' watching him 'with the innocence and the costume of Eden'.

Back in Tokyo he found himself the guest of the Japanese Alpine Club at a romantic dinner looking out on a moonlit river, and he was asked by them to carry greetings to the parent club. 'The viands were choice and rare, the speeches models of brevity. May I venture to quote that in which my own health was proposed: "One has come down to us from 20,000 feet, but the love of Beauty and Pure Colour will soon carry back the mountaineer to his own sphere."'

During the time between the death of Gussie and the outbreak of war, those who were close to Douglas noticed a change taking place. Almost slyly, just peeping out, a new charm was daring to show itself. There was a softening and a broadening of his attitudes, and a more apparent kindness and tolerance, and a kinder humour. The Ritchie women and their friends with whom he had so long associated were sharp, witty, intelligent and perhaps a little condescending, but intelligent good looking women certainly attracted him and called forth his kindness. His favourites, sisters-in-law Pinkie and Nellie, Mrs Carruthers and later Violet Needham were often his companions as he drove around Wych Cross. Old associates noticed what they had always suspected, as did Arthur Clough and many others who came to discuss matters concerned with geography, mountaineering or business.

During this time he brought his thinking on the old teaser of Hannibal's pass up to date, and prepared a book on the subject; he translated into English verse some Greek poems, and published his own collected poems in 'Unto The Hills', something which perhaps he might not have done had Gussie still been alive, as she would not, possibly rightly, have placed them in a high literary category, but they gave his friends much pleasure at the time.

Now at nearly seventy years of age, what more was there he could do for mountain geography? There was still the projected visit to the mountains of Chinese Turkestan. As he said in his address to the British Association: 'For fifty years I have loved and at frequent intervals wandered in the Alps. I have had something of a grand passion for the Caucasus. I am on terms of visiting acquaintance with the Pyrenees and the Himalayas, the Apennines and the Algerian Atlas, the mountains of Greece, Syria, Corsica, and Norway.' So what more could there be? Mountain literature of the old kind to which he had been such a great contributor was in danger of becoming a bore. In the same lecture he hinted at this: 'What boulders, or rather pebbles, can we add to the enormous moraine of modern alpine literature – a moraine the lighter portions of which it is hoped for the sake of posterity, that the torrent of time make away with.'

But already he had started a major project, he wanted to write a full life of the father of all mountaineering, Horace Benedict de Saussure (1740–99) and to this end he was already in correspondence with H. F. Montagnier in Switzerland; but the war came and with it a more demanding task.

CHAPTER 13

Over twenty years after he had given up effective office in the Royal Geographical Society, and had relinquished the post as Honorary Secretary, which had enabled him to move the Society forward into a more progressive stance, he was called upon once again to exert his influence over its affairs. The Battle of the Ladies was now over, and as Vice President Douglas Freshfield had witnessed the complete triumph of his views; not before time, when the President, none other than Curzon himself was placed in the embarrassing position of having to welcome the first lady fellows.

His taking office as President in 1914 was not the first time that he had taken the chair at a General Meeting of the Society. There was a tragic occasion when the news was brought to the Headquarters of the Royal Geographical Society of the deaths of Scott and his companions in the Antarctic. Curzon was away ill, and, at the request of the Council members, Freshfield took the chair at the General Meeting that followed, gave details of the telegram and made a most moving speech, at the conclusion of which the meeting broke up.

It was to be a great personal disappointment to him that his taking office as President should coincide with the outbreak of the First World War. There were two particular ambitions that he would have liked to have seen come to fruition during the period that he was in office, and which had to be postponed until later. In the first place there was the Society's new building, for which Edmund Fisher had already drawn up plans; second, and above all, there was his desire to see a full scale exploratory expedition in the Everest area – though at last he had recognized that he would not lead such a project himself. But by the time the war was over Fisher was dead and Fresh-field's Presidency was passed – for no man holds the office, by custom, for more than three years.

During the war Freshfield moved to London so that he could give the Royal Geographical Society his daily attention, for many demands were placed upon the Society and its staff by the fighting services. Since his wife's death his two youngest daughters had centred their lives on Wych Cross, particularly the youngest, Kather-ine, who was keen on hunting and was involved in local country pursuits. Olivier was the more politically minded and was in revolt against the lifestyle of her parents and was becoming more and more involved with charitable work in the East End of London. Under the management of Katherine, Wych Cross was converted into a hospi-tal for the wounded and convalescent from the front and Katherine herself trained for the V.A.D. and soon found herself behind the lines in France at an advanced dressing station, as was her brother-in-law, Edmund Fisher, who had volunteered as a medical orderly.

In a war that in all its aspects covered such a large area it was essential that the Headquarters of the Royal Geographical Society, with its Map Room and archives, should be at the disposal of the War Office, and it was fitting that someone with Freshfield's experi-ence and dedication should fulfil the office he did at the time. Apart from deciding to continue, as far as possible, the instructive activi-ties and publications of the Society, which he considered even more important in war time, he had placed the whole resources of the Society at the disposal of the Admiralty and the War Office, both of which made continual demands upon its services. Freshfield's orga-nizing ability and steadiness were of great assistance to the hard pressed staff. Under his guidance the 1/million map of the world, which the Society was preparing for the War Office, was pressed forward – every detail, even to printing and colouring, came under his scrutiny. Accelerated by the war, new information about all kinds of features of the globe were being sent in to the Society's headquarters, where it would be checked and recorded. Papers were still being read, to much diminished audiences it is true, and some-times under difficulties. There was one occasion when General Smuts was due to give a lecture and there came an air-raid warning, and although the lecture was given, some of the Fellows remained in a shelter, including Freshfield's old friend and confidant, Sir John Keltie. This incident gave Freshfield an opportunity for a few moments relaxed fun:

> Sir John, dark things have come to light,
>   If I am told the story rightly,
> Your conduct on last Monday night
>   Fell somewhat short of being knightly.
>
> The legend runs around the Town
>   That you and sundry other Fellows
> Were found at a late hour down
>   In Oddenino's deepest cellars.
>
> We all have read of one Sir John,
>   Who mostly spent his life in taverns;
> His record you improve upon
>   Lurking in subterranean caverns.
>
> For boon companions underground,
>   While shrapnel out of doors grew hotter
> And German airships hovered round,
>   You had our worthy friend Coutts-Trotter.
>
> And someone adds – I fear it's true -
>   A tale that hardly bears repeating;
> Yates Thompson too was there with you,
>   While his brave wife was at the meeting!

And their shelter was the Oddeninos' restaurant.

This light digression apart, Freshfield's pen was fully occupied in giving the kind of service for which he was particularly qualified because of his wide personal and detailed experience of odd corners of the world, particularly of the mountainous regions of the southern frontiers of Austria.

In his final address to the Society as its President, at the Anniversary meeting of 21 May 1917 he spoke of some of the hopes and aspirations for which he had strived throughout his life. Television was still undreamed of, but it is interesting how he seems to forecast the nature and travel documentaries that have become such a feature of the small screen. He started with a summary of the exploratory activities that had been in progress when he took office, and some of

Douglas William Freshfield, President of the Royal Geographical Society

the lessons that might be learned from them, and then moved on to a summary of the many and varied tasks upon which the Society was currently engaged, and the more interesting lectures and discussions they had held. Then he came to one of his favourite subjects – geographical education. Edmund Fisher's brother, H. A. L. Fisher had just been appointed Minister of Education: 'Another branch of our activity in which progress has been hampered by the war is education. In the universities the students have gone; the men to the wars, the women to the farms. The national mind has been too much occupied for any serious reforms to be brought into practice in the schools. But if men's minds have been occupied, they have also been stirred, and there is a movement in the higher circles of education and even in Parliament which should tend both towards broader principles and to improvements in working. The appointment of a Minister of Education who brings to his task not only Oxford traditions but intimate acquaintance with a great working centre, Sheffield, raises hopes in many quarters. I learn with much satisfaction of one contemplated step in the right direction. In the new scheme under consideration for Civil Service examinations, it is proposed to assign a very much larger proportion of the possible marks to geography. Geography is the knowledge of the world we live in, and must be taught, as Lord Bryce recently put it, as a link between the natural sciences and the humanities. The physical facts of geography must be treated not only in themselves, but as elements in human history, politics, and commerce.

'I can even conceive in the future the Society sending forth distinguished travellers, or authorized educational lecturers, with sets of cinematographic views, showing for instance, not only the icebergs and seals of the Antarctic, but a camel caravan passing through the Great Wall of China, or the procession of the Holy Carpet travelling across the Arabian desert on its way to Mecca. The minds of our future fellow citizens want stirring; they need to have the wonders of the world and its capabilities for human effort and human happiness brought home to them. They want, not long queer words, but lessons which leave behind them pictures of objects which though beyond their parochial surroundings may nevertheless affect their future from many aspects. We must begin young and not stop too early. Our education has failed to civilize in the sense of making men fit for citizenship of a world empire. It has stopped short at a critical moment in the youthful mind. It has tended to dwarf any natural shrewdness of observation and put little in its place but a desultory interest in the lower forms of literature, or the horrors and crimes of the Sunday newspapers.'

It seems that in spite of advances in teaching technology we have not advanced as he would have hoped. In his speech he went on to describe how the Society began as a dining club where travellers could meet and swap stories, but soon grew into a somewhat small select body that in turn gave way to its proper scientific role, concentrating on the nature and structure of the globe and the interaction between man and nature.

The Royal Society, the Royal Geographical Society, The British Association: how often it was that gifted and not so gifted amateurs contributed to the great explosion of knowledge of the physical world that took place in the nineteenth century, rather than the Universities, where the classics, the law and theology remained the obsession for so long.

Douglas Freshfield disliked personal publicity and self-advertisement, and for this reason he was almost unknown outside his own chosen circles, yet his friendship and opinions were sought long after his retirement. Ronald Clark in his *Victorian Mountaineers* describes him as a grim and palisaded figure, but this was not so, as all those who approached him found.[1] In fact there are many descriptions of his courteous attention when his opinion was sought by some young explorer seeking advice and information. He was honoured too by geographical bodies all over the world; ironically, some of them attached his name to newly discovered peaks and glaciers. The Royal Geographical Society made him a trustee in 1924.

When the war was over Airlie Gardens was disposed of (as was Dimbola which had been let since the family had ceased to visit), and from then on Freshfield used the Athenaeum when in London. Wych Cross Place was returned to him, and once again, under the supervision of Katherine, was refurbished in its old role. Katherine had

---

[1] Some of his contemporaries would have agreed with Clark. There is a startling description of D.W.F. during his time as Hon. Sec. of the R.G.S. by one of his most adamant opponents, telling of the curious shape of his head, wide at the top with diminutive chin and glaring eyes with apparent humourless ferocity.

inherited her father's qualities of indifference to personal discomfort as well as his organizing ability. In France she had been running an advanced dressing station, and during an enemy attack the place had been heavily shelled. She had managed to get all her wounded charges under their beds to protect them from falling masonry, when the building collapsed, severely damaging her head to the extent that she suffered from bad headaches for the rest of her life. Her fiancé had been killed and somehow after the war, when Wych Cross had been restored, she found herself drifting into becoming housekeeper and manager of Wych Cross and the estates. This was not entirely to her taste, for she saw how much the world had changed, and the organization and richness that still continued, even on a lesser scale, now that they were back in the great house, irritated her as wasteful extravagance. She was given to occasional outbursts of temper towards her sisters and what she regarded as their over-cosseted lives. Even Eleanor admitted to feeling shame after one such outburst when they all received a tremendous 'drubbing' at the lunch table. This did not apply to Olivier, however, who had started her own home for orphaned and deprived children in London and devoted her life to this often thankless task. But her father supported the home privately, and the kitchen gardens supplied fresh vegetables and fruit.

There was an amusing sequel to the wartime activities of the family. Freshfield was asked if he would accept a knighthood in recognition of his services to the country in allowing his house to be taken and used by the Red Cross. He refused, saying that had they wished to honour him for his services to geography, he would have accepted, but the loan of Wych Cross had been his daughter's idea, and he had left to her all the work of carrying it through.

But retirement did not mean stagnation for Freshfield. His collaboration with Montagnier on the subject of the Genoese professor de Saussure was resumed. H. F. Montagnier was an American who had long been resident in Switzerland, was an experienced climber and as Freshfield says 'was an accomplished student of the literature of mountain travel'. Freshfield had contacted him before 1914 and he industriously spent the intervening war years on the latter's behalf searching family and private collections for material. He was very successful, and was able to present Freshfield with a mass of neatly organized sources when their contact was resumed. In 1920 the *Life of de Saussure* was published by Edward Arnold in English, and then, in 1924, in French. Freshfield had personally covered all the tracks of de Saussure and had taken an equal interest in the scientific activities of this pioneer from the eighteenth century, and this, as well as his own skills as a writer of mountain travel, made him possibly the most qualified to undertake such a task. The completed biography was a new summit which he climbed successfully and which earned him a doctorate from the University of Geneva, an honour he very much prized.

Where de Saussure had trod Freshfield followed and went further. Freshfield looked for views and geography, De Saussure was exploring the geology and formation of the mountains which his Genoese neighbours had ignored. He was a much respected teacher and lecturer at his University, and a writer on natural philosophy who was well known in Paris and in England, where he addressed the Royal Society, as well as the great universities of Europe. In England he had toured with his wife which, apart from the sea crossing, had been a great success, and he was welcomed in many of the great houses. The main difference between the lives of the two men was de Saussure's close involvement in the politics of the independent State of Geneva. Both he and his popular, intelligent wife were wealthy, owning a very substantial town house, and a pretty farm outside the city. But by 1790 the infectious unrest that was stirring in Paris was inevitably spreading to complacent and wealthy Geneva. De Saussure strived with his friends through the existing institutions of the government to preserve peace and order and satisfy the increasing demands of the populace. For some time the great respect in which he was held, combined with his persuasive oratory and energy, kept the situation in check, but as in Paris, to no avail. He and his wife, whose fortunes were mainly invested in Paris, lost almost all, and only avoided real poverty through a loan from a friend. At one time the family were in danger of their lives, but in spite of a number of executions the situation never by any means equalled that of the Paris 'Terror'. Their situation was not restored by the time of his death, but Madame de Saussure regained some of her fortune after Geneva acquired the independence from France which the revolution had stolen. The couple were openly devoted and supportive of one another throughout their lives in spite of all their troubles, including his long final illness. One is reminded in one respect of Douglas and Gussie in that Madame de Saussure disliked being left when her husband departed on his mountain expeditions. On one occasion at least he was so upset by the thought of her tears at his departure that he slipped away without a farewell. But she soon recovered and her subsequent letters to him continued to overflow with her concerns for his safety and news from home.

It is hardly the business of this biography to attempt a full review of Freshfield's *Life of de Saussure*. Students of mountain literature must be well aware of it already. It is enough to say that it remains today as the crown of his achievements as a writer and a lasting tribute not only to de Saussure but also to the book's septuagenarian creator.

He was now serving as a Justice of the Peace, and continued the work which his father had started as Chairman of the Conservators of Ashdown Forest. For a time he was Chairman of the Committee of the Society of Authors, was active within the C.O.S. and was treasurer of the Hellenic Society. But his first love was also his last. At the formation of the Everest Committee he was invited to attend, and continued to do so almost to the end of his life, as a consultant member. It was Freshfield, who at the Alpine Club's Jubilee Dinner in 1907, had made the prediction that 'The Company who dines here fifty years hence, will include the conqueror of Everest' and every facet of those early expeditions drew his attention and sometimes his comment. His devotion to the British Empire was Victorian and Kiplingesque, and he saw in its future a great hope for the world, and therefore it was only fitting that Englishmen should achieve its highest summit. After the fatal expedition of 1924 he wrote an epitaph to Mallory and Irvine on the flyleaf of his own copy of his book of published poems:

> Climbing in air too thin for mortal breath
> These men stood poised on the world's parapet:
> Watched by the stars on the last height they met,
> Content in Victory, the Kiss of Death.

Now, with old age, he increasingly preferred old and tried friendships. Young mountaineers of a new generation and school would come, sometimes from the other side of the world, often bearing letters of introduction, only to find that arrival at the Alpine Club or at the Royal Geographical Society did not necessarily mean that they got the coveted invitation to Wych Cross. Sometimes his family, knowing of a request for an interview perhaps from American visitors, would combine and prevail upon him to break his rule and see them. When this happened he would do so with an old-world charm, listening to their problems with courtesy and offering assistance from his great store of knowledge, and sometimes using his influence on their behalf. He still liked to know what was happening in the realms of the Royal Geographical Society, and even now and again to have his say. He collaborated with H. R. Mill on the *Record of the Royal Geographical Society* that was published in 1930, and, still in 'historical' vein, in that same year he spoke at the centenary meeting on 'The Society Sixty Years Ago'.

His shyness, his age, and his connections with the past gave him a formidable reputation among the younger geographical circles which was not entirely deserved. Those who were now running the *Alpine Journal* and the *Journal of the Royal Geographical Society* on the other hand, found they were always sure of a willing response to their requests for help.

The physical limits of increasing old age irked him. He undertook an extensive tour of the Rocky Mountains in 1920, and the previous year had seen him crossing his last high alpine passes on foot. But if ever a motor car qualified for the title of Mountaineer it was his. With his faithful chauffeur, Doble, at the wheel they thrust upwards into all kinds of seemingly inaccessible alpine corners, in an attempt to recapture the thrills of his youth. On one such expedition he was accompanied by his two daughters, Eleanor and Janie. They remembered the problems they had when their father insisted on driving with the hood down so that he could see the peaks and experience the cold wind, even though it was pouring with rain. But his physical powers still remained remarkable. He was never ill; spare and fit as ever though somewhat stout, he was often seen running from the Athenaeum to go about his business when in London; while at Wych Cross he would sometimes startle Katherine and the servants by vanishing for hours down the steep valley, negotiating streams, bridges, tangle and wet as though reliving Abkahsia or the jungles of Sikhim.

There is a story told, for which there is no known authority, of his time on the Bench. It is said that for some years a tramp lived in a home-made shack buried deep in a hollow on the estate. He lived by snaring rabbits, and no doubt poaching the odd pheasant. So long as he caused no damage or trouble, and apparently he never did, the estate workers were told to leave him alone. But the situation used to worry Douglas, especially at Christmas, when the thought of the tramp out there in his hidey-hole possibly cold and wet was against the spirit of the season. But the old man had his pride, and was not going to accept charity. Then a plan was hit upon that saved face all round. Just before Christmas the keepers would go out with the local constable, and bring the tramp into the village lock up. There he was made warm, comfortable and dry, and a fine Christmas dinner sent down to him – normal gaol fare of course. At the first session of the magistrates court after Christmas no evidence would be offered and the case dismissed by the stern unsmiling chairman.

Wych Cross was by no means a dead place. Katherine saw to that, for waste and extravagance were her enemies. It was not a museum to house a failing old man and his memories. In spite of his inclination to merge into the rich, sombre background of his study, lined as it was with richly embossed Spanish leather, the house was often full of people, including children. They were his grandchildren and even towards the very end, his great-grandchildren. One old friend of Katherine's was allowed to start a small school for very young children in one part of the house, and he never objected to their high spirits. There is a story told of the day when a younger grandson came tearing down the main staircase and in his hurry knocked over a priceless vase that stood on a stand close to the forbidden study door. Sure enough that door opened, and in silence 'Gompy' supervised the collection of all the pieces. Perhaps a year later that same boy once again came down the same stair, and stopped short in surprise. 'Goodness!' he exclaimed, 'that looks just like the vase I broke last year!' From the shadowy depths boomed a well-known voice. 'It IS the vase you broke last year!' Furthermore it seemed perfectly natural to him, when he was showing a distinguished visitor round the beautiful gardens, that a large stone urn should start to gyrate apparently of its own accord just as they were passing. A natural phenomenon for 'Gompy', though what the visitor made of it is not known.

Close attachment to his distinguished lady friends continued to their mutual comfort. One of them received a book from him within which he wrote:

> The Book To Its Mistress
> When you espy me on your shelf
> Perched, like a small, brown, friendly elf,
> Lest out of sight prove out of mind,
> Be, as you always have been, kind,
> And wing a message through the air
> To him who gave me to your care;
> A ready ear you're sure to find,
> Love is not deaf, though often blind.

Perhaps the most pathetic tragedy of extreme old age is that no one can believe that you were ever young. The conqueror of Kasbek and Elbruz did not strain credulity by telling endless stories of his past mountain exploits, though he sometimes referred with amusement to the Battle of the Ladies. In his books, his pictures and his home he found interest and pleasure. Only occasionally was his peace destroyed, as when Arthur Clough arrived unexpectedly, bringing with him the odour of crisis and unease. Eleanor never knew that on several occasions her father had to meet the wages bill to keep Arthur's sinking empire afloat for a few weeks longer.

As late as 1927 he embarked on a formidable motor tour of southern Europe, feasting his eyes once again on the works of art and architecture that he had once shared with Gussie. He liked intelligent and unemotional company and on this occasion it was again Mrs Carruthers. While he was away, one of his increasing number of great-grandchildren was christened at Wych Cross and present as one of the godparents, was Admiral William (later Sir William) Fisher, another of Edmund's brothers. In the breezy, salty way of one of his calling he remarked loudly at the tea party that he had heard that old Douglas was sporting on the Lido with a dashing widow. The remark did not go down well with Freshfield's daughters – the old undeserved reputation died very hard.

When the time came for his last climb in the winter of 1934, into 'air too thin for mortal breath', he was ready. He called for his climbing boots, he called for the faithful François to come and help him up this last slope, and died painlessly and peacefully in his eighty-ninth year.

On 13 February 1934 his body was carried from the quiet of his study, where it had lain surrounded by the evidence of the richness of his mind, and the blue, ethereal Carrara mountains over the fireplace bid him a last farewell.

Now elderly, with their own troubles pressing in upon them, his daughters stood, fur-coated against the cold, within the enclosure where they had stood so long ago in mourning for a lost brother, and closed the tomb on an era.

But to the survivors of that day there is a picture that remains vivid. It is of a thin, wiry old gentleman, trotting rapidly along the terrace at Wych Cross, eyeglasses dangling, in the familiar cut-away coat, a style that he never abandoned, taking the corners too fast, deep in his thoughts and memories.

Today, many years after Douglas Freshfield was laid to rest with his wife and son at Brookwood, the deer still wander amongst the pines and seedling birches, flocks of small seed-eating birds hunt their way through the pine tops with feint but audible chatter. There is a distant rumble of traffic now, and the family plot is overgrown with brambles and young trees. But Hal's portrait is still discernable through the branches, and when the moss and dead leaves are brushed from the top of the marble sarcophagus beneath, there revealed are the words:

'I WILL LIFT UP MINE EYES UNTO THE HILLS'

APPENDIX

In 1934, amongst the many tributes paid to one of the last links to the grand age of Victorian mountain exploration, a number of senior members of both the Royal Geographical Society and the Alpine Club contributed their memorials to his long life and his contributions to their deliborations For those who are interested in the itinerary of D.W.F's life long travels, I quote below some of the major items taken from the Alpine Club's 'In Memorium' to which a number of his friends had contributed. I am grateful to the Alpine Club for their permission to quote from their publication '... gathered from "Mumm" and forty-five volumes of the *Journal*.'

1864. Monte Rosa, Alphubeljoch, Rheinwaldhorn, Lenta Lucke (first crossing and ascent), Piz Sella and pass, Piz Palu (first traverse of all the peaks, first ascent from the south), Konigsspitze (second ascent), Presanells (first ascent), Passo di Cercen (first crossing), Bocca di Camosci (first crossing), etc.

1865. Marmolata (second ascent), Obere Oedelwinkelsscharte (first crossing), Mosele (first ascent and traverse), Oetzthaler Wildspitze (third ascent), Mittelbergerjoch (first crossing), Langaufererspitze (first ascent and traverse), Weissgugel (second ascent), Ortler Pass (first crossing), Punta San Matteo (first ascent), Pizzo Tresero (first ascent), Adamello (second ascent), Pizzo di Verona (first ascent). First crossings of Passo di Mello and West Passo di Bondo, Piz Urlan, etc.

1866. Wetterhorn, Aletschhorn, Bietschhorn (new route), Todi (including first crossing of Ruseinlucke), Piz Cengalo (first ascent), Pizzo del Teo (first ascent), Cima di Castello (first ascent), Tinzenhorn (first ascent), first attempt on Porta Roseg, Pizzo and Passo Zembrasca, E. peak of Cimadi lago Spalmo and passo d'Avedo (all first ascents and crossings).

1867. Dent Blanche (not quite to the top), Tour du Grand St. Pierre (first ascent), Tour Ronde (first ascent and traverse).

1868. Journey from Egypt through Palestine to Constantinople and on to the Taurus and Caucasus. Attempt on Ararat to 16,000 ft. (D.W.F. was ill), Kasbek (first ascent), Elbruz (first ascent of E. peak), many Caucasian passes (all first crossings); the first exploration of the Caucasus.

1869. Uri-Rothstock, Schreckhorn, Monte Rosa, Rutor, etc.

1871. Orttler, Cima di Brenta (first ascent), Piz Quatervals (second ascent: new route), Piz Zupo (new route), Zupo Pass (first crossing), etc.

1872. Cima di Vezzana (first ascent: guideless). Julian Alps: failed to 'find' Montaschin Sseisera glen (!), etc.

1873. New high level route over Monte Cevedale to Veneziaspitze etc., Cima Tosa (traverse), Care Alto (third ascent), first crossings of Lares, Lobbia Alta and Mandron Passes, Campo Tencia (second ascent).

1874. Vignemale, Pic de Sauvegarde (both guideless), Glenstock, first ascent and crossing of Monte and Passo di Gleno, Re di Castello (first ascent), etc.

1875. Abruzzi. First British ascent of Gran Sasso d'Italia, etc.

1876. Punta Tersiva (new route), many new E. Graian cols, Col de Sea, etc.

1877–8. Maritimes and Dauphine, many ascents and cols, Cima di Nasta (first ascent), Lysjoch.

1879. Mittelhorn (from Rosenlaui and alone with two ladies one of whom was his sister-in-law Nelly), Monte Leone, Gr. Nesthorn, etc.

1880. Corsica: many ascents, Monte Rotondo, etc. Sasso di Mur and many ascents in the Dolomites; Col d'Olen, etc.

1881. Graians: Grand Casse etc., Ponte Percee du Reposoir, etc., Maritimes, etc.

1882. Besimauda, Cols de l'Argenbtiere, de la Traversette, etc., collecting material for *Hannibal's Pass*.

1884. Scotch Hills.

1886. Algeria and ascents in Atlas; Ras Timedouine, etc.

1887. Caucasus: many new passes, Gulba (first ascent), Tetnuld (first ascent), exploration of Shkara, Skoda (first ascent).

1888. Bernese Oberland.

1889. Caucasus: search party for Donkin and Fox. Many new passes including Freshfield Pass. Finding of Donkin's last bivouac on

Koshtantau. N.W. peak of Laila (first ascent), Abkhasia region, etc.

1890. Buet, Mont Blanc, etc.

1891. Dent du Midi, Mont Blanc, etc.

1892. Pyrenees: Mont Perdu, etc.

1893. Campo Tencio, Basodino, Brenta group, Adfamello, etc.

1894. Corsica: Monte d'Oro, etc., Bernina: Pizzo Scalino, Piz Bernina (guideless), Monte Disgrazia, Piz Badile (Masinobagni, Badile, Val Coders, Chiavenna in one day), Sella Crast' Aguzza, Beramasasque Alps.

1899. Himalya: first circuit of Kanchenjunga.

1900. Piz Gallegione, Schwestern (Pontresina), Piz Morteratsch (traverse all guideless), etc.

1901. Bernese Oberland.

1902. Pizzi Corvatsch, Margna, Palu (traverse: the party including Miss Katherine Freshfield, aged 17, and another lady). Ortler, Ifingerspitze.

1903. Soracte, etc. (*Classical Climbs*), etc. Norway: many peaks.

1904. Greece: (*Classical Climbs*) Pentelicus, Taygetus, Parnassus, Olympus (attempt defeated by brigands), etc.

1905–6. S. Africa: Table Mountain. Ruwenzori, first attempt to climb Mountains of the Moon – defeated by 'mud bath' and weather.

1907. Dinaric Alps: Bosnioa-Herzegovina: Prenj, etc. *Mountains of Dante*, etc.

1911. Canada: Rockies. Alleghanys (U.S.A.).

1912. Pyrenees and and Picos de Europa.

1913. Siberia and Japanese Alps.

1920. Canadian Rockies and Selkirks. [Ironically the Canadian Alpine Club named a peak in the Rockies 'Mount Freshfield'.]

The titles mentioned in italics are those publications amongst many others for the Alpine Club.

THE PUBLISHED WORKS
OF DOUGLAS FRESHFIELD

Thonon to Trent, Spottiswoode, 1865
Central Caucasus and the Bashan, 1869
Exploration of the Caucasus, Arnold, 1896
Round Kanchenjunga, Arnold, 1903
Hannibal Once More, Arnold, 1914
Unto the Hills, Arnold, 1914
de Saussure, Arnold, 1920
Quips for Cranks, Privately printed, 1923
Below the Snowline, Constable, 1923
Italian Alps, Basil Blackwell, 1937
A Tramp's Wallet – a privately printed collection of sundry notes and poems.

D.W.F. made numerous and some lengthy contributions to the *Geographical Journal* (the journal of the R.G.S.), the *Alpine Journal* (journal of the Alpine Club), on serious subjects, viz. his report on 'The Southern Frontiers of Austria' in 1915 and many others. Many were illustrated with both maps and photographs.

INDEX